Sz...

Wista

Bug

Klein-Koenisberg

Warta

Lodz

Lublin
Maïdanek

Oder

...dt

...sko

Gross Rosen

Monowitz
Buna

...eresienstadt

Zwodau

Gleiwitz

Auschwitz

Elbe

Ratibor

Birkenau

Wista

...eischen

...ausen

Melk

...en

Amstetten

Vienne

Danube

Wiener
Neustadt

The Deportees' Camps

Camp Annexes

0   100   200   300 km

CAMP
FOR WOMEN

CHRISTIAN BERNADAC

CAMP FOR WOMEN

Ravensbrück

FERNI PUBLISHING HOUSE

This book is dedicated to the women of Ravensbrück—all the women of Ravensbrück.

To my mother, who should have been deported like my father, but finally "avoided" Ravensbrück.

To André Malraux, because he knows "the weight of death in man".

"The dead rule the living."

Auguste Comte

Saturday night. End of another week,
One more, alas, that brought nothing;
The month is already wasting away, as empty and morose
As all those other uneventful months of the past.

All day they killed them,
And the last with rifle butts;
The wounded and the dead bedded down together,
In the same hole.

The next morning, the earth so palpitated
With obstinate signs of life
That they ran a heavy, furious roller
Up and down and back and forth so that
Crime was the victor.

Françoise Babillot

(unpublished poems written
at Ravensbrück)

—They've recaptured Odette.

— I said they would.

— Maybe, maybe. But Odette had the courage to try. She's the first Frenchwoman to have a go and her attempt will give ideas to others who will succeed. She proved that you can escape from Ravensbrück.

— For three days.

— For three days, yes, but three days of liberty count....

— Particularly for her because "her three days" would have been the last. In the meantime, your Odette is in for fifty whacks on the buttocks; and if she's not dead after that, solitary confinement, where—nude and without food—she can spend ten or fifteen days; and if by some miracle she still has any breath of life in her, "company discipline"....Let's face it, she's finished—really finished. She'd be better off if they gassed her right away.

— I know her; she'll hang on.

* *

Undressed,[1] I'm attached by the wrists, the neck and
the ankles to a sort of "torture table." The officers are
grouped around me; one of them, with a cape over his
shoulders, wears a monocle. An "appeal" had gone out
for volunteers to do the flogging. Three strong, solid
young women, probably tempted by supplementary food
rations, presented themselves for the job. Since my
detention, I kept my wedding ring on and, during critical
moments, hid it in my mouth. Naturally, I cannot scream.
A medical officer checks my pulse after every ten lashes
to verify, undoubtedly, the condition of my heart. Each
time he tells a Polish interpreter, the only person authorized to witness this unbelievable scene (so unbelievable
that I was living in an unreal world where all suffering
was spared me), to ask me to explain the reasons for my
escape attempt....

My only reply, always the same, is that a return to my
home suddenly tempted me more than a prolongation of
my visit among the mad and the dying.

At the end, when I was picked up, the S.S. said to me:
"You didn't scream, madame." All that I found to answer
was: "I'm French," a remark which brought on so many
kicks I fainted.

— And Odette. Did she hang on?
— Sure, she held on. She didn't scream and when
they asked her "why?" she simply replied "I'm French."
— I'm French. If she said that, she'll survive solitary
confinement.

When[2] I recovered consciousness, I found myself
stretched out nude on the floor. God knows how long I'd
been there. In the room was a sort of wash basin, like at
Fresnes, with a faucet, a chained-up chair and an
overturned bed that was hooked to the wall and locked. I

1. Unpublished manuscript, Odette Fabius. January 1970—April
1970.
2. Odette Fabius. Already quoted.

stayed on the floor for ten days without eating. I must have howled and moaned. It was the water that I could drink which permitted me to hold on. I was delirious. I saw the Lord Mayor of Cork (reminiscent of a story I read as a child) on a hunger strike. And I saw Gandhi. But above all, in my half-conscious state, I saw a white paper flying before my eyes. It was the little note that, from the train, I was able to pass to my 12-year-old daughter— promising her to return. After ten days, I was thrown a striped dress and a letter... it's a card from my daughter, the only one I would receive at the camp.... As a result of wounds opened up by a "cat-o'-nine-tails," one of my legs became infected; naturally no medical care was available.

— Odette held out. She's not very pretty to look at but she's alive.
— Quite a woman. Do you know her well?
— Nobody knows one another well here.... Her name is Odette Fabius.

During the last twenty-five years,[1] these events have, little by little, attached themselves to me like photos to a kaleidoscope, resulting in an intense whirlpool of contra-dictions; it's now even the essence of my feelings....

My souvenirs go back to June 1940. Sometimes I ask myself if my real birth in this life did not take place at that time. Certainly I lived before, but... what did I know about liberty? about duty? about self-respect?

I had what some people call "a pampered youth," without problems. Daughter of a successful lawyer, married at 18, mother of a little girl at nineteen, I led an agreeable life. I was not interested in politics in general, nor in the politics of my country in particular... but only in the daily problems of my easy existence—and without fervor.

1. Odette Fabius. Already quoted.

I woke up in June 1940 when I heard Marshal Pétain proclaim the armistice. I was 28 years old and a member of a motorized section of the Red Cross. Everything collapsed for me. The notion of "country" which this swift, odd war awoke in me caused such intense personal revulsion that, thirty years later, I still find myself engulfed by it.

What good is this work apprenticeship of the last few months going to do me? I had been "drafted" by Suzanne Crémieux, a family friend and now a senator of the Gard Department, to aid in the evacuation of children from Paris—to which her section in the Public Health Ministry had consecrated much time and effort since March. I had also enrolled in the motorized sanitary sections (S.S.A.) and participated in the evacuations of Rethel, Soissons, Sedan, Laon and Château-Thierry.

I felt incapable of taking up the semi-idle life that was mine up to the dramatic events of 1939. In this state of mind, I devoted myself to the service of the S.S.A. with desperate eagerness and defiance. I made visits to temporary prison camps: to Châteaubriant, Savenay, Saint-Lô, etc. I even traveled to certain camps for black prisoners in the Bordelais region.

This activity brought me to Marseilles in 1941 where, through the intermediary of Commander Raynal, I met Commander Faye who had just arrived from London. Commander Faye put me in touch with Colonel Alamichel and later with Marie-Madeleine. The "Alliance" and "Centurie" networks had made a new Odette Fabius out of me—one that was to be arrested April 23, 1943, at the home of Monsieur Amphoux, a coal dealer in Marseilles, whose office served as a "letter drop," and where I had gone to warn of the dismantling of our network. Three Corsican resistance members from Marseilles, Pierre Ferri Pisani, Jean Secco and Mathieu Anfriani, had been arrested at our command post in my home that very morning. Unfortunately, the Gestapo was there before me.

After spending two months at the Saint-Pierre prison in Marseilles, nine months at Fresnes, of which five months were in "solitary," a month at the Romainville Fort, a month at the prison in Compiègne, and then three days in the town's Royallieu Camp, I found myself on January 29, 1944, at five in the morning, singing "La Marseillaise" and the "Song of Departure" in a cart (as old as the French Revolution) which was taking me to the Compiègne railroad station for the great voyage east...towards Ravensbrück.

We were only one thousand, but our registration number referred to us as "the twenty-seven thousand."

The trip, in sealed cattle cars, took four nights and three days during which, 80 to a car, we all sang and divided up the provisions which some of us had been able to bring along (a marvelous supplement to the almost inedible bread and sausages which had been distributed back on the Compiègne railway platform. But despite its horror, the journey did not in the least prepare us for the calvary of the days we were to spend in the concentration camp.

Along the way there were disputes. Some wanted to smoke, others opposed because of the danger of fire. The floor was covered with straw and there would have been no escape from our rolling prison if, while en route, it suddenly burst into flame.

We went through various rail stations and temporarily halted alongside other trains crammed with prisoners with whom we tried to communicate; at such times a few lucky women took turns peering through the railroad car's skylight "to see." Others just wanted to breathe for a few seconds air that was less polluted than that which permeated the car's stifling stench—an unavoidable odor when 80 women have only a few sanitary soil-tubs to use for their natural wastes—particularly since they were only emptied once, at the "official" stop which our train made at the frontier railroad station in Saarbrücken. (This halt enabled the S.S. to count us again, and distribute another ration of whacks with waistbelts and clubs.)

In a few other stations where the convoy made short stops, at least to the frontier, some charitable souls...the Red Cross, without doubt...tried to fill all our utensils with water through the bars of the skylight; this brought on more squabbling between the thirsty and those privileged enough not to feel such pangs.

Our arrival at Ravensbrück still sticks in my mind as a hideous nightmare. One woman had died in our car from an attack of diabetes...and when we saw the camp, which was just coming to life (it was about five in the morning), it was like something out of Dante—only the night was white with snow.

The high kitchen chimneys and, without doubt, those of the crematorium, vomited forth their smoke into a sky of pure winter.

Women, without any definite age, young, old, some very old, in blue and grey-striped costumes, seemed to our eyes—still unaccustomed to such physical misery—to be personages that had escaped from portraits of the Apocalypse.

The women lined up to be counted, shuffling their feet to keep warm...several couples of them passed carrying immense buckets filled with a blackish liquid.

And we advanced, numb with cold, frightened, exhausted and shaking under our kit-packs, surrounded by the S.S., dogs, women in uniform, and petrified with anxiety.

The days passed...first a period of quarantine, then work...roads to be constructed for the German Fatherland. From freight cars arriving from all the occupied cities of Europe the prisoners unloaded the modest treasures that had been stolen as fast as their owners were arbitrarily arrested....

In the port of Fürstenberg they also had to pile up coal briquettes into huge heaps which eventually were to nourish the camp's chimneys and warm the armada of

An interior of the Drancy camp. All over France, the Gestapo, aided as of 1943 — by French Militiamen, tracked down resistance forces and Jews. The internment camps multiplied: Agde, Aincourt, Aurigny, Argelès... certain ones like Drancy and Compiègne were set aside as centers where the selection of prisoners to be sent to the concentration camps could be made. From October 1941 to November 1944, ten tousand French-women were deported to Ravensbrück.
Bernadac Archives

S.S. troops, the officers and soldiers of the Wehrmacht, S.S. women and, in a word, all the chain-gang guards who lived on the backs of this pitiful mass of human refuse which we were becoming, little by little....

Then there is the flow of innumerable, heartbreaking, dramatic and revolting memories—although some were touching, moving and redeeming.

It is difficult to forget the expressions of moral and physical pain on the faces of the dead.

It is also difficult to forget the debasing moral level to which the guards lowered our companions. Whether from Poland or Russia, from France or Belgium, from Hungary or Romania, or from one of the fifty-two countries which had citizens stagnating in the camp, there were always guards about who were ready to accept the abominable mission of watching, beating and denouncing us....

This was, I believe, Nazi Germany's most corrosive and cynically-successful undertaking: to provoke, by supplementary food rations, or by certain favors (that is to say, by appealing to such primitive needs of man as survival), progressive degradation within the already corrupt-minded.

How could one forget the young prisoner who rushed up to Himmler during one of his visits to try and explain to him the misery in which we were living—and who totally disappeared the same day.

Although mysterious voices confirmed the rumor circulating within the camp during the last week of August 1944 that Paris had been liberated, it was still difficult for me to imagine the city free again and my loved ones reunited—and not be among them to live, think, love and forget...and I decided, almost unconsciously, to escape.

Actually, from the day of my arrest, I had always thought of escaping; but what seemed impossible to do in the prisons of Marseilles and Paris, or in the camps of Romainville and Compiègne, now appeared to me to be much more feasible in Germany—even though I knew neither the country nor the language.

It is probable that, subconsciously, the time I spent in French prisons and camps nourished hope of escape. For example, I knew that, one day or another, I would be incarcerated elsewhere and that just the physical shift itself would, for a person with such an optimistic outlook as mine, open up a thousand possibilities: ways of escape, better treatment, the possibility of becoming useful, etc.

At Ravensbrück, on the other hand, I felt that only the end of the war would permit me to return home—if for no other reason than the notation written on the decision to condemn me to prison: "Dangerous terrorist, imprisonment until the end of hostilities." The question which I never ceased to ask myself was: "When will hostilities end?" In addition, when I learned that hostilities throughout France were about to end, I became haunted with this vision of a free, though convalescing, France, and I could no longer resist plotting the escape project which had been in the latent part of my mind for the last 16 months.

Now I had to find a way to bring it off. I began by dropping hints of my desire for evasion in all my conversations. I was soon approached by numerous comrades who wanted to break out of the camp with me....I must admit that my "level-headed" friends begged me to drop my bold idea to flee. But nothing could hold me back.

It was thus that I volunteered to go with a group of prisoners to a place called Templin (I think that's what it was called), only a few kilometers from Fürstenberg; we were to clear up the rubble around a hospital that had been evacuated just before being demolished during an Allied air raid.

A camp acquaintance, Betty Smith, also volunteered to go on the work detail...(though of English origin, she had lived many years in Germany)....Along with some thirty other women, we were accepted and scheduled to leave for Templin in two days. The following night, however, Betty came to say she had been chosen as an interpreter in the camp's Political Office and that she would not be able to leave with me; nevertheless, she had talked one of her friends in the workshop into replacing her and she would come around the next day before the convoy left to introduce the two of us...which she did.

Since then, I neither met nor heard anyone speak of Betty Smith again. Had she really been given work in the Political Office? Or did she get cold feet? Or was she just an instigator? None of my friends ever saw her again either....She left her barracks and the workshop and simply vanished....The replacement to whom she had introduced me, Sylvie Paul, was around my age and pretty, but very authoritative and common; I built up an immediate antipathy toward her, but she spoke German very well and...since I had no choice....

We left at five in the morning for the Fürstenberg railroad station; there we boarded a tiny suburban train. We were accompanied by women whom we called "little grey mice"; they were all volunteers, but we didn't know them. It was easy enough to pick them out from the regular guards, though. The latter wore leather-like army boots, while the former generally wore their own shoes. Usually, most of these volunteers were more brutal and cruel than the standard guards—probably because it was work they had chosen to do.

This time, however, all the guards were amiable and smiling enough. A few of them chatted with us; one that had her eye on me offered me a cigarette and, in bad English, spoke of her life as a journalist. She had asked to accompany our group in order to write an article on prisoners held by the Reich.

After a twenty-minute trip through a ravishing region on which the sun shone radiantly (it was August 28, 1944), we arrived in a small provincial station, crossed the tiny adjacent town and, after again being counted, were taken to the work site which we were to clean up.

We began work around seven; it was hard labor but everyone was generally in good humor; we had had a change of scenery...the weather was splendid...the political news was good (at least for the prisoners)...the guards were still more or less friendly...and the few S.S. troops standing about watched us with indifference.

At noon, a small mobile kitchen rolled up with soup that tasted vaguely of turnips. Fifteen minutes later we were sent back to work. Soon after, Sylvie Paul and I realized that, because of the torrid heat, all the guards had slumped down in the grass around us for a siesta. Slowly we eased away; our evasion had begun.

After passing through several strands of barbed wire, which left us with some nasty scratches, we found ourselves in a superb forest where we stripped down to the "civies" we wore underneath our prison rags. (I, personally, had "bought" a loose-fitting jacket for four rations of bread from a comrade who was assigned to a work detail that unloaded "recuperated" clothing and goods from trains arriving from various occupied countries of Europe.)

We hid our ugly camp garb under some moss and, finally finding a road, began our walk to hoped-for freedom. Shortly, we decided to separate because we easily imagined that as soon as our absence was detected, an alert would go out everywhere for "two" fugitives. We also decided to wait for each other at the exit end of each village through which we would pass in order to "confer" and make sure we were walking in the right direction to Berlin—some eighty kilometers to the south. There I naively believed I could contact a prisoner repatriation center or Ambassador Scapini whom I knew very well as a leading lawyer and friend of my father.

After an hour's walk during which, for the first time in many months, I felt infinitely free, I had to admit to myself that I was very tired; I had fallen behind Sylvie because I was greatly suffering from an abscess on one of my feet. I sat down to rest for ten minutes at the bottom of a haystack and watched Sylvie plod on up the road. She was nearly out of sight when I suddenly realized that a loaded haywagon with two men riding on top was coming up a little lane through the nearby field. Not being able to dash back out onto the road without being seen, I buried myself as much as possible in the hay so they wouldn't see me.

Moments later, I furtively looked up and saw the wagon had stopped; one of the men was coming toward me. I pretended to be in a deep sleep. Suddenly I felt a tap on my shoulder, and then a voice asking "krank?" My knowledge of German was not that meager; the word meant "sick." I stretched, sat up and looked directly into the eyes of the man who had been leaning over me. He repeated his question, "sehr krank?" (very sick?). I shook my head and said, "nein." Then he asked, "Deutsch?" and I again answered "nein." But this game could go on for some time, so I risked saying to him, "Ich Franzose." I never saw a man so startled. Then he said in perfect French, "Well, I'm French, too." "Auguste, come on down here," he shouted to his friend. And the three of us all began talking at once. It turned out they were two French prisoners from Brittany who had volunteered to work on a farm; but, though delighted to run into a compatriot, they seriously doubted I could walk through the German countryside with so little linguistic baggage....They knew of the existence of Ravensbrück; they also knew something about the camp that I did not: the Russian women prisoners who had escaped from it were recaptured and hanged....

First they asked me if I were alone. I said no and pointed to Sylvie Paul's distant silhouette. Auguste decided to run after her so that at least I would have a traveling companion who spoke German. When he got near her, I told him to whistle "On the roads of France," the signal we used to "recognize" each other at night or in "emergencies." Off he went, but, by this time, Sylvie had seen me with a man, and—now with another one running after her—believed I had been recaptured. She turned and ran in the direction away from us as fast as her legs would carry her. That was the last time I saw her until after the liberation when her photo appeared on the front pages of a number of newspapers. After being mixed up in an incalculable number of swindles, which—after her return from deportation—had put her in prison after prison, she had been arrested for a particularly odious murder.

My two "friends," saddened to see me thus abandoned, decided to go ask the farmers who employed them, and with whom they seemed on excellent terms, to extend me hospitality for the approaching night. They came back shamefaced...their employers, fearing that I would denounce them if I were recaptured, had refused—but they had sent along some coffee, boiled potatoes, a compass, 25 marks and an empty potato sack to keep me warm in my haystack...and I had a banquet....My two lifesavers then left but promised to come back at one o'clock to get me started again. As they suggested, I planned to walk at night and hide during the day....Sure enough, they returned and escorted me to the road leading to Berlin. Our parting was sad but we exchanged addresses and promised each other to meet again after the war.

Auguste never came back; he was sent to Russia; Francis, however, was able to escape and came to see me one sunny day in the winter of 1945-46. At first we did not recognize each other—but what joy we experienced when we did.

After leaving them I walked in rhythm to my favorite songs, lowly humming them to myself...."On the roads of France," "Oh, how beautiful was my village," "Jeanne of Lorraine," etc. I ate apples that I picked from the trees and dug up some potatoes and ate them raw....I had had worse meals in my life...and, after all, I was free....I was finally going to get home where I would be able to explain to General de Gaulle, or to the proper ministry, what was actually happening in the concentration camps, and I was going to see my little girl again. I was 32 years old...and I was a heroine. The third night I managed to get myself lost in a forest. While wandering around, I came upon a group of animals with piercing eyes which I took for dogs (I later learned that they were wolves, but that, at that time of the year, they didn't attack humans). Thinking back, I get faint imagining myself being devoured by wolves; what an anonymous end that would have been. Finally, just at the break of dawn, the hour when I usually began looking for a place to hide, I found my way out of the forest near a sign which said: "Berlin, 18 kilometers—Tempelhof, 2 kilometers." Being now only a 3 or 4-hour walk from the suburbs of Berlin, where I hoped to lose myself in the crowds of foreign workers, I decided not to wait for night to fall to continue my journey. That was my undoing....

Around six that morning I passed through a sleepy little village; it was so quiet I was almost afraid my footsteps would wake the inhabitants. Suddenly a door opened near me and out came two policemen. They were momentarily astonished to see me, and then approached and politely asked for my papers. "Nix Papier," I answered. Just as politely, I was taken into the building—the local police-station. They gave me some coffee and bread and put me in a small, fairly comfortable cell. At nine o'clock I was taken before an officer who spoke fairly good French. In the same office, a young girl sat behind a typewriter.

Of course I was interrogated about my presence in the neighborhood. I concocted a story that seemed perfectly plausible to me: I was a collaborator and had come to work in the Siemens factories in Berlin, but the constant Anglo-Saxon air-raids so terrorized me that, two days ago, I ran away to the countryside—which explained my shabby appearance.

All this was listened to with interest and typed up by the young secretary. When I had finished, I was asked my identity; I gave a false one. Then I was asked to sign the typed statement I had just made. At that moment the officer opened a drawer, looked me square in the eye, and said: "Mrs. Fabius, isn't it?" Undoubtedly, my description had been given to all the surrounding police-stations (I still don't know why I was asked to sign a statement which my captor knew was phony). After a telephone conversation in German, the officer had me returned to my cell where, for the next two hours, I tried to pull myself together. I consider those two hours to be the saddest and most dramatic of my entire deten-tion. I had just counted too much on the success of my escape.

Two hours later, the Ravensbrück Camp Commander appeared, accompanied by the notorious Oberaufseherin Binz and two soldiers carrying rifles with fixed bayonets. They prodded me into a convertible sedan and sat me between two S.S. troopers; the commander drove, with Binz alongside—smoking, laughing and kissing him. We took less than two hours to drive back on the same road that I had taken three days to cover. Upon my return to the camp, I was given fifty lashes with a whip and then thrown into "solitary" where I remained nude without bed, blankets or food.

Ten days later, I was judged by the camp commander and several superior officers, Binz and the Super-Schwes-ter Martha who served as an interpreter. I was very arbitrarily condemned, once again, to a prison for con-victs until the end of hostilities; I was also made to put a red circle on the front and back of my clothes which would identify me to camp authorities as a prisoner requiring particular surveillance.

My "return to life" in this awful prison atmosphere was very difficult. Here I was suddenly deprived of my prison-camp companions with whom I had established rare ties of friendship—a friendship which remains solid

with those who survived the last months of deportation and the passage of the years. Their acts of solidarity, comradeship and moral support were true and profound....

I was put on the most difficult and distressing work
details imaginable: road-building, scraping up excrement
from around the camp, picking up bodies to take to the
crematorium, cleaning the toilets in the wards which
housed those afflicted with typhus....

Nevertheless, despite the last twenty-five years, I still
look back upon certain acts with identical emotion—
upon gestures which were gifts of love given amid much
meanness and contempt which permanent promiscuity
made even more intolerable.

That is why the gentle gesture of a little factory worker
once took on such importance for me. After watching me
clumsily swing a pickaxe on a road-building construction
crew laboring near Fürstenberg, she came over and said:
"Pretend you're working and let me do this job; you
know, I get up every morning at five and go to the
factory, so, whether it's here or somewhere else, I still
have to put in my time; besides, I'm certainly more in the
habit of doing this than you are."

I also think of "Kiki" and Mrs. Michel, from Marseilles,
who always found a way to slip me a little supplement
from the Blockowa for whom she cleaned...

and Micheline from H., a young Belgian prisoner and
mother of four children who, every time she received a
package (I was not permitted to), slipped a small can of
food under my pillow...

and T., from F., arrested in Bordeaux, who, after many
weeks, received a package and waited until seven that
night for me to return from an outside work detail so that
I could have the pleasure of opening it with her—while
putting off the joy she always had when she extracted
news of her loved ones from the hem of the skirt they
sent her...

and P., from R., an anti-Nazi German arrested in Paris,

who worked as an interpreter in the camp's Political Office. Working in close contact with the prison
directors permitted her to keep us abreast of all the
latest news which, in turn, raised our morale and
made it a little easier for us to wait for the end of our
calvary....

and Susan S., from Nice, who never tried to get out of
any work which another prisoner would have had to
perform...

and Marie M., from Paris, who, while on her deathbed,
prayed to God (even though she had always been
a Communist) to ask him to exchange what remained
of her life for mine so that I could see my little girl
again...

and Paule D., from Isigny, who, knowing that I often
complained of not being able to remember any verses
and of not having read anything for months, spent part of
one night writing out, by the light of a candle, Rostand's
"Hymn to the Sun" which, in a feverish moment while
lying sick with typhus in the infirmary, I had manifested
the desire to re-read; she brought it to my hospital bed at
four, just before the morning roll call....

— O, Sun, you without whom things....

And, oh, how many others...who, by such acts, gave
us reassurance by not permitting us to doubt that love
still existed, that life could still be beautiful, and that we
must continue to struggle....

The days, weeks and months of my deportation have
been, without doubt, abominable. The experience of
being in concentration camps is difficult to express and
get people to understand....Only those who have lived
through such hell can possibly know....

The horror and the grandeur, the disgrace and the
noblesse that we have seen and endured return unceasingly to stir and agitate our memories; however,
because our country had to undergo this ordeal, I feel
privileged to have been able to go through it, even under
the circumstances in which I experienced it, and to

have survived and still be here to tell you that the profound bitterness of those hours has often been compensated for by the feeling of solidarity and the discovery of deep, mutual respect and love for one's fellow beings[1].

1. Yvonne Pagniez, another escapee from Ravensbrück, told her adventure, and that of a Swiss friend who accompanied her, in *Evasion 44*, Flammarion, 1949.

PREFACE

So they will be, triumphant members of this herd of "disfigured shadows," marked by indifference and oblivion, the seal of wisdom. Geniuses. Geniuses of a time when the grandeur of every second was measured in faith. Faith in man. Man creature and spirit.

So they will be, scabby women with blue eyes dotted with white, the resuscitated of torment and of storm. So they will be, as they return to the world, this grey chalk which cements beating hearts.

So they will be, having escaped the massacre in the slaughterhouse, with their flavorless, musky sweat, the saliva of our new language.

Heretic authors of an enslaved century, they are the mildew on our stones, the praying figures of our desires.

Women they will be.

Mother-women of another generation. The naked puppets of Ravensbrück, the utensil-woman of Zwodau, puppet of the Scheisskolonne (the shit detail), stück (piece) of the bowels of the mine or the sand, feet, arms, hands, fingers, and lever, and muscles, and pincers, and thread; needle, lathe, shovel, pickaxe, hands, feet, fingers and hammer and scissors. Cranes, bridges, wagons, etc....

— Kaffee holen: go get the coffee.

— Raus! Schnell, Schweinerei! Get out! Quick! Garbage!

— Gas chamber! Crematorium!

— Raus! Zu fünft: Get out! five at a time! Zu fünft! always by five! Groups of five. Work zu fünft! On your knees zu fünft!

To die zu fünft! Die a million times zu fünft!

Yes! Shadows of another world, of another life astride death.

Dreams of red meat, of laughs, of caresses, of Venus-like silhouettes, of home, food, bed, the cemetery....

Tomorrow they will be. Today they are.

Today they are and their "flag," this standard on which Constantine had a cross placed with the inscription "In hoc signo vincis" (By this sign thou wilt conquer), has fallen into the dust. Poor red triangle of forgotten deportees:

— Old tales!

— Exaggerations!

— Psychopaths!

— Ridiculous pajamas of July fourteenth.

They aren't any more. They have been.

And history will not find them again until tomorrow, tomorrow when reason will want to know, understand. Tomorrow, because today is still our history. Tomorrow yes, more than today.

These women, as these thousands of men—fringe survival—are depositaries of a secret. They only have known and perhaps found man. If they have not always known how to understand him or account for him, if they have deformed him—beautified or blackened—one thing is sure; they have seen him.

Designated, chosen to be nothing more than a number in a series, of a ward, of a camp, of a work detail, a "thing," a piece; considered as veritable puppets without life, without soul—naked puppets engaged in a gigantic work force of drudgery on a scale comparable to the New World, New Conquerors—they have found themselves in this primitive tribe which the greatest anthropologists would like to discover in their research and which they had there, open, welcoming and gaping since 1933.

Man is there.

Never has man been more present than in a concentration camp. Stomach-man, thing-man, sorcerer-man, spirit-man, object-man, victor-vanquished-man, love-man, lone-man, hope-man, woman-man, man-woman, dream-man, sometimes devil-man or God-man, exhausted man, cadaver, skeleton, light ash carried up the chimney or "non-skidding" on patches of ice. Muscle-man, Guinea-pig-man, barter-man, suffering-man, dead-man, free-man. Avenger, indifferent.

Forgotten men or women.

Yes, forgotten. Thousands of forgotten witnesses. One sole testimony is an approach to the concentration camp system, more profound than a thousand-page thesis[1], than kilos of paper, of notes, abbreviations, footnotes, lists, statistics...that day she died as she entrusted me with a hairpin. That day she gave birth during roll call, that day she was hungry and stole a piece of bread from her best friend, that day she felt like laughing, that day she wrote a poem, sketched the guard on the margin of a magazine...that day, like all the other days, like all the other hours, she was afraid.

That day....

But that day is not a historic fact.

1. I am obviously not speaking of the theses presented by deportees upon their return, because these documents are witness-type theses based on "direct" observation....The works of André Lettich, Paulette Don Zimmet-Gazel, Suzanne Wenstein-Lambolez, etc. will remain as the fundamental pillars in the study of the concentration camp system.

Perhaps tomorrow, thanks to "those days," one will be able to recreate historical facts.

This volume is part of a series consecrated to concentration camps, rather consecrated to the deportees of these camps and their torturers. I think it is very different from the others, not because it is reserved to the women incarcerated in Ravensbrück, and the personnel there, but perhaps because the horror and the bestiality are in the background. A diary that reads like an obituary? A diary of life, work, suffering and hopes. Diary of the largest group of women ever put behind barbed wire. Diary of nationalities. Diary of differences and of unions. Diary of Ravensbrück.

In the first volume of *Naked Puppets*, which dealt with the women's camp at Auschwitz, I wrote:

— One does not "recount" Auschwitz. Each deportee, each commander, each guard, each Kapo only knew a little of Auschwitz. Since 1945, every military investigating officer, every judge, every witness, every lawyer, every defendant, every writer, every journalist, every condemned person has (or had) "a certain idea" of Auschwitz.

— Today, each one "imagines" Auschwitz with the knowledge that it is a part of man's bad conscience, because this crime—perhaps the greatest in our history— has been committed by man. And man cannot pardon man for Auschwitz. And man knows that man, in certain circumstances, is capable of re-inventing other Auschwitzes, other naked puppets.

One does not recount Auschwitz.

But nevertheless....

Ravensbrück has often been "recounted," and one can easily believe that it is the best known concentration camp. Above all, it is famous—but its notoriety is more discreet, less horrific... "only 92,000 dead, whereas, at Auschwitz, in just one day!..." Most of those who died at

Ravensbrück were not shoved into the gas chambers to suck toxic chemicals up into their nostrils. Days, weeks months—a few days, a few weeks, a few months were enough to recreate all the stages of a life: youth, adolescence, respite of adult power, the shipwreck of old-age; and the camps do not tolerate the elderly, even if they're only twenty years old. Of the ten thousand Frenchwomen deported to Ravensbrück, eight thousand died there, one day or another.

The dead and the survivors, this book is their book.

C.B.

1

The Bridge of the Ravens

— Yes, there are firs. Strange looking firs: Stunted, with deformed branches and trunks that look like they have leprosy.

— The bark?

— It's peeling off in strips. A gigantic congenital disease of some kind. I have the impression they're all infected.

The young blind girl—not yet 25 years old—trips.

Hélène Rabinatt takes a firmer hold on her infirm friend's elbow. A guard screams out something. Perhaps: "Faster!"

The blind girl smiles.

— So it's here that the end is?

— The end?

— Ravensbrück is the end of the journey. The end, period. Except, perhaps, for you who are better equipped to defend yourself—you might be able to hold on. Me, I'm condemned ... my eyes .... Haven't we changed direction?

— I don't think so.

— So then it is Ravensbrück. In Strasbourg, I was told about this camp. People talked to me about it in almost religious terms... with anxiety and everything I was told about it was so different from the suppositions and the rumors that the women in Romainville spread about. I realized that what I was told was true when you described the firs to me. My guard in Strasbourg said: "In Ravensbrück, even the fir trees are dying."

— But what is Ravensbrück? A camp? Like so many others?

— A camp, yes! The camp for women. The camp for all the women that Germany wants to eliminate. Ravensbrück is oblivion. In Strasbourg he told me: "Above all, above all you, a blind person, try to escape from Ravensbrück. There a prisoner cannot hope to live more than three or four months." He also talked to me about the ravens. Do you see any ravens?

— Yes, there are a few around.

— Dirty ravens? Grey? The ravens of Ravensbrück are like the trees: without elegance... sick. Ravensbrück means "The Bridge of the Ravens" or "From where the Ravens come." It appears that all the ravens in the region, when they feel they are about to die, choose these forests. We are the dead ravens of Ravensbrück.

*   *
*

In the province of Mecklenburg, eighty kilometers north of Berlin, a slope of lakes surrounded by marsh lands. Dunes and "beaches" of white sand, chestnut-colored mires, isles of ash-grey birch trees, clearings made at the beginning of the century by naturalist sects.[1] Wind. Snow. The rugged provincials of Fürstenberg adore their little Siberia and Jerome Klorst, a "song-

1. The "Artamane Company" reclaimed several acres of land for cultivation from 1925 to 1935. Rudolph Hoess, the future commander of Auschwitz, worked for three seasons with his wife in Mecklenburg.

writer" in the early 1900s, immortalized this desolation in a poem of 750 lines:

— O, my forest, my sweet Siberia....

Heinrich Himmler, who liked the company of naturalists, "camped" several times in this lake region and, in 1936, bought a vast piece of land at a little place called Ravensbrück. Investigators and historians have never found titles for the property owned by the Reichsführer S.S. and it is probable that he allowed the concentration camp's administrative authorities "to acquire" the area as a hedge against "what this ungrateful world could become." It was near good roads and rail routes and a training camp for young recruits.

On September 17, 1938, twenty-odd "common-law" Germans from Sachsenhausen-Oranienburg, led by an S.S. lieutenant, Ernst Kögel, arrived in the Fürstenberg railroad station. Ludwig Diederich, condemned to 30 years of hard labor for having embezzled several million marks from the treasury of a public works firm in Berlin, would be the head of this new work site. Kögel, who had the title of commander, had only three months to complete the central administration's project: "a re-education camp able to hold five to six thousand prisoners." He learned that Ravensbrück was destined to group all the women held in German prisons only fifteen days before the arrival of the first convoy.

In order to put up 16 barracks around an assembly area, and build watch towers, a double-wire electric fence, and administrative buildings, Diederich regularly demanded reinforcements. In two months, Oranienburg sent 600 "specialists" to Ravensbrück. Ravensbrück was Himmler's "golden-haired child"—and, according to his secretary, he would visit it "at least fifteen times" during the period of construction; he wanted it to be a model camp—just like the one for men at Oranienburg.

On May 13, 1939, Commander Kögel welcomed the first 867 prisoners to Ravensbrück: 7 Austrians, 1 Spaniard, 1 Italian, 1 Greek and 857 Germans. For the most part they are "criminals" who are serving sentences requiring only temporary detention; they have no trouble smothering the minuscule knots of "political" prisoners, who, alone, could undoubtedly be re-educated and saved: opponents of national socialism, imprisoned like the Jehovah's Witnesses or the Scrutinizers of the Bible since 1933.

The experiences of Dachau and Oranienburg have taught the instigators of the concentration system that, to be effective, the responsibility for surveillance and repression should be given to the greatest criminals. Ravensbrück was not an exception to the rule. The first "Kapo" chosen, "cousin Angèle," a former waitress in a Hanover café-dancehall, had, on the same night, strangled her father, her mother and an old grandfather. She handled the "Gummi" with virtuosity and when she slapped someone, an average of one out of three ended up with a broken ear-drum. This speciality earned her the nickname "The Deafener."

The "grounds" for having concentration camps in the first place, at least between 1933 and 1941, were very different from the "reasons for existing" which French deportees came to know a little later. When these open-air areas were first set up, as opposed to closed penitentiary centers, they were expected to mould an individual's physical and moral components into one perfect form. Every human being, provided he is of pure birth and pure blood, deserves to have the community take care of his future by giving him the means to mend his ways and atone for his sins and errors. It is curious to note that, in May 1942, only one month after Oswald Pohl, chief of the S.S.'s Central Economic and Administrative Office, had put the camps on a wartime basis[1] and defined the

---

1. The war has manifestly changed the structure of the concentration camps and fundamentally modified their task as regards the utilization of prisoners. The guarding of prisons for the sole reasons of security, correction or prevention is no longer a priority. The center of gravity has now shifted to the economic

new policy, "Production first, the means are unimportant,"
Himmler wrote him:

— On the whole[1] I am in complete agreement. But I
think it would be well to underline, in one way or
another, the fact that the policy of verifying incarcera-
tions, as well as planning the educative goals for those
who can be educated in the concentration camps,
remains unchanged. If not, we could be accused of
arresting people, or of maintaining them in detention
once they had been arrested, just to have workers on
hand—which explains why we must underline and make
clear our determination to keep our verifying policy
unchanged and not dependent upon the economic con-
juncture.

— In addition, and I am well aware that we must get
the work done at all costs, with a 100% effort, I am of the
opinion that the camp commanders must take on the job
of educating the "educables."

This dream of concentration "seminars" will haunt
Himmler until the day he commits suicide. To save,
"despite himself" of course, the opponent, the criminal,
but also the homosexual and the prostitute. This is an
important mission of the Party which is the guide, the
friend, the truth and, in the most desperate situations: the
torturer.

side. The prison workers must be mobilized to perform the tasks
of war. The camp commander is solely responsible for the work
performed by the prisoners. This work must be, in the real sense
of the word, exhausting if the maximum profit is to be obtained....
The duration of the work is not limited; it depends on the
organization of labor in the camp and is determined only by the
camp commander. Any nonlabor activities which shorten the
duration of the work period (meals, roll calls, etc.) must be
reduced to the strict minimum. Moving about from one place to
another and pauses at noon, no matter for how short a time, are
forbidden if their sole purpose is to have meals.
1. Letter addressed to Oswald Pohl, May 29, 1942. *Himmler
aux cent visages*. 387 letters from and to the Reichsführer S.S.
presented by Helmut Heiber. Fayard, 1969.

* * *

The Ravensbrück correction camp is, therefore, the object of much special attention: rich and healthy food (experimentation with wheat, soya, barley, oatmeal, and maple syrup which will be served at breakfast to the S.S. shock squads out in the field), meticulous cleanliness, scrupulous order, respect for property—each prisoner has a bed, a mattress, two blankets, a cupboard—and respect for the prison's organization.

For all these women,[1] the camp rules had become second nature. One closet resembled the other, on each door hung a dish cloth, folded like a man's tie. The aluminium basin, the cup and the plate shone like a new coin: in each closet were stowed six sanitary napkins and a belt with embroidered initials; combs were washed every day; with pieces of glass, every stain on the shoe brush handles was carefully removed; there must be no finger marks showing on the closet door. The stepladders were all lined up, and well washed down. Each "Bibelforscherin" knew and followed the rules: in order to avoid getting shoe polish stains on the stepladders, it was forbidden to brush one's shoes on the rubber rungs. I was given the secret of having a highly-polished table top: using the pointed edge of a shoe brush handle, I pressed down on the surface centimeter by centimeter!!! The tiles also shone brightly and the floor was immaculately white; we got down on our knees and washed it every day.

— But the dormitories, with their 140 beds, were the grand attraction. Mattresses absolutely flat, blankets perfectly straight, folded to the same dimension of the checkered pillow cases—so that they would be of the same width; even the squares of the bed clothing were counted; one pillow the same as the other, like the footlocker-type wooden boxes with their pointed corners.

1. G. Buder-Neumann: *De Potsdam à Ravensbrück*.

On the dormitory door was a detailed drawing of the location of all the beds; it corresponded to the prisoners' numbers; that way, the "Blockowa" could easily detect the one whose bed was badly made.

As for the work—extenuating and useless—it generally consisted of transporting, eight hours a day, sand from one dune to another dune. When the first dune had disappeared, it was built back up again with the aid of sand from the second dune—and so on....

— Work just to work.

— Pleasure!

"Pleasure" also for certain "recipients": the application of sentences. Five, ten, twenty or twenty-five blows of a bludgeon on the buttocks. Corporal punishment which camp rules stipulated must be inflicted only in the presence of a doctor and a nurse. The Bibelforscher, followers of the bible, conscientious objectors, are the regular customers of these public sessions.

— They had built the camp several years before.[1] They were among the first victims of the Nazi regime; victims who were simple souls, wrapped up in a fanatic faith, with hardened features and the large hands of solid peasants who evoked God knows what primitive statues by their awkward, clumsy stance and attitude. Their group, partly composed of Germans and partly of Poles, belonged to a dissident sect of Protestantism: they saw in Hitler the Anti-Christ announced by the Apocalypse. They were arrested by the thousands on the advent of National-Socialism and they worked with all their force to erect the tomb of Ravensbrück: their hands were scraped to the bone as they raised the walls of the camp and the S.S. villas outside the compound; the gravel and rocks made their nude feet bleed. They died by the hundreds every day, at that time, falling from the top of

1. Testimony of Violette Maurice in *N.N.*, S.P.E.R., Saint-Etienne, 1946.

scaffoldings from where some of them were occasionally thrown intentionally.

— Then came the day when, their work ended, they were parked behind the very barbed wire they had strung. When we arrived at Ravensbrück, nothing was left of them except a handful of old ladies who could only be distinguished from the other prisoners by the violet triangle they wore on their right arm; the rest had been massacred. We knew they had refused to do any work which would help the war effort. In the long run, their inertia caused their torturers to pity them; because they were scrupulously honest, they were put in positions of trust throughout the camp; they could go and come as they pleased and leave the compound without being hounded: the idea never came into their heads to profit by this situation and try to flee. Some of them worked around the S.S. farmyard, and others took care of German children. On many occasions, the commander promised to liberate them immediately if they would disavow their doctrine; their refusal was unanimous.

— Unfortunately, they often took it into their heads, on the spur of the moment, not to obey some rule or regulation; for example, not to show up anymore for roll call; nothing could change their minds; I have seen the S.S. guards drag them by the hair; I have seen them fall on their face in the snow rather than give in and, while lying prostrated there, remain completely insensible to the lashes that rained down upon them. Confronted with such stubbornness, which nothing could overcome, the guards, on several occasions, had to throw them on carts in order to get them to roll call. I still hear the raucous yells of the S.S. and the crunching thump of clubs that used to break the stillness of the morbid morning air. After throwing them off the carts, furious dogs were unleashed to attack them; but they didn't move or whimper. These women, whose heroism is confined to the superhuman, make me think of trees about to be felled with an axe....

— One day they decided they would no longer wear their immatriculation number. The commander gave the order for them to stand at "attention" until they submitted: they refused to give in; every morning we caught a glimpse of them lined up in front of the commander's office, standing like totem poles in their voluntary obstinacy. The hours passed, and they could almost no longer stand erect on their swollen legs. I still see their busts hanging forward, their bodies ready to collapse with weariness. They stood up like this for about a week; we don't know the end of the story....

2

The Green Spot

Hélène Rabinatt contracted the muscles of her lips. All the flesh of her yellow face is slowly coming to life. Under the chapped, pudgy fingers that outline the mouth, the lip fibers vibrated; the underlip is irritated and swells at the contact of teeth. The tongue, soldered to the soft palate, is suddenly loosened by little waves of saliva. Invaded, drowned, it seems to float between two layers of thick water.

The pinched nose takes on a ruby color before the nostrils expand:

— What strikes me even more[1] than these cud-chewing reflexes is the trembling that seems to work up from my toenails, making my legs and stomach quiver (the gurgling in the intestines is tragically grotesque in a camp), my arms shake...the whole of the body, while the head, motionless and drooping slightly over the right shoulder, still belongs to the dream it has just had.

1. Unpublished testimony of Hélène Rabinatt. Lausanne, November 1971.

Hélène Rabinatt is tall. Tall, skinny and bent over. Large slices of wrinkled skin flap around her chest and at the base of her kidneys. The hidden brown eyes appear to be washed out by the cold and the tears; they are not much more than two bewildered little buttons. For almost two months now Hélène Rabinatt has not washed. As her "comrades" say: she has "thrown in the sponge," it is not very far from this point to the last stage of downfall: the "mummification." Did she want to surrender? She only knows one thing: one morning she just didn't bother dipping her hands in the washbasin. And there it was! One morning. Some morning. Perhaps tomorrow! But tomorrow she'll be dead....So what difference does it make if you clean yourself like a cat; hygiene, their diabolical, stupid, useless Germanic hygiene. The others said:

— Pull your socks up. Get ahold of yourself. You're on the skids.

She answered:

— I'm tired. I'm hungry. I can't go on anymore. I'm 33 years old, and I'm old. And old people in this camp....A stupid, fat "bigwig" threw in her two bits' worth:

— 33 years old? That's young. That's the age when Christ threw in the towel.

A barracks orderly shouted:

— Shut up, fatty....

Hélène Rabinatt slipped under the humid blanket and began to cry. Perhaps that night "bigwig" and the barracks orderly could have saved her. It was just a matter of a little love, of a hand placed on the back of the neck, of a kind remark or a minuscule little hunk of bread recuperated out of "solidarity." Alone. Alone in this uproar. The yammering of the "bigwig." The insults of the barracks orderly. Alone in this December cold. Alone in the middle of the mob falling out for roll call. Alone in the depths of this desolate dungeon of humanity, in this primitive tribe recreated by some ethnological genius.

She cried in the morning.

Other mornings.

And this morning: the last morning....

— The shaking started again.[1] I am frozen, planted in the earth. Enclosed in a halo. Beyond this circle, nothing....Perhaps a few silhouettes. A fog. That's all! But here, from my nude feet to the unraveled strand of my shawl, prisoners of the circle: all the silence of the world, all the light of the world. My eyes have witnessed this forgotten life for many long weeks now. No snow; but there should be snow in December! I know that, before my attack, there was snow. A dirty snow. The color of mud with flakes of ashes. No snow. Are we really in December? Drops of sweat at the roots of my hair. "My dear, you're going mad!" The crackled earth, shriveled by the frost, resembles the tiles of a sink-hole that my mother made by herself a year before the war. Little by little, the borders of the circle take shape, underlying this almost unreal light, sweetish but spicy and aggressive. A large ring, perfectly placed on the stage, just behind the footlights. A perfect ring, with a greenish spot in the center, very small but well in evidence...so much in evidence—obsessively even—that it develops by branches, by tentacles. Green circle. Beyond, green haze—green eye—green camp—green world.

Also, green dreams. From this acid green with glints of yellow, placed on a brownish base. And this green, these clashing greens, dilute before recomposing behind the prism, before projecting forgotten images, of forgotten places to the epicenter of the eye. Crazy sequences running from white to blue—crib and sea, milk and sky, sugar and a baby's waddling pants—while hesitating on the red of a sucker, the washed-out bisters of partitions, the black of slates on the Rue des Platanes—uncertain and lost colors: lithographs of does in the Brazilian

1. Unpublished testimony of Hélène Rabinatt. Lausanne, November 1971.

rosewood room (naturally, the reflections of the bed
spew forth in purplish-blue sprays, but the delicate does,
chased by a Borzoi, with a neck too long and hair too
short, were they grey, reddish, heather or fern, autumn
leaf? And the Borzoi? Beach sand? Milky scum? Perch
bark?) and Aunt Louise's shawl, and Mama's cat and the
jams, and the greenhouse? and...? So many more
forgotten memories, transparent, as though, without
obstruction, I could stare through walls and off into
infinity. Colors without color: absence.

Immobilized for less than two seconds, Hélène Rabinatt
suddenly becomes conscious of the cold reaching into
her bones, of the racket made by these hundreds of
women running out for roll call. For her, these two
seconds have, without doubt, been the richest since she
set foot on the gravel of Ravensbrück. Two seconds
during which life clung to life; odors, feelings, memories,
"the shakes," palpitations—all the sensations that sweep
through or over the lost woman.

— It was then,[1] at that precise instant, in front of this
green spot on the ground, that I realized I had to forget
all that had ever been before. Perhaps because I immediately understood what the green spot was. This flow
from the past which swept through my body had
transformed me. A miraculous remedy. One had to
struggle. To fight hour after hour, day after day, in order
to witness the fall of the "heroes," to go back home and
hug Lucie, my little Lucie, mama, papa, all the family,
rediscovered and reunited. It may seem highly improbable
that two or three seconds are enough to transform a
woman at death's door. Surrender, renouncement are
sometimes easily made to vanish. And what a lesson for
the others when I tell them: Listen, listen. I was finished,
washed up. If I had had the strength, I think I would have
looked for some form of committing suicide, but it was
easier for me to let myself be devoured bit by bit by

1.   Hélène Rabinatt. Already mentioned.

despair. Death by despair, at least, was certain, whereas
last week a "suicide" was "resuscitated" in the infirmary.
Listen! Listen!. I was dead, but on the steps of the
barracks I saw, lying on the ground, a green spot, a
twisted, crumpled, round green paper. You can't guess?
A green spot! Palish green! Transparent paper. Give up?
It was a piece of candy! That's right, it was a piece of
candy. I spotted it. It's true. I swear it. I tell you it's true.
Believe me, I was there. A piece of candy lying on the
ground in a concentration camp, two meters from a
barracks, two meters from a path worn down by thousands of women's feet each morning—going and
coming—dragging their feet, without any imagination, in
the same tracks. Feet shuffling along in wooden clogs,
wrapped in rags, stuck into high boots...a universe of
dirty feet, deformed and screaming for relief. Extracted
toenails, swollen tissues, pus, blood. And there in the
shadow of these feet, a tiny piece of candy. Green mint.
Mint candy. Local fairs and elderly aunts, school play-
ground, last pew in the church. "Say thank you to the
nice lady!" Mint tea. Chinese salad. Mint syrup. Mint
poultice and camphor alcohol. Mint preserves. Mint from
the peach liquor bottle. And that dry, sharp voice of
Suzanne: "The praline is always too sweet and the
almond inside is often bitter. The soft caramel is too dry
and the hard ones soften up with heat, but, on the other
hand, chocolate candies...." Say, Suzanne, chocolate
candies—and shit! With your kitchen recipes, your sauces,
your sweets. They give us a pain in the ass. One must
never talk about food and sweets to women who no
longer have any taste, stomach, or intestines because
they have swallowed so much garbage while trying to
deceive their hunger pangs. Suzanne never mentioned
the word mint. Why? This piece of candy, there, on the
ground, in front of me, at my feet, I already feel it nice
and warm in my mouth and tucked up into the hole in my
wisdom tooth. On the left. The back left obviously. I
should only suck it once. Just once. Then put it back in

the paper. Forget it. But how can one forget a piece of mint candy in a camp.

— Without doubt, this is probably the only piece of mint candy that has been lost by a guard, a Kapo, an S.S. trooper or a German prisoner who receives packages. Lost? A person must be crazy to lose a mint candy. Crazy? Yes! Even criminal. It's a crime, all this wealth in front of our misery. A crime that should be punished by death. Others should be told that the rich still exist. Rich people with mint candy. The richer the rich get, the poorer the poor get...everywhere. So here, naturally....

— It's mine! I only have to bend over and stick out my hand. There. I bend over and grab it. My fingers open up and I use them like a hook. It's there. Imprisoned. All my fingers. My skin, all my skin, inhales it. It's not possible! It seems....No! It does not seem! I'm sure it still tastes of blood. My thirsty pores are pumping. Quickly, into the pocket. Now it's in the pocket. My hand holds it tightly. I have a piece of mint candy. Just think. A piece of candy. A piece of mint candy. A treasure! The treasure of the camp. Shall I cut it in two? Should I really cut it in two? Half of it would also be a treasure. Yes, I'm going to cut it in two. I'll keep one half and trade off the other half. With half a piece of mint candy, it will be easy for me to find one or even—why not—two slices of bread. Not black bread. Brown bread. I must choose the brown. It swells up more and it seems sugary. With one half I'm even certain to trade it for a sweater. Those who receive packages stock their woolens, but they are certainly deprived of candy because the "superfluous" has no place in a package of "necessities" for one's survival. And the superfluous is the spice of life. So it follows that they would like to have my half piece of candy and I'll put on the sweater. Warm. Warm in winter! At the end of winter, inasmuch as we will have passed our last winter as prisoners, it will be easy for me to resell it. Two parts equal: one for the bread, one for the sweater. That will be the end of the candy. Question: Who is capable of

determining the weight of half a piece of candy? Answer:
well! inasmuch as.... "That's enough!" I say, I affirm, no
one. That depends on the candy. Of the form of the
candy. Of the size of the candy. Of the brand of candy.
Small footnote: "In winter, candy is like human beings,
squat and shriveled. But put a piece of candy in the sun.
You'll see how quickly it stretches, spreads and runs. It
doubles—sure, certain, I swear—in volume." You con-
clude? Conclusion: "I'm going to suck both halves for an
equal amount of time, one after the other, naturally, while
counting...let's say to five, and hop! presto! back into
its paper." Who will see, who will know? Those on the
receiving end of the trade will be too happy about the
exchange to even notice. Five seconds in my mouth will
not take the coating off the hard surface. Five seconds is
not enough. I'll start the operation over again, three or
four times. I'll play it by ear: "Not too much sucked off?"
"No, not too much!" "Good! Once, one little time...."
Oh, what a sublime taste. Don't tighten up. Don't bite
down, teeth. Back! Paper. First half: experience to be
carried out over four days. Second half: Watch it! It
might be better to let a week go by before attacking the
second half in order to forget the taste, then hope for and
re-find it. Therefore, if I've counted right: three weeks:
three weeks for a ridiculous little piece of candy. It's
fantastic, but mathematical. Let's recount.

— Annie! I've forgotten Annie. I should let Annie in
on the deal at least once. Once on each half. Annie
deserves it. Before my attack, she gave me three soups.
Yes, Annie deserves it. I said to you that this candy was a
miracle. I hold off for three weeks just thinking of the
"five seconds," I give pleasure to Annie, and I get at least
two slices of bread and a sweater out of the bargain. All
that for just two little chunks of mint candy. Absurd
world! Ignoble world! To get to this point. This candy's
going to push me down even more. By saving me, it
exterminates me. I'm going to give up the whole idea.
Let's go back to square one. I am going.... Will I have

Ravensbrück. The end of the journey. The end, period.
It has strange, stunted fir-trees. Ravensbrück means
"The Bridge of the Ravens." It seems that when the ravens
in the region are about to die, they choose these
forests.
Bernadac Archives

the courage? I am going....It will be a victory over myself. The first. I am going....

Hélène Rabinatt delicately unrolls the paper. There is no inscription on it. The green sugar glimmers like a thousand crystals. A stone marked with glittering pinpoints. It rolls between the thumb and the index finger. Without hesitation, Hélène Rabinatt places it behind her rows of teeth. From left to right. The tongue, pushing it about ever so slightly, describes its volume. The throat receives the first vapors. Emanations. The jaws unlock. A storm. The temples relax. The molars set themselves. The candy grinds against them. A sharp blow. Juices. Teeth dug in. Holding on. New opening. The cheeks and the tongue assemble the debris. The "coup de grâce." Down the hatch!

The scene involving the "green spot" did not last more than ten seconds.

— Roll call!

A little piece of transparent paper will provide memories and hope until the day of liberation.

A little piece of paper in a pocket, a green image inscribed in my visual memory, a slightly refreshing, pungent sensation on level with my mucous membranes.

— Thank you, little green spot.

3

Discovery

How many approaches to Ravensbrück? And how many discoveries can be made there? All things equal, two sisters do not see, hear, feel or register the same scenes, the same images, the same sensations. The "roads" that take one to this barbed-wire enclosure are so different....

After the stupor one feels at being arrested, the terror of the interrogations, the isolation—the cold—of the cell, the anxiety one feels after being condemned, the camps in which we were first grouped (like Compiègne and Romainville in France) were almost relaxing. Like being liberated from prison. A peaceful community; very administrative, but good-natured and fond of gossip. We had come out of the tunnel. Here, everything is possible: escape, exchanges, letters, packages, maybe even a visit....Departure for Germany is for "tomorrow" and tomorrow may not come for a month.

Tomorrow is now. Baggage. Good-byes. On foot or by bus. Railroad platform. For the most part, the hallucination of the unknown (which keeps getting bigger and bigger) replaces all the other depressive moments spent in cells, and the list of bare facts facing each person—a list of accusations and an inventory of one's true responsibilities—shapes a world in proportion to the indictments, imagined, trumped up or otherwise: work camp, work sites for "youth," crematorium chimney ("but I swear, I've been told, it exists").

The train, the overcrowded freight car, the promiscuity, the heat, the need to perform natural functions, the indecent assaults against human modesty, well-mannered though they may be, reveal the true essence of human nature. A freight car full of goods is like a miniature concentration camp.... It is already a revelation of one's "self." Egoism, friendship, hatred, indifference, one's all, in a word. The train stops.

— After a seven-day-long trip,[1] it is almost with relief that we were led to a permanent residence, and full of optimism that everything we had heard about Ravensbrück's bad reputation was undoubtedly exaggerated.

— It was a beautiful day, that 21st of August when, around 10 in the morning, we left the railroad station and entered a pine wood which would take us to the camp. We were not yet accustomed to the rigid "five by five" and our guards ignored the disorder in our marching ranks. Several women, heavily loaded down with baggage, were following way behind the others—not hurrying at all. After days without air, this morning stroll seemed ideal. We couldn't keep from admiring the lovely, carefully kept villas surrounded by eye-pleasing flower gardens, in which beautiful half-nude babies played....

— Little by little the woods thinned out and we could see the Fürstenberg belfry, around which little toy-like houses were grouped. The roofs reflecting in the waters of a peaceful lake. A few rowboats were slowly gliding on its surface. Suddenly we came upon a prison camp whose inmates work in the woods. Their shaved

1.   Unpublished manuscript, G...H...

heads and striped tunics gave them a weird appearance (these were the first "pajamas" we had seen), but our guards explained that we were looking at German deserters on whom the Reich had taken pity: not only were they not shot, but they were not sent back to the Russian front. It goes without saying that we were quickly informed of the identity of these so-called deserters.

— After walking another three or four kilometers, we found ourselves in front of a large walled enclosure guarded by sentinels. As we approached, an enormous door opened; we were about to enter the camp.

— On each side of the entrance,[1] there was a guard post and probably a garage because several prisoners had their heads poked under the hoods of automobiles. In the middle an immense main gate was wide open, but passage through it was controlled by a barrier which could be raised and lowered (like those I used to see at the railroad crossings back home when we would joyously leave by automobile to go on vacation). This huge door suddenly made me think of the poor priest of Cucugnan waiting in front of the entrance to hell.

— We stop and they count us. Are they afraid someone has escaped?

— "They're count-crazy," one of our group called out.

— During this short pause, I felt tired all over. As long as I walked I didn't really notice how weary I was, but as soon as I stopped I had the impression my legs were going to let me collapse completely.

— We enter. With a dull thud the barrier closed behind us. There, it's finished, we're really in their hands, consigned to their mercy. Without hope of escape. A vise tightens in my throat. Herded like cattle into the middle of a field, we wait, standing up, under a torrid sun. I can no longer even think; I am literally drained, emptied,

1.   Unpublished manuscript, Madame J. Brun.

annihilated; I feel animalistic; nevertheless, a hope as powerful as the weight of the world supports me: to see my mother, because I have learned (news flies fast in camp) that she's here. Oh, if she could just take me in her arms and rock me as she did when I was a child: to be able to hide my suffering and my fatigue in the hollow of her shoulder. But she must be exhausted too. Poor mama!

— For the moment, the only distraction we have is to watch the columns coming in one after the other. They must be coming back from working somewhere because everyone has a tool: some have shovels or pickaxes slung over their shoulders; others are dragging along rakes which make a scraping sound on the coal-like earth. I was thinking, because almost anything becomes a distraction, that someone in that mob out there is going to end up stepping on the upturned teeth of the rake being dragged along in front of her. I was right! At that very moment, as if I had become clairvoyant, a woman got the handle smack on her forehead and let out a scream of pain. The scene was comic enough for me to burst out laughing. Yettoun, who was shuffling along beside me with her head down, looked up and said in that tone of reprobation (perfumed with her Mediterranean accent):

— "So you think this fix we're in is funny; it makes you laugh?"

— Do I offer an explanation or do I let her die an idiot? Oh, hell, to explain what she didn't see wouldn't have the same charm anyway—and, besides, it kills me to talk. Although they were irritated by the burning light of the sun, I strained my eyes to try and find my mother, or friends from Rennes, in this ever-growing massive mountain of women. But without results. Damn! I'll try tomorrow! What I want most of all is to sit down, even on the ground. What a delight that would be! The grandmothers with us are falling prostrate one after the other. It's fatal; we, too, are stunned with fatigue and

hunger, but they don't have our resistance. What gets to
me is thirst; I have been thirsty before, but never like
now; it's awful!

— Then, suddenly, I see her; it's her all right, I would
recognize her in ten thousand. Thin, drawn expression,
seeming to be even taller in her striped dress. Oh, darling
mother, how did you get like this? When I get very near
to her, I must show no signs of astonishment. When I
think of how you looked only two or three years ago; you
were so beautiful, in the prime of your forty years, and I
found you old! What have they done to you in so little
time? I feel only love for you at this instant, the love of a
child who has, and will always have, need of her mother
for protection. You are there, so near and yet so far.
Forgetting everything, I leap forward to join her; I hadn't
taken two steps when a powerful hand harpooned me by
the arm, turned me around and gave me an earshattering
clout which quickly convinced me I should stay where I
had been told to.

— "Don't try again," she cried from afar, "I'll come see
you in quarantine."

And then nothing, nothing more than the emptiness
around; she and others had been chased away by a
guard.

— "Well, little lady, how does it feel to be baptized
into the camp?"

— "If I knew all the answers to everything, I wouldn't
be here in the first place, right?"

— Revolted? I certainly am. All my being bristles,
suffers a thousand deaths by not being able to say
anything. I have the impression of crawling. I am crawling. No! I refuse. Come what may, I am going to rebel.
Unfortunately, it's only the beginning for us. What will it
be like later on? Can I hold together like the others? After
all, why not? I have to, but I also have to beware of
myself, of my tendency to fly off the handle; I'm going to
have to learn to keep my trap shut if I want to survive and
take my carcass back to France.

— After a "pause," which lasted I don't know how long, we were taken to a brick building where we were told the showers were located. We all looked around at each other, and a few of our group even panicked, refusing to go in because they had already heard about the "showers" in Auschwitz. I am also afraid. A fear that goes right down to my guts; then I reassure myself: after all, I saw my mother in the camp; therefore, they're not going to gas us—not yet anyway!

— Here one enters the kingdom of organized theft. Nothing more in the hands, nothing more in the pockets; they take everything: knapsacks, toilet articles, jewels— real or false—rings, symbols of love-pacts, every-thing.

— Good-bye to you, lovely and precious ring of my sixteenth birthday, offered to me by my parents; it was a valuable pearl set in gold—it was the first piece of jewelry I'd ever had that was worth anything. Good-bye, my watch, my little bracelet; had I known, I would have left them with the court clerk of the Roquette prison back in Paris. Oh, well, as someone said, it was in the cards.

* * *

— Here come[1] two women dressed like the "deserters" seen earlier. They are certainly criminals. They are pulling a cart loaded with a long wooden box; there is no doubt about its contents. Although it is a sad sight, it is not a surprising one; if, as it has been said, we are in a camp of 30,000 to 40,000 persons, it is not astonishing that there is a death per day. Maybe two or even three die daily. The little convoy passes the barrier and disappears in the direction of the crematorium oven.

— Then we hear some singing off in the distance. It gets nearer. This is going to be interesting. We concen-

---

1. Unpublished manuscript, G...H...

trate all our attention on it. Into view comes a weird-
looking group of women wearing wooden clogs. They all
wear the same blue-and-grey striped dress; their legs are
as bare as their completely shaved heads. They are
carrying garden tools on their left shoulders as they plod
toward the exit barrier, keeping in step to a German
chant. If their appearance is strange, even more bizarre is
their physiognomy. These women have no age; none
of them are young; their eyes are dull, without expression. Almost all of them have sores on their legs
and walk stooped over; it is frightening to see how
pale and thin they look. These must also be German
prisoners serving prison terms. We have no time to
exchange our impressions. They pass and don't even
look at us—soon followed by another chanting group
with identical characteristics; if there is a difference between the two, it is that their tools are not the
same.

— Then a third column comes along; immediately we
see that they are not the same women: first of all, they
are not singing, and if their garb is the same, their allure
is younger and more determined. Although their faces are
pale and their cheeks are hollow, their eyes glow with
life. They look at us and shout out:

— "French?"
— "Yes."
— "Where are you from? What's the news?"
— Then, seeing a policewoman arriving on the double
with a club in her hand to shut them up, they hurriedly
added:
— "Eat all your reserve food, don't keep anything,
they'll take it. Eat everything."

We were moved by their concern for us; no one had
any further interest in the rest of the long procession,
always the same. We had found a little bit of France here.
It is evident, however, that our situation is less precarious
than that of these Frenchwomen, certainly condemned to
severe sentences on some serious grounds.

— Around four or five o'clock, a rumor circulated among us: "There's drink." Sure enough, two women were walking toward us carrying a heavy drum. Within seconds, we were all on our feet. It was no longer a question of 10 by 10, but a rush toward the precious liquid: women were knocked down and the drum was jostled: nobody could open it, and there was nothing to drink out of. It didn't matter, the point was to reach the life-saving coffee. More containers arrived and were also knocked about. I got hold of an empty can, but I preferred to wait and not get crushed; however, as soon as I could get near, I also began pushing everyone aside to get my share of the burning fluid—and then I drank, like I don't think anyone could drink—so much that I thought I would be sick; perhaps five liters, six liters, I don't know how many, without being able to quench my thirst....

— Towards evening, some large cans of clear soup appeared; they had little bits of sausage chopped up in them; six or eight persons had to share a disgusting mess kit—we didn't even have a spoon. None of us were very hungry, anyway. We had followed the advice of the column of Frenchwomen we had met earlier and eaten all of our food reserves.

— One woman appeared at a window;[1] she was emaciated, the skin glued to her bones, the eyes set back in their sockets, and the head covered with her Kopftuch "kerchief." She was dirty. Her legs were wrapped with strips of filthy paper, all covered with pus, and she was begging. One of our group, a girl from Brittany, called her Skinny. Then others came, one by one, to stand next to her. The unfortunate ones with neither paper bandages nor rags to hide their sores were utterly repugnant. The Blockowa and the Stubowa (barracks chief and section chief) pushed them back, screaming at them not to come

1. Unpublished manuscript, Léone Bodin.

near us. They said we were plague-stricken, but these suffering souls were holding out their mess kits, anyway. On the other hand, we thought the reason the barracks chief didn't want them to get near us was because they were lepers or syphilitics. Then the section chief shouted to us: "If you don't like your soup, they'll be glad to eat it; they've been here a long time and they're hungry." We asked if they were contagious. The Stubowa told us these women weren't any sicker than we were; they had just been in the camp longer, that was all. "When you've been here awhile," she told us, "you'll understand better, you'll be like they are." We still poured our soup into their mess kits and then watched these wretched women gobble up the mess with their fingers, and then lick the metal plates clean with their tongues.

— Two months later we were in the same shape. Our faces and the rest of our physical being had significantly changed. And when the 22,000 from Romainville arrived in Ravensbrück, they didn't recognize us. Our mentality and even our dignity had also changed terribly. Of course we kept our dignity, but it was immeasureably modified now; there was much less pride in our stride, and we closely resembled our sisters of misery. The new arrivals from Romainville asked us many questions: What's happened to you? Have you been sick? Why are you so down in the dumps? Do you have less to eat here than in Romainville (where, if she received no packages, an inmate was in bad shape in any case)? Bits of news were passed back and forth among us until finally all the women in the barracks were whispering and exchanging gossip with bunkmates to whom they had hardly ever said "hello." We had seen and spoken with Belgian women and knew that conditions here were worse than in France or Belgium, and that everything was simply terrible. The discipline or the work? Which of the two was worse?

*   *   *

— After having gone through[1] what passed for administrative formalities (a comedy from beginning to end), we shucked our clothes for the now famous striped uniform—complete with a number to indicate our "civil status." I fastened my overshoes and headed in the direction of Barracks No. 22 which, with some of my convoy comrades, had been designated as my "new home."

— Well before our arrival, I heard screams and the sound of people being thumped.... Had I heard right?...

— I stopped in my tracks—horrified—as soon as I'd entered the building. Later on, such spectacles became familiar, leaving me indifferent. But even today, the sight of that berserk woman, standing on a stool, with her face deformed by hate and, with only a soup ladle, indiscriminately beating a group of women and children huddled around a kettle, is hallucinating.

— This furious beast, who had been given a 22-year term for murder, as people later said, and who reigned in terror over this barracks, was, as I soon learned, Choura.

— Taken out of a Central European prison to carry on the functions of a Blockowa in Barracks 22, she exercized her omnipotence, encouraged by the S.S., on a lamentable cluster of women and children, some of whom could hardly walk. They were gypsies, and all were destined to die; but Nazi sadism had allowed Choura to "work them over beforehand."

— It seems that, as the soup was about to be distributed, the mothers had stormed the large tubs like animals to get as much as possible for their urchins.

— While the beating went on, I slipped into the building's central room with my "companions"; there, on three floors, were the bunks to which we had been assigned.

— Driven half-crazy by the screams, worn-out, shocked by the persecution, the insults, the harassing that we had

1. Unpublished manuscript, Madame Bisserier. June 1970.

undergone, plus the anxiety and the hunger, I had no other desire but to rest—despite the infernal atmosphere of this nightmarish place.

— This short respite gave me the occasion to examine my new universe: the beds were disgusting, smeared with excrement; they had no blankets, and some didn't even have mattresses. The occupants were lying on the bed-springs—which threatened at any moment to collapse (sometimes three people would lie in a space only 90 centimeters wide).

— Windows broken during the fights among mothers had not been replaced. Tiny tots, too weak to move, lay whimpering on their mean little beds, sometimes in the throes of death.

— Faced with such horror, I didn't even react when the owners of the beds that we had unthinkingly occupied savagely knocked us to the floor. It was in a gloomy little corner of the barracks, huddled against each other, that—afraid, incredulous, and sick with fatigue—we finally found a place to sleep that night. The day had indeed revealed much to us about life in the camp.

The Schnauzer

It's not so bad!

Kapo Sylvaine—blond, 30 years old, salesgirl in a Parisian library, multilingual—designates Wanda Carliez Lambert from Loulay for the soup detail.

— It's quite a little chore[1] having to carry an enormous kettle to the center of the camp where the kitchens are; it's not the first time, though, and there's not much to see.

— The alleyways are bordered with ghettoes that are tragically monotonous, as are the pimply vagabonds hanging about; the return trip is no better; on each side are walls crowned with barbed wire....Around the corner of one barracks comes a group on the way back from the potato detail. The women in the front row stare at us. I unexpectedly heard one rolling her Rs, just like back home. Then, in the back row, I thought I recognized (and I made a little sign to her) Rosine Deréan.

1. Wanda Carliez Lambert, *Déportée 50440*. André Bonne, Paris, December 1945.

— No, this soup detail isn't so bad! However, it does involve a long wait, with similar delegations from each of the barracks. If only we could converse! But the S.S. troops, escorted by dogs, smack you without warning.

— Dogs! On the second day I waited near a giant, blue-grey schnauzer, whose resemblance to Lolotte was striking. Monster Lolotte! A Lolotte who curls back its cruel, pendulous lips and seems ready to jump on you— as it is taught to do. No doubt about it: the way the ears stand up, the tail sticks out—and that little white tuft of hair around the throat—make me think of my little Lolotte.

— The schnauzer's master, a very tall S.S. soldier with a scar on his cheek, had him on a leash. We were, as the military say, "at ease." I don't know why I was tempted to do it, but, through tightly-closed lips, I made a little clucking sound...like I used to make to Lolotte when I gave her permission to hop up on the bed. I should have expected the dog's reaction. He turned toward me with a suspicious look and growled.

— The scarred S.S. approached. He belched a sentence in fury. We understood well enough that he didn't want anyone to bother his dog: my neighbors looked at me in reprobation. I asked myself what I did!

— The next day, I was again waiting around in the same place; the animal was not far away and his sea-green eyes met mine. To amuse myself, I looked him square in the pupils and playfully tossed my head. As his master wasn't watching me, I took him into my confidence and silently murmured a few words to him: "Big dog, why are you angry with me? You look just like Lolotte, the prettiest dog in the world. I loved her; she loved me; and you...why shouldn't we love each other?"

— His eyes grew large and he fixed me with a stare. I tried to say something about my love for animals in my little speech. The schnauzer again showed his fangs, but without conviction. I got a kick out of looking at him, looking away, and then quickly looking at him again. Our little flirtation remained there for that day.

— This type of meeting attracted me. Whatever has come into my head? Chinon, the girl in my resistance network with whom I could never get along (we hardly spoke; but there's a long story behind it all), caught on to my antics and manifestly condemned them. What harm was I doing anyway? It's so exhilarating to try and use what little charm I have left.

— Another morning (the schnauzer had gotten in the habit of sitting down next to me), I made the clucking sound again. His head pivots; his large eyes are less harsh as they gleam at me. I'm content for the day. The following morning, still more progress. Two days later, I even permitted myself the luxury of patting his head! What temerity! But he tolerated the contact.

— This went on another two days. I wouldn't let anyone take my place on the soup detail—not even for one of those little sacks which the rich pay for with bread. The gratifying sensation I get from this relationship. This feeling of velvet, this warm life! The dog does not look directly at me anymore, he is playing a clandestine game. A simple wag of the tail when I leave him, or he moves off elsewhere.

— Finally, one morning when I was coaxing the dog in our secret sign language, some of my prison mates stepped, as always, between me and "Scarface." But this time, someone purposely diverted the trooper's attention to what I was doing. Was it Chinon? In any case, my heart sank as he brusquely wheeled toward us and came and stood just in front of me, face to face. He raised his arm, then let it drop; but he took the schnauzer away.

— I can still visualize how calm he was when he drew a revolver from his fatigue jacket and Bang!.... Right between the eyes. The dog rose up on its hind feet before falling, howling to the ground. I could no longer breathe. And though she didn't stoop so low as to smile at the dog's death, Chinon had, nevertheless, reaped sweet revenge for the loss of a dancehall partner!

5

Initiation

Brutal incorporation into the camp for all new arrivals: Everything is controlled. Forgetting and abandoning this envelope which "soils" the nude body, projection into the first circle: "the dehumanization." The attribution of a registered number, of a triangle corresponding to a nationality, to an ethnic group, social, religious, to a condemnable "category" (a rose triangle, for example, for homosexuals), the uncalled-for insults, the imbecilic medical visits and the prophylactic measures taken, the screams, the pushing, the blows, the orders, and the questions asked in unknown languages cannot but break down personalities and resistances. A petrified skin, a "Stück" (piece) of an entire tool kit or machine to utilize recklessly because it is easily replaceable.

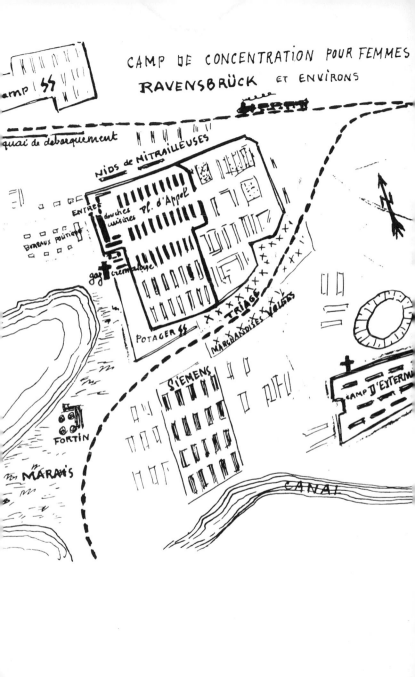

CAMP DE CONCENTRATION POUR FEMMES
RAVENSBRÜCK ET ENVIRONS

Camp SS

quai de débarquement

NIDS de MITRAILLEUSES

Entrée
douches
cuisines
Pl. d'Appel

Bureaux politique

gaz crematoire

Potager SS

TRIAGE

MARCHANDISES VOLÉES

SIEMENS

CAMP D'EXTERM...

FORTIN

MARAIS

CANAL

This map, drawn by France Audoul, a deportee, outlines the perimeter of what was the Camp for Women: Re-education, Work and Extermination—the closed universe of a prison in "Mecklenburg's Little Siberia."
Famot Archives

BARRACKS 22

The first fifty on the list[1] were taken out of ranks and escorted away by police. After leaving the showers, our comrades were directed to Barracks 22, which was reserved for our group. Although I belonged to the first contingents, I had to wait until evening. Fatigue crept over us and, as the time passed, we saw the perspective of having a bed that night fade; it's been more than a week since we've been able to stretch our legs. At last my turn came.

Once again, by rows of five, our cortege crossed the camp but in the reverse direction to that which we had taken the memorable night of our arrival. We were walking in double time when an anonymous herd of women called to us. It was with difficulty that we recognized our companions who had just come out of the showers. The heads of almost all of them were shaved; they were dressed in striped dresses and their nude feet were stuck into wooden clogs. They no longer had any baggage with them; each carried a little bundle. They were trembling with cold. As their column went by us, several cried out: "They're taking everything. Try to hang on to your sweaters." We were floored. What was the reason for clipping almost everyone's hair? We still didn't recognize that the most rational pretexts, and generally the most favorable to our well-being, always concealed a more or less refined machiavellism. Thus it was that, under the cover of impeccable hygiene, our hair hád been cut because it was supposedly infested with fleas.

But they had omitted to tell us that the mattresses which were going to be put at our disposition were veritable fleabags, and that the daily examination of our clothes would never be unfruitful. In fact, I always asked myself afterwards why the camp authorities took so

1.   Denise Dufournier: *La Maison des Mortes*. Hachette 1945.

much trouble to justify their behavior when, all along, we had the ostensible proof that the motives they invoked were a pack of lies.

I apprehensively stepped through the doorway of the building and went directly into the shower room, on whose ceiling large nozzles were suspended. We saw a certain number of our companions there, sadly sitting around waiting to be called into the office where our transformation from human being into convict took place. We were pushed over next to them and watched one of the acts in the show: fifteen or so nude, frightened women, who had lost not only their hair but their personality as well, not to mention the loss of their humanity, shivered under a spray of tepid water. Out of bravado, the young laughed at the revolting lewdness of this exhibition, but the old women could not hide the humiliation that their haggard eyes revealed or the trembling of all their arms and legs.

How could I forget the look of that young woman with the long blond hair (by miracle, it had been spared)? She was holding up her aged mother (who didn't have the same luck). I didn't have the courage to follow them with my eyes when they went up before the camp commander—who had insisted on seeing for himself how the work was advancing.

I thought to myself, the moment has come for us to abandon the role of spectator to take, with the uniform, a role in this drama—whose final act would be our defeat or our victory, our death or our life. But, at the same time this hideous atmosphere permeated my mind, I felt within me the throbbing certainty that another danger, just as deadly, threatened our individualities, our intelligences and the very essence of our personalities.

What good would it do to struggle to safeguard our lives if we were not strong enough to safeguard our souls? Naturally, it's not because you are suddenly put into a dress that resembles a sack, or are obliged to have your hair cut to the roots, that you betray the principles which, during a long number of years, were the basis for your very character. But I didn't doubt for an instant that this was the application of the first article of a system, minutely worked out, which, by stages, had our moral decay and ultimate downfall as its goal. Unfortunately, the future justified our fears.

Were we destined then, to become like the spectres we glimpsed the other night? Feeling momentarily dizzy on the edge of this terrifying chasm into which I had the impression we were going to be thrown, one of Gide's phrases, which I had etched on the sordid wall of my cell, came to mind: "Nathanael, may the beauty be in your gaze and not in the object of your attention."

It was already late when we were told that the day's work had terminated and that we were going to spend the night where we were; once again, we installed ourselves, and once again, blankets and bundles were made into beds. We had enough room, and I was so comfortable that I immediately fell asleep. The next morning, while I was waiting for my turn to go into the little room reserved for the pillaging of baggage, I could see on the wall of the barber shop next door the moving shadow of scissors in action.

The handling of mail, as well as all the work in the camp, was done by prisoners who, in turn, were watched by the Aufseherinnen, that is to say, the German guards, sisters of the "grey mice" which were well known in all French cities. They constituted a kind of army, held grades, were subjected to severe discipline (up at dawn, residence in barracks situated close to the camp), obliged to fall out for roll call, etc.

At their head was an Oberaufseherin whose role was one of general supervision. No sooner was I in the room (where mountains of objects stolen from those who had preceded me were heaped high), and even before I had time to open my suitcase, my blankets and sleeping bag were taken from me; while I was getting undressed, I watched the integral pillage of my baggage: papers, photographs, rosaries were thrown on a pile that was probably destined to be burned; on another pile was what they didn't want; as for the rest (eau de Cologne, linen, a leather belt, etc.,) they were the objects of a lightning raid made by the guards. They grabbed at the items, calculated their value, the weight, the quality, and, within the space of a few minutes, I found myself completely nude with only a piece of soap and a toothbrush in my hand.

Then I was ushered into the barber shop. My hair was lopped off as soon as they saw it. This operation done, I submitted to the second examination—which centered around a particularly susceptible part of my body and which, so they said, was also infested with fleas. This examination was done with a toothbrush....I was still flabbergasted when I went into the shower room. After a quick rinse, I went over to where the clothes we were to wear were piled. I quickly snatched a dress, a jacket, a shirt, a pair of pants, and a pair of wooden clogs called "pantines." I hardly had time to put all these things on before being thrown out of the building and expedited with others, in ranks of five, towards my new residence: Barracks 22.

When I wasn't tripping (I wasn't used to my new footwear), I looked around at the other prisoners, our fellow creatures, our sisters.

It was then that I had the impression that, from now on, we were stamped with the same seal they were, that our future was definitely chained to theirs, that their lives, their suffering, their hopes were becoming our lives, our suffering, our hopes—the punishment dealt out to one unit could result in punishment for the whole barracks, the punishment given a barracks could reverberate throughout the entire camp—and, at the moment when we entered this new communion of saints, I felt, in my confused way, that the last vestige of liberty which we still thought we had was now being taken from us.

Each barracks was administered by a chief prisoner,
the Blockowa or Blockälteste, who ordered two or more
Stubowa or Stubenältesten about who, in turn, were in
charge of one of the two sides of a barracks. Most of
them were Poles. They could be distinguished from the
other prisoners by the green armband they wore on
which their barracks number was sewn. The barracks
was divided into two identical parts: side A and side B.
Each side consisted of a dormitory of triple-bunk beds, a
room furnished with tables, stools, closets and a washroom.

When our little group arrived in Barracks 22, it was put
on side A where a large Polish woman, who appeared to
be very harsh, was shouting and gesticulating at everyone like a traffic policeman. We were given a table at
which to sit—only we sat around it on the floor because
there weren't enough stools; there we waited.

The Stubowa told us we'd have to wait there like that
during the entire period of quarantine, forty days. She
explained to us that we were not going to participate in
the life of the camp except for roll calls from morning to
night, and that our only obligations during this period
would be the last formalities relative to our incorporation.
The prospect of having to work was thus happily put off,
enabling us to gain time and save our energy. The
convoys that followed didn't have this chance; they
multiplied and succeeded themselves at such an accelerated rate that there was no longer any question of
quarantine. We chose our spots in the dormitory: the
barracks had previously been inhabited by Gypsies, and
the mattresses were seething with fleas. We installed
ourselves, two to a bed—which, in fact, turned out to be
the only available heating system because we had not
been issued any blankets.

BARRACKS 26

At the end of the black camp streets is a new vacant lot;[1] the buildings surrounding it are larger. We were taken to the last one: "Barracks 26." Entering it was difficult because our baggage kept banging into the sides of the narrow corridor. We were led into a fairly large room, about 10 meters by 10. Two women in striped clothing wearing red police brassards on their arms made us stand up against the walls. With their shrill voices they screamed "Zurück! Zurück!" rolling their Rs with exaggeration. Then, when our cries of protest became too strong: Ruhe! We are already as packed together as we were in the train, but it appears this does not suffice; finally, we realize with horror that 980 women have to fit into this room. The heat is absolutely stifling; women are swearing and climbing all over each other. Finally, the guards succeed in stuffing them into the hall. It's the most frightening case of humans being compressed together that I have ever seen. In the doorway, a policewoman asks for an interpreter and then, with a strong Slavic accent, made more or less this little speech:

"You are here in a concentration camp. We get up at 3:30 in the morning; we work for 12 hours; we go to bed at seven in the evening. You will work in the camp or in a nearby factory. If you disobey, you will get 25 thumps with a club or you will go into the bunker (dungeon). You do not have the right to keep your personal affairs; all religious practices are strictly forbidden. Do not try to escape; the walls are strung with electrified barbed wire and the S.S. troops have dogs. Oh, yes, one more thing: there are around 20,000 women here, and every week three people are liberated. That's all."

We had not had the time to digest all this when a siren began hurling and, amid screams and disorder, all the

1. Testimony of Elisabeth Will. Publication from the Faculty of Letters in Strasbourg, *Témoignages strasbourgeois,* Les Belles Lettres 1947.

lights went out. The policewoman shouted: Ruhe!
Ruhe! Ruhe! The sentinel outside began rapping on the
windows, yelling: "Fenster zu!" In the midst of this
uproar, the interpreter transmitted the orders: there was
an alert and we had to maintain complete silence and
shut all the windows or their glass panes would be
riddled with bullet holes. Because they were very high
and difficult to get at, it was a small miracle that we
finally succeeded—what with everybody pushing and
punching one another. Ultimately, though, a heavy terrifying silence settled over the room. I was unsteadily
standing on one foot while heavy-breathing and
sweating bodies were hanging on to me and shoving me
about. If I opened my mouth, my neighbor's hair flopped
in. Minute by minute, the atmosphere became almost
unbreathable. We were sinking in an abyss of anxiety
and despair. Outside, the sentinels were still making the
rounds; then the planes passed over, very high. Slowly
the light filtering through the windows grew dim. With
the next scream of the siren, activity in the camp returned
to normal. We learn that the alert is over and that a
second room, similar to this one but at the other end of
the barracks, is going to be opened up. Sure enough, two
hours later our vital living space has doubled: we now
have room to sit down on our luggage; we also have the
run of an overcrowded corridor and the convenience of
two washrooms and 5 toilets. But the traffic is so heavy
that one only uses them in moments of absolute necessity.
Those among us who are doctors have installed an
infirmary in the washroom: there are several bad cases of
sickness, not to mention nervous breakdowns and fainting
spells. If one wants to wash, or use one of the toilets
(only four of the five work), it's necessary to stand in
line. Little by little, law and order is organized: barracks
M.P.s are chosen among us to exhort the other prisoners
to be patient and good-humored. During the course of
the morning, a coffee substitute is brought to us, it's the
first time that we've had anything to drink for eternities.

Toward 2 p.m. the guards with the red armbands reappeared:

— Everybody out. With baggage!

Frantically grabbing her bundles, everyone made a mad dash for the windows and the only door. When the operation was half completed, a counter-order came:

— Everybody out, without baggage!

It was just as tumultuous getting our bundles and baggage back into the barracks.

We were lined up on the vast area of sand in front of the barracks. For an interminable time, an "Aufseherin," the interpreter's aide, proceeded to call off all our names. On these transport lists, we were classed by order of arrival at Compiègne, but here we go by alphabetical order; the confusion that follows is monumental. We're beginning to appreciate German organization. It is cold, the air is brisk, and it's snowing a little. After two hours of standing there, everybody is sent back into the barracks: another battle takes place to recuperate our beds and baggage. Each woman defends her little corner as if she were going to live there forever. The atmosphere is stormy, the hullabaloo of voices becomes a bellowing sound, even worse to put up with than the heat of the room and the odor of dirty humanity. Today is Thursday; I stayed there until Monday night.

Our food ration is brought to the barracks, home delivery! Turnip soup, black bread and margarine. But we have our packages from the Red Cross, which we devour with relish. The policewomen coming and going to and fro consent to stop and chat: for the most part, they are Czechs and Poles who know quite a bit of German. They see that we have a lot of nice, good things in our baggage and begin a little discreet blackmail: "In any case, you'll be left with absolutely nothing. So, give me a scarf, a little perfume, and I'll make it up to you during the search sessions.... If you give me your sugar, I'll hide your watch and they won't get it.... You want to save your photos from destruction? I know someone who will keep them for you, but I need a pair of silk stockings...."

And so it went, for five days. The Frenchwomen panicked and walked into the trap—thus preparing future complications. In the meantime, our suitcases miraculously reappeared. One beautiful morning we were told to go and get them. They were lying around in the sand—broken or split open and partly covered with snow. Anything that looked like a can of sardines, toilet articles or silk underwear had disappeared. The rest would serve to clutter up Barracks 26 a little more, and add to the confused game we played each morning and evening:

"Everybody out, without baggage . . . no, with baggage!"

This would become proverbial. But I blessed these hours when we could get out into the fresh air, where at last we could stretch our legs. Little by little, we came to some definite conclusions: we were not expected at Ravensbrück; so many women were pouring in and out that the personnel was overwhelmed and supplies and material were insufficient; they didn't know where to lodge us, and the workshops couldn't sew enough striped dresses fast enough; they could only put out enough daily to outfit a small group which, as we noticed during roll call, just as quickly disappeared, thus augmenting our vital living space. The first night, I slept standing up; the second, with my knees under my chin; the third, with one leg carefully outstretched on the floor. Inasmuch as I am under the Ws on the last list, I know that I'm going to end up having two square meters of the floor just for me. But the atmosphere in Barracks 26 is becoming more and more unbearable, so much so that simply taking a shower and putting on my striped dress, which, at the beginning, I did with disgust, now becomes something which I look forward to. Then things became nightmarish again: several women among us had looked out the window and seen a group of friends coming back from the showers. Almost all had their hair shaved off. It became the subject of all our conversation. We asked the policewomen about it and they affirmed that only those who had fleas had their hair cut off. Everyone in Barracks 26 suddenly joined a delousing campaign: the few that were captured would never justify shearing the hair of all the women in our barracks. So what is the real reason for this mass head-shaving?

Monday night it's my turn at last. My name and number—27,856—are called. I surrender my jewels and a few hundred francs; they are put into a little pocket-envelope and I sign a series of forms and the receipt. I had sewn most of my money into the lining of my hand-bag and my mountain sack; whatever happens, they won't get it. Then we are taken to the showers. It's a very vast room, surrounded by smaller ones. We are searched and deloused. Because we were so numerous, our guards told us to stack our baggage in the center of the shower room and wait there while they went off to dinner. After they had gone, we organized ourselves in such a fashion that those who had not yet already been searched gave their precious objects to those who had.

When the guards returned, they looked tired and were visibly impatient to finish the chore at hand. One police-woman rapidly explored the contents of my suitcase, contemptuously tearing up a pack of papers written in German. I had done these translations during my two months of prison and they were perhaps the best work I had ever done. She threw them all on the floor, and my books were about to follow when the "Aufseherin" on duty stopped her:

"Are these German novels?"

"Yes, Madame."

"Is that right; do you speak German? Are you German?"

"No, I'm French, but I'm a professor of German."

"Is it interesting, this thing here?" (A large historical novel numbering 786 pages.)

"Very interesting." (I strongly doubt that it would amuse an S.S. woman.) She puts it in her pocket.

"All right, leave her alone."

And the policewoman then showed rare magnanimity. Into a large paper sack she stuffed my coat, dress, a pair of shoes, and some underwear—clothes that I would not be ashamed to wear in the improbable event that I would be liberated. I said to her:

"You forgot the stockings."

She winked her eye:

"Don't need them. So you're French, eh? You'll be liberated sometime in the summer months."

Once again I signed a receipt. Then she quickly sorted through the rest of my belongings. She left me my mountain shoes (work shoes, she explained to me), two sweaters and some laundry. She put everything into my rucksack which she then handed me. I nearly cried with joy. Then I took advantage of a discussion with the "following client" to stick in a few more small items. The rest is thrown on an immense pile of odds and ends which was growing like a mountain at the end of the room.

Dragging my sack I must now pass the most feared test of all: an examination of the nooks and crannies of my body that might conceal vermin; the operation ends with the hair: it seems to me they're shaving less now than before; the barber must be tired! I have the time to make a few observations: the fleas (or the S.S.) don't seem to like dyed or discolored hair. They have a marked preference for long blond tresses which they cut and carefully put into waste baskets. It's my turn. A wan-looking Finnish woman sticks my head under the projector and looks and looks interminably. Is it because she has found nothing? She tells me to go: "Los!" I'm saved. I go into the showers. In all my life, I was never so confused as I was when I appeared in front of my bald comrades with all my long hair hanging down....

BARRACKS 27

October 18 1943.[1] From No. 5, the small barracks
where we underwent our quarantine, we were transferred
to Barracks 27. It was the last one built at the time—over
there, at the end of the camp, in the sand, behind the
barbed wire fence.

Here are the circumstances:

After several officers had made an inspection the day
before, we all sensed a "surprise" in the air. That night,
our theatrical Blockowa—Madame Brandt— announced
that we were to move, triumphantly exclaiming:

"These gentlemen want you to be more at ease; you
will have a very large barracks, a personal bed, good
blankets for the winter, an immense washroom and a
spacious dining room—so clean you can eat off the floor."

I still hear these enthusiastic but misleading words. For
the moment, we have to get out, leaving in the dormitory
all our still-new bedclothes which we owned and used
during the quarantine period and which we kept as clean
as possible; it was forbidden to take them with us. We
quickly formed ranks and marched to the famous barracks 27, passing through a guarded barbed wire door
which had been opened for us. Some 1,500 Gypsies and
Russians had just left the building and were sent elsewhere. The odor of an unwashed crowd filled the rooms.
To our great stupor, everything is putrid; in the corridor,
urine ran as far as the "Dienstzimmer," our general
assembly area; the washroom is full of refuse and
without water; the electricity does not work and the
water pipes are plugged up; the toilets are in such
wretched condition that they cannot be used; the bowls
are overflowing, the doors are demolished and the odor
is enough to make one choke. We had all run into the
dormitory to make sure we got a bed. It's ridiculous, we

1. Rosane: *Terre des Cendres* ("Earth of Ashes"). Les Œuvres
Françaises, Paris 1946.

will never be able to sleep in them; they are broken and rickety and what passes for mattresses are greasy sacks that are split open and alive with fleas; the sleeping bags are unbelievably dirty, blemished with blood and matted with mud brought in on the feet of their former occupants. This is what they offer the "Frenchwomen."

Naïvely enough, we were expecting clean linen and fresh bedclothes; we had been waiting for them for three months—the time to get scabies. I got a case of them immediately, the day after my arrival, and eventually everyone got them; as a result, the limbs of many prisoners were infected and became abscessed—a condition that was attributed to vitamin deficiency; some of these horrible sores lasted until a person's death. We had no cloths or rags to protect or even clean the abscesses, which dripped and stuck to our dirty shirts; the accompanying scabs were torn off while we walked or worked. It was pitiful. We looked awful undressed. Some used paper wrappings, some greased their pimples and blisters with margarine while others brought the abscesses to a head with plaster made of turnips from the kitchen; but no one could help from scratching herself unceasingly night and day.... Soon we were invaded by fleas, and no one escaped; those who labored in the workshop never had a free moment to kill them. At night, after we had come in from roll call, we dropped with fatigue; the lights were not on for very long in the dormitory; and below, at the back, there are beds where one can't see. Above, under the electric light, several prisoners actively crushed the animals between their fingers; however, cries of protest arose because the remains were falling into mess kits below.

With the vermin came the dysentry; it was very cold and we were still lacking water; those that are sick more or less clean their own clothing; we had no right to dry our clothes so we had to put them on wet.

Towards Christmas, some 30 women died in the space of 15 days.

At this time of the year (1943), we were certainly the unhappiest women in the camp. Why did these officers come to see us? Why did they play with our emotions and our hopes?

How could they have been so cynical as to even dare make such deceitful promises? We had not asked for anything, but they took pleasure in trampling their victims; these Krauts respected nothing....

Our suffering and sorrow accumulated. We could not write letters to France; all the other prisoners, including the Belgians, are authorized to receive and to send one letter a month. There is no question of us receiving a package because our families don't know where we are and the Vichy government, like the Red Cross that is in its corner, cares absolutely nothing about deportees. We are being eaten away by worry for our loved ones who have no news of us; we are hungry, more and more of us have fallen ill, punishment has doubled without motive, and we have had seven successive Sundays without soup; instead, we had six hours of standing at attention and a forced march. We pass for "nothing" women, young girls; we are threatened with roll call under jets of water, with the dogs.

During the months of October and November, our barracks overflowed with prisoners. We were more than eleven hundred instead of five or six hundred. First of all, we received a group of "Mischlinge," half-Jewish survivors from Birkenau; then, hundreds of Hungarian, Romanian and Turkish women and children, among the last Jews to be tracked down, ranging from two-year-old babies to tall 14-year-old boys; 33 different nationalities; every imaginable jargon was spoken in our barracks. There were some very old women; six were nearly eighty, three were aged 76; and they used the washroom alongside nude boys.

The lack of hygiene is alarming and every night new contingents arrive; we must huddle increasingly closer to each other; it's easy to say, but we're already seven on

two little mattresses! After the roll call, we run to our
beds out of fear we will find them already occupied. It
often happens! The pushy prisoners are the greatest
offenders; but who could we complain to? We lie down
on the floor, using our dresses as sheets. Any dirty or sick
unknown person can try to lie down on our straw mats.
Those isolated off in a corner who have still not made
any real friends are in a precarious position because, in
this huge crowd, one must be prepared to struggle,
defend and fight every minute. For a month, two young
students from Lyons shared a litter of rags belonging to
an old Jewish woman covered with fleas and afflicted
with typhus; the night they arrived there was absolutely
no place whatsoever to lie down, just a tiny place on the
floor. In one corner of the dormitory, complaints were
made about a certain Marcelle, a loud-mouthed, repugnant girl who once worked in a shady cabaret. One of her
neighbors said with disgust: "You could germinate potatoes on her feet."

BARRACKS 32

In Barracks 32 at Ravensbrück,[1] we had a group of
Belgians from prisons in Belgium and Germany. Almost
all of them belonged to the Belgian resistance movement.
Like us Frenchwomen, they wore the red triangle without
any initial to indicate nationality (Belgium was undoubtedly considered, along with France, to be under a
German protectorate). As I also once belonged to a
Belgian network, I fraternized with many of them. Several, having traveled throughout France, talked about the
different parts of the country they had gone through and
the long leisurely trips they had taken across the Alps
and...above all, Paris! I happened to be in Brussels the

1.   Suzanne Busson: *Dans les griffes nazies* ("In the Claws of
the Nazis"). *Maine Libre* Printing Shop. Le Mans, 1952.

day a Belgian holiday was being celebrated and they were proud to learn that I had seen the Manneken-Pis decked out in his best attire. They were also proud of their succulent delicatessen stores, of their delicious pastry shops (which I so appreciated during my stay) and laughed to hear me reel off some of the names of streets in Brussels that had a culinary origin: Rue des Harengs (herrings), Rue des Radis (radishes), Rue du Fromage (cheese), Impasse de la Moutarde (mustard)....

Belgium was right next to...China. In Barracks 32, there was a Chinese girl called Nadine who, having lived for many years in Peking, initiated us into the ancestral customs of her country; she also told us about the dwarf-high trees in the lovely countryside, the paper houses, the bamboo furniture and the fun and joy everyone had during festivals—such as the one celebrating the arrival of the first cherry blossoms.

Next to her was Blanchette, a poor little Negress who had tuberculosis. She suffered greatly from the rigors of the Nordic temperature and she coughed night and day. Like a child who cannot understand the injustice of man, her large eyes, full of fever, always seemed to be questioning—and naïvely she once asked: "Why did these bad men take me away, and what are they going to do with me?"

She took care of some children whose parents were active members of a resistance movement. She knew nothing of their secrets or activities but, nevertheless, she was sent here to Ravensbrück after having spent two months in the Fresnes prison—where she was not even so much as interrogated.

Kouta

Ｗith a superhuman effort,[1] she raised herself a few centimeters. She lifted her arms like a baby sparrow trying to fly. The blanket slipped. The nude body, more an immense wound, fell back to its hollow in the befouled straw mattress. Two large black holes fixed me with a stare, looking right through me. She opens her mouth, closes it, opens it again. In the hubbub of cries, coughs and the throat-rattles of the Revier, the sick-room, I thought I heard the word: "Kouta."

This is the first time that I saw a woman die. A woman? It could be a man (an old man), a young girl (a child). I think she's Polish. I think she's about 35 years old. I think she is new in camp. She came to the Revier three days ago. I don't even know if a doctor has had the time to examine her. She was put up here on the second floor, in one of the four bunks reserved for "the dead." I don't think any living prisoners have been put in one of these four "death" bunks and survived more than five days.

1. Unpublished testimony of Josette H. (December 1971).

I live on the frontier of the "dead sector." The authorities, who fear the stains, the odors and the microbes—
particularly the microbes—never come around to this end
of the barracks. Instead, the prison hierarchy takes
advantages of this "no man's land" to hide those condemned to die.

— Kouta! Kouta!

The raspy voice drivels on.

— Kouta!

"Shut-up" and "silence" are called out in seven or
eight languages.

— Kouta!

— Again.

Who is Kouta? What does this "Kouta" want to say?
I'll bet she won't hold out an hour, that she won't be able
to pronounce her "Kouta" more than ten times. The arms
rise up. Desperately the fingers try to grip part of the
bunk above, but only manage to claw thin air. Die! The
Pole is going to die. Alone. I'm too much of a softie
to remain indifferent. I have to get up, to get over and
help her, to be present. Will I be able to look into her
eyes...?

— Kouta!

She squeezes my hand. A yellow hand, a refined,
unscathed hand, a cold hand with shiny fingernails.

— Don't move, the doctor's going to come.

I have the impression of seeing her blood running
under the transparent skin. Blood that has almost
no color. Just the blue of the veins and the blood
vessels. And these wounds? These horrible wounds?
Certainly erysipelas....One doesn't die of erysipelas,
even if it's spread all over. Shingles, something else
more serious?

— Kouta!

The voice is now nothing more than a breath. The face
is calm, peaceful. That's how she wants to leave. Maybe
she's able to imagine, to see within herself. A nurse
shakes and pushes me.

— Quick! To bed. If they see you standing up, they'll make you leave but you have to stay here at least another two days.

— But she's going to die.

— It's not the first one. She was already dead when she came.

— She's still alive!...

— For us she was dead. We're not even able to save the slightly sick, how can we save the others? Go on, get up.

The black eyes. The hand. The hand that agitates....

— Kouta!

— One second, wait, she wants to tell me something.

The dying woman closes her eyes. The cheeks puff out slightly. The hand goes up to her kidneys. The nurse pinces my arm.

— Quick!

— Wait! Look, she's trying to give me something. A belt! It's a belt! It's for me.

I take a step forward. The half-open eyelids blink, the hand holds out the belt.

— Kouta!

I know that it's the last "Kouta."

— Thank you! Thank you!

I'm already on my straw mattress, the belt hidden under my thighs. I don't dare turn my head toward the "death" corner. "Who is she?" I can usually spot the face of a Polish woman....She is not all Polish. Maybe the cheek bones....

She "endured" another six hours. Six hours of immobility, and silence. Six hours....And then nothing: a simple relaxation of the muscles. An exemplary death, without any noise. I saw and experienced the split second when everything suddenly ended for her; on the other hand, I have never fully understood the meaning of the thought that ran through me like a sword in the following few seconds and which today—almost thirty years later—I still remember when I look at the belt from

"Kouta." I am ashamed to say that when my neighbor died on that infamous bed so many years ago in Ravensbrück, an immense joy mounted within me. An explosion of joy. Perhaps the happiest instant in my life. "She's the one who's dead! And I'm living." As if the death of this unknown person provided me with an additional chance. "She's the one that's dead! And I'm the one who's alive." Seconds in time which will follow me to my own death. Seconds of oblivion. It's difficult to believe: simple seconds during which man's true "inhuman nature," deformed by internment and deportation, rose to the surface.... Several of my friends from Ravensbrück have "felt" this unimaginable second while watching a deportee die. That for me is the greatest crime of Ravensbrück.

7

Dialogue

Madame de... (the countess): Ladies, we would very much like to go to sleep. It's late.

Louisette (the shepherdess): You've forgotten your gymnastics.

Madame de.... What gymnastics?

Louisette: You know very well that you snore (laughs).

Madame de...: Snore? Me?

Louisette: You do it every night. You snore and you keep your bunkmates from sleeping.

Madame de...: All right! I snore! I forgot the movements.

Louisette: Do it with me, Madame de.... I'll begin (she sings softly). And one and one, I pinch my nose. And two and two, my shoulders flat on the bed.

Madame de...: Not so fast!

Louisette: Good and flat, and two and two. And three and three. I cough three times. And four and four....

Louisette's neighbor whispers into her ear.

— So it's for tonight? Are you going to do it to her tonight? She's going along with it. She's already fallen for it six times. Tomorrow she'll think something's up.

Louisette lowers her head.

— And five and five, I suck in my stomach five times. And six and six....

Madame de...: Not so fast!

Louisette: And six and six....I raise my right leg. And seven and seven, repeat with me, and seven and seven.

Madame de...: And seven and seven.

Louisette: So I won't snore while I'm sleeping.

Madame de...: So I won't snore while I'm sleeping.

The neighbor: Go on....Now!

Louisette: And seven and seven, I fart seven times. Laughs. Lots of laughs.

Madame de... (indignant): Oh! Oh! Ah!

The neighbor: Bravo! You got her!

Madame de...: Oh! It's unqualifiable, inadmissible!

Louisette: It's not so nasty.

Madame de...: Inadmissible, I tell you. I know we're in a pigsty, but after all....I'm not going to talk to you again. Good night!

8

Present Arms!

Mouth. Ear.
— Can you imagine!
And mouths, and ears.
— It's unbelievable!
In less than an hour, "the event" made the rounds of the camp.
— Impossible! Impossible! Who could imagine such a scene in a concentration camp?
— But it happened. I was there. Thousands of women saw it. It was right after roll call, just when the work teams are formed. In front of everyone, and everyone saw.
Mouth. Ear.
And mouths, and ears.
Beyond the camp—you pass the Revier kitchens and the bunkers—on the Kommando grounds:
— Me, I saw. And Bernadette, and fat Louisette, and Angèle. Angèle even spit on the ground. It was disgusting!
— It's unbelievable!

— Impossible!

— But of course you know her: the big tall sour-puss....She's around 45 or 50. Always a little stand-offish....On the defensive.

— A stinker?

— A stinker? A stinker, no! I'd say distinguished. Lots of education. In fact she's a noblewoman. You can't miss her.

— I got it! The woman from Bordeaux! Yes, that's her. Denise de Mar....That doesn't astonish me. And so? Give some details, give us some background.

— Well, it's a simple story. Everything began with "Action Française," and then afterwards, when these gentlemen arrived, she started collaborating with them. She would have sold her family for a superior officer's smile. She profited, and so did they. They first began to balk when she insisted that they arrest her boyfriend: a real gentleman, very "correct," very "indifferent"—politically indifferent, of course—but "very well off." To have peace all around, the Germans finally arrested her "pro-tector." A few months later, Madame de Mar changed her mind. She missed having her battery charged—and asked the Kommandantur to free him. "Very well, Madame!" The next morning the Gestapo arrested Madame de Mar....At the Fort du Hâ, she received certain benefits: she even had her dog in the cell. I traveled with her on my way up here. In the cattle car, she was very depressed. She just couldn't understand what had happened to her: "To do this to me....Me, who...me that..." and she showed us a photograph of her son who is serving in the L.V.F. A very good-looking volunteer! A very good-looking uniform too! Members of our little resistance group were nauseated. That's it! You know the rest. This morning, after roll call, an S.S. trooper called out Madame de Mar's number....The S.S. was escorted by 10 or so armed men. Prisoners in the first row thought it was a firing squad. The S.S. said to her: "Madame, your son has been killed on the Russian

A comfortable chalet in a countryside setting for the
Lagerkommandant and the Kommandantur. Promoted to
the rank of ruling lords, the S.S. install themselves.
All of them have been formed at the Eicke school and
believe they are ready to put Hitler's words into action:
"It is not a matter of doing away with the inequality
among men but, on the contrary, to deepen it and, as in
all great cultures, legalize it and protect it with impassable
barriers."
Tallandier Archives

front." Madame de Mar...closed her eyes, then straightened up. "On my command!" The soldiers presented arms. For a long moment. "Order arms!" "About face!" Finished. She remained alone, then a Kapo helped her back to the barracks. Since then, I have never heard of such an honor being given to a deportee imprisoned in a concentration camp.[1]

1. Unpublished testimony of Madame G...L...(Bordeaux, December 1971).

Dialogue (sequel)

Madame de... ("The countess" and Louisette, "the shepherdess," are back on friendly terms): How do you like my new dress?

A long patched gown, made up of at least seven different pieces of material.

Louisette: For length it's fine; it's even too long.

Madame de...: The collar?

Louisette: It hangs over.

Madame de...: And the pockets?

Louisette: They're shitty, and I mean real shitty....

Madame de...: You're not going to start all over again, are you, Louisette? Must you always resort to vulgarity?

Louisette: Vulgarity? That's not vulgar. In fashion circles "shitty" is an everyday term. When a dress has badly-made pockets that bag, they're said to be "shitty."

Madame de...: It's not possible!

Louisette: I'm telling you. I know. I worked with the Molyneux dress-making house. And Molyneux himself, who spoke like a poet, always used to say "those pockets are shitty." He did.

Madame de...: I could never say a pocket is "shitty."

Louisette: But I'm telling you....

The neighbor: You got her again!

Louisette: No, it's true. I really did work with Molyneux and a sloppy-looking pocket is one that's shitty. At least I've taught the countess something.

A voice: Silence, you bitches.

10

Louise

I said it to myself, and I swore it to myself[1]: "I'll never forget that day"; and today I don't know if it was in June or August. In any case, on that lovely sunny morning, of what was to be the last summer of our long "vacation," we were all assembled for roll call. Louise, the little freckle-faced Belgian, was lined up just behind. Suddenly she grabbed me around the back of the waist with her two hands. I didn't dare turn around. I thought that my large shoulders would hide her frail form from the eyes of the guards, and that, probably "out" on her feet, she had leaned on me to rest. Fifteen or so seconds passed. My neighbor to the right, another Belgian, was bubbling over with laughter just as Louise dug her ten fingers into my back and began tickling me...stopping and then kneading my clothes down to the flesh like a roll of dough. She kept this up until I couldn't stand at attention without giggling convulsively, which brought

1. Taken from an interview of Margarett Breitmann. Lausanne, November 1971.

on hiccups. I tried stamping on her foot and twisting my
waist about to make her stop. I had a pain in the pit of
my stomach and I muttered to her: "All right, that's
enough"; but she kept on: "Just a little bit more!" To
stop laughing I looked at the ground. My two neighbors
were laughing. I had the impression the entire camp was
laughing. "That's enough!" I repeated. Louise drawled
into my ear: "Itchy-coo, itchy-coo; been a long time
since someone went itchy-coo to you?" I was shaking
with so much mirth I thought I'd cry when....Wham...a
swagger stick cut across my jaws and made my facial
muscles prickle and smart. More blows rained down on
those around me. Then the Belgian on the right said:
"Shit, if you can't have a little tickle among friends"—and
the giggling began again, turning into a crazy laugh that
came in uncontrollable waves.

— It's over, finished now. We're surrounded by howling
mouths. Our barracks is punished: ""Two hours!" Two
hours of standing at attention in the roll call assembly
area. Two hours during which, at least every two minutes,
I had to contract the muscles of my bust and neck to
keep my nervous system from setting off another laughing jag. This laugh in Ravensbrück is my laugh. I feel and
see it again. We were able to laugh there. We caused an
uproar at Ravensbrück. I was happy to laugh. I never
again saw Louise after she left on a kommando work
detail....The little freckle-faced Belgian died, crushed
with the weight of a railroad tie that she no longer had
the strength to carry.

11

Everyday

THE ROLL CALL

Roll call is a spectacle.[1] Its colossal and tragic aspect should be recorded on film for Doubting Thomases. But, unless a famine sweeps Europe and the continent's population is subjected to the criminal punishment meted out by the Nazis, I doubt any film director will ever be able to recruit suitable extras for the crowd scenes.

An hour after reveille, the striped columns of prisoners, who were hooted at by a siren at 3:30 in the morning, arrive in the vast Lagerstrasse—which stretches from one end of the camp to the other. Only the Frenchwomen look like they still have a little life left in them, with a spruced-up appearance that sets them apart from this assembly of beggars—from whom they will soon separate. The Gypsies, with their black hair and olive complexion, can hardly be distinguished from the Germans, Russians, Poles, Czechs and Dutchwomen—all miserable-

1. Anne Fernier: *Chronique de Minuit.* Paris 1946.

looking creatures, humped over and sagging under the weight of the appalling atmosphere which continually hangs over Ravensbrück. Eyes hardly visible in a bony, waxy, greyish face, the mouth half open, they cling to little sacks made of rags and clutch battered mess kits under their skinny arms. They shiver in the cold, early morning air, badly protected from the elements in their dirty old, frayed and streaked clothes and their feet stuck into the remains of what were once galoshes or clogs.

The prisoners who have been in the camp the longest wear an unbelievably small three-striped cap, tied under the chin, which makes them look like serfs out of the Middle Ages. "Ah! says our comrade Bella,[1] when I wear that hat, you can say that I've given up the struggle, that I'm a member of this mass, and that my downfall is complete."

Often the most hideous of masks stand out among the pitiful faces: envy, hate, lust, theft, vanity, slander and crime.

The Lagerstrasse is filled with these sinister columns that the policewomen push into orderly ranks with insults and fierce blows. When everyone is in place, the Aufseherinnen rapidly pass by in their grey costumes and black capes and form their own rank. The awful silence hovering above us is broken when the Oberaufseherin comes out of her office. (Under no pretext can a prisoner speak to her.) She's a hefty woman, dressed up like an animal trainer in her grey uniform with stripes to show her grade, a short skirt and high boots. She wears neither cape nor tie and her shirt collar is open—even when it's very cold. As her kepi-like hat inclines sharply to the left, an enormous tuft of fuzzy red hair sticks out on the right. When she puffs herself up, her receding chin disappears into her neck and her long pointed nose thrusts up between her grey, set eyes...she is horrible. She calls to mind the evil ogress in the fairy tales that

1.   Denise Dufournier.

frighten children. Later I saw the Ober of Auschwitz in
action. Her laugh was demential, particularly when she
amused herself by sending prisoners to their death or
reprieving them by pointing and saying: "Sympathisch.... Nicht   sympathisch.... Sympathisch.... Nicht
sympathisch[1]...." I also knew the little Ober, Annie
Schmidt, with the saucy and charming features which
ambition, little by little, transformed into a monster....

The Oberaufseherin struts about with a swagger stick
in her hand, and sometimes gives a little lecture to the
guardians, lined up like black crows (shades of Ravensbrück!), before waddling back to her office. But the
worst of the roll call comes after she has left. For a long
time the sea of yellow, lined faces must remain immobile,
hardly showing the strain that their bodies, badly in need
of rest, are under—even though the narrow, verminous
straw mattresses now only have two occupants each.
Daylight appears, sometimes pale, sometimes in all its
glory, bringing to eyes that can still marvel the first
magnificent, carmine-colored rays of dawn, immense
clouds hemmed with brilliant gold, and daybreak adorned
with supernaturally pure colors in the semi-transparent,
cold light of Baltic skies. How far away France is!

Don't turn the head towards this arid land that drinks
all feeling, keep struggling; the sky is open to every
appeal. Later on, overwhelmed with too much evil and
suffering...you will forget, haplessly, that you are
deprived of liberty....At last, the siren rends the air, the
prisoners move off except for those designated for work.
They must march interminably, group by group, for a
beast wearing eyeglasses, the work director; then they
have to stand in line in front of the sheds that contain the
tools, then get back in ranks again, shovel or pickaxes on
shoulders, ready to go off in cadenced step to some peat
field or sandpile. They walk in rhythm to the chant of the
"inmate" who, by an order handed down daily, must

1. "Likable...unlikable."

express his joy of work; a German chant whose melody is absent and is nothing more than jerky, harsh sounds of despair.

* * *

— Several of us[1] formed ourselves into sort of a "family" and, in order to bear up under the interminable morning roll calls (from minus 28° C. to minus 32° C. in winter), we had decided to take turns telling each other about the kind of day we would like to live through if we were at home. We had to imagine a complete day, and try not to talk too much about "food" (unfortunately, it was hard to resist). From morning until night we described

1.   Unpublished manuscript of Cecile de Majo, June 1970. "Condemned to death, I had been sent as a hostage (N.N.) to the Lübeck fortress where I stayed from October 1943 to April 1944. Well treated, as a political prisoner, dependent on article number 5 of German law (espionage). That permitted me to survive, having had fewer concentration camps to endure. In fact, being condemned to death saved my life! When the Germans felt they were lost, they sent all the hostages (N.N.) to various concentration camps (it cost them less and we would die sooner). Leaving Lübeck, we were first sent to the Cottbus fortress. There were about 200 N.N. women at Lübeck and Cottbus. At Cottbus, there were some Frenchwomen who had arrived before us, and we saw them walking around in the courtyard; they were handcuffed, and had been, it seems, for the past two months. The cuffs were only taken off for two hours out of twenty-four—just to eat and go to the bathroom! They never knew why they had to undergo this inhuman treatment! In this fortress, we were still more or less well treated. We had to weave dried corn leaves into rope for the navy. Instead of that, we made summer sandals for ourselves, and we all put them on the same day for the daily walk. At first the guards were stupefied, then furious, and they wanted to punish us. However, inasmuch as we had turned out such ravishing little sandals—(in color, thanks to some potassium permanganate, black-lead graphite, etc.) they had second thoughts...instead of being punished...we had to make sandals, buskins and slippers for all the guardians...and their families! It was still more enjoyable than weaving kilometers of braids!

walks in the woods (with dogs), painting exhibitions, visits to see the new fashions (for the coquettish), a good film (for the frivolous), a conference (for the intellectuals), a bridge game (for the cardplayers). It was practically impossible to ignore lunch, a snack at the home of one of us, and dinner. Those marvelous days that we concocted and told each other about helped us to get through the long hours of standing in the night, the cold, the odor and in the sinister gleam of the crematorium.

.*.

A stork[1] passed over our miserable ranks this morning and the faces lifted as one towards the bird as it glided, marvelous in the blue sky...under the all-white clouds, and our sunken cheeks blushed because our hearts had beaten faster. Perhaps it was returning to Alsace!...Our eyes followed it for a long, long time....A trail of light was left in its wake and it seemed we could read: "Hope." During the roll call, in the freezing morning, a stork flew through the sky of Ravensbrück.

HUNGER

Who among us[2] has not had a bellyful of being hungry at Ravensbrück or at Mauthausen? Throbbing hunger, hunger that twists the intestines and leaves you without strength and a prey to constant dizzy spells.

I have always had a ferocious appetite; my comrades at Montluc remember it well! More than anyone else at Ravensbrück, I knew obsessive hunger, furious hunger that never dies down and gets even worse at mealtimes.

We had begun by having soup morning and night, the eternal cabbage and turnip soup which was often dehy-

1.   Denise Leboucher. Unpublished.
2.   Violette Maurice: *N.N.*, S.P.E.R., Saint-Etienne 1946.

drated. If we looked forward to Saturday because of the little piece of margarine and the slice of sausage allowed us that day, we dreaded the quarter cup of tepid coffee which was served to us in place of the soup. The ball of black bread mixed with straw didn't last long. It was mouldy, but we ate it with relish! We got to a point where our ration was reduced and the soup at night was definitely abolished. As for the soup served at noon, it was more and more unsubstantial: it was nothing but cloudy water in which the debris of a few vegetables swam. The pangs of hunger were terrible: when we got out of our beds, the head spun and we nearly fell down out of sheer weakness. In those days, numerous women fainted at each roll call. The slice of bread allotted us was getting thinner by the day; we tried in every way to get the maximum amount of nutrition from it; some prisoners said it was preferable to eat it all at one time because the stomach could hold up better with this regime; others economized it, gnawing at it crumb by crumb all during the day. We also noticed that, when we swallowed without chewing it, the impression of being hungry momentarily subsided; most of us, however, ate it very slowly, making the pleasure last as long as possible. The last mouthful was terrorizing; it had the bitter foretaste of renewed hunger; it marked the beginning of the suffering we went through while waiting for the next bread ration to come. On those prodigal days when we had an additional potato, the Russians went to look for the peelings in the garbage cans; but they didn't find many because few women still peeled their spuds.

Dreadful dramas continued to multiply: in the infirmaries, the sick who were too feeble to struggle died of hunger—and their rations of bread and soup were stolen. Prisoners even began stealing from one another; some, who prided themselves on being members of high society, surreptitiously stole food belonging to comrades and even friends.... I remember one, S... (who was later gassed), who, with the skeleton-like allure of a mangy greyhound, used to slump down dejectedly on my bed to talk. She came from a good Parisian family; she had always led a gay life and had had everything in profusion; she was intelligent and refined; she had read and traveled extensively; but in camp, her soul turned into that of a petty merchant and she would have given anything for enough to eat; she later told me that she could not stand being hungry. At night she silently slipped onto the straw pallets of her neighbors, from whom she was caught stealing on several occasions. Everyone pushed her away and jumped down her throat; this extreme degradation (due to the camp and general misery) compelled me to extend to her what little compassion I still had left.

There were even prisoners who went as far as selling clothes from the workshop to their comrades. In winter, a sweater could be traded for four rations of bread. We started a campaign to stop this infamous commerce between Frenchwomen; did a person have to die of hunger to keep from being cold? Such suffering made us mean and pitted us against one another; outsiders were the object of mortal hate. We who had made it our duty to wrong no one began to be perversely jealous of those who had more than we did; we were a hair away from hating our neighbor because, one day, she received a ration of something or other that happened to be larger than ours.

On the days when we were told to take sand over to the kitchens, we literally jumped for joy; we searched about in the refuse for rotting cabbage leaves or potatoes that had been thrown into the garbage; we formed a theft squad that we called "the cabbage-core team"; the motto was: "Right to the Core."

We would have risked our life for a piece of turnip buried in the heap of rubbish that came from the kitchens. The common punishment for "taking" a turnip was the bunker.[1] I was literally beaten senseless

---

1. "The disciplinary barracks, the prison."

one day after being caught with a turnip hidden in my dress.

On several occasions, large containers of sour soup, considered inedible, were abandoned in the camp. Marie-Jeanne gave me the high sign; we ran over with our mess kits and gorged ourselves on soup until we were satiated.

Encroaching hunger, debasing hunger, hunger that makes one stupid: the women talked of nothing more now than menus, and tried to assuage their pangs by copying food recipes. I swore I'd never go as far as that and promised myself to hold to my word. I tried in vain to think of other things; the thought of how hungry I was kept coming back.

We[1] are waiting for bread. It's late; the noon soup was very clear and, to everyone's consternation, the Blockowa has just announced that it might not be distributed tonight.

Near us, in the same wing of the barracks, Andrée is doing the best she can to take care of a very sick friend; she's hardly eating at all and Andrée asks if it would be possible for me to get her a cup of milk.

I reluctantly get out of bed. I don't even know her friend, and to go to the end of the dormitory where the painters[2] sleep is a veritable expedition.

Anyway, off I go with some bread and an empty container.

As I figured, the corridor is mobbed. Continually jostled, I had a lot of trouble reaching my goal.

One woman is making her bed. In order to move about, she put all her stuff in the hallway; she only moved it so I could pass after a lengthy discussion.

At last I reached the painters' corner!.... I climbed to the third floor where they're lodged; they still have what

1.   Maisie Renault: *La Grande Misère.* Chavane, 1948.
2.   Painters received a milk ration to combat the toxic effects of the paints.

I'm looking for. I gave them the bread and they filled my container.

But when I see the beautiful white liquid in my possession, I am sorely tempted....I'm so hungry! If I had just a gulpful, I think I'd feel better and no one would know the difference.

Besides, I've gone out of my way for someone I don't even know and, ordinarily, anyone who consents to serve as an intermediary deserves to take a little commission.

Will I drink...or will I not drink?

I'm still hesitating; to put myself right with my conscience, I finally make a decision; if the passageway is free, I won't touch it; but if it's still clogged up, I'll take just a little sip.

All the odds are on my side because there is still an intense amount of traffic in the dormitory. I have only one thing in mind: the milk...it seems I can almost taste it. Cautiously I descend to the ground floor and look up the aisle....

The passage is free, right up to the refectory. I took the container, intact, to the sick woman.

I'm hungry.[1] It's the leitmotiv, the conversation gravitates only around soup. The hopes of the prisoner are limited to the spoonful of marmalade and to the full ladle of soup on Saturdays. Then she describes the abundance and variety of the food packages received by other prisoners. She is always complaining; she bitches about having the smallest bread ration, etc. All the rest of the conversation is along the same lines.

As with boys aged 8 to 14, the swap is the thing. It's a mania, and for some it almost reaches scandalous proportions. The daily bread allowance is legal tender and a true trading standard. The female prisoners of Eastern

1.   Dr. Paulette Don Zimmet-Gazel: *Les Conditions d'existence et l'état sanitaire dans les camps de concentration de femmes déportées en Allemagne.* Imprimerie Franco-Suisse, Ambilly-Annemasse, 1947.

Europe are the experts in this type of commerce. We French had absolutely no respect whatsoever for comrades who entered into such swap deals. The fact that the bread ration was used as a means of exchange was repugnant to us. The transaction: its sale, particularly its sale, seemed to us to be antisocial and inhuman because it meant taking the bread form a neighbor. On the other hand, we were often obliged to "purchase" with our bread. This operation seemed less immoral to us than the other because it was ourselves who were being deprived.[1]

In certain barracks where food packages were distributed, the women exchanged their bread for a sardine which, in turn, was transformed into three pieces of sugar which was then traded for something else until finally the bread had turned into a scarf—even an elegant scarf.

Those who smoked exchanged their bread for tobacco—and what tobacco! It had been taken from the bodies of soldiers slain on the front and brought to camp by the Ukrainian women who specialized in this type of pocket-pillaging. The tragic end of a number of inveterate smokers was hastened by this passion for cigarettes—not because of the quality of the tobacco within nor the harmful effects on their health from smoking, but because they preferred to deprive themselves of their bread and soup in order to scrounge a cigarette butt and satisfy their need to smoke, a need which they found to be impetuous and impossible to resist.

My male friends told me that the exchange of food for tobacco was much more rampant among men. According to some male camp inmates, a large number of deportees died because of their obsession for tobacco—which

1. In the barracks where I lived, the barracks of the French N.N., the morale was fairly high because we were the most unfortunate women in the camp—not having received any food packages. As a result, we were partially liberated from this mania for swapping and exchanging goods.

they satisfied by trading away their thin, daily food ration.

Nevertheless, we withstood the pangs of hunger fairly well with the help of a little gumption. The stomach was used to receiving the same quantity at a fixed time. We continually had an appetite. At night, it was rare that I or any of my close friends felt that we had a "hole in the stomach"—a sensation that others in the barracks experienced. As I said, we had a constant appetite which became hard to set aside when the hour at which soup was to be served went by and we had received nothing. It was then that the psychological factor of having to wait, combined with the exasperation involved in waiting, undoubtedly prompted a psychic reflex on the stomach which made it secrete prematurely. Coupled with the contractions of the unstriped (*sic*) gastric muscles, this secretion caused a very unpleasant sensation of hunger.

As soon as anyone even mentioned the name of certain foods, a psychic secretion immediately started and our mouths began to fill with saliva.

Each of us used to cite the foods that we would like "to eat if, suddenly, we had the possibility." For me it was: a soft-boiled egg, a piece of buttered bread and well-sweetened coffee. However, it wasn't at all the evocation of these foods which made me practically froth at the mouth but merely hearing certain alimentary words pronounced—like "ham and lemon" which made me positively drool. Was it because our organism especially suffered from a vitamin deficiency due to the absence of two vital food elements: meat and fruit?

Almost at the same hour, my friend Lucienne Idoine would see before her the same image. It was clear as a bell: it was "a large slab of bacon—rose-colored and almost quivering on a platter of red beans." She said she could even whiff its odor. Lucienne announced the apparition of her vision with a: "there it is, I see my piece of bacon again!"—with a mixture of amusement and disillusion in her voice.

Very frequently our dreams took on a gastronomic character; if we awoke in the middle of such a dream, we immediately had an attack of stomach cramps that were very painful. In fact, it was probably this sensation of painful contractions in an empty stomach that so brusquely woke us. There were also times at night when we dreamed we were cooking cutlets and we woke up smelling the odor of the crematorium which gave off a stench that permeated the air—the smell of meat that had been forgotten on the grill! While discussing their various dreams the following morning, several women found they had had identical dreams; some said, "I dreamed that I was grilling lamb chops."

I call another mania derived from the preoccupation with hunger "magiromania": it's the passion for cooking recipes. Each prisoner has her "cook book" in which she scrupulously enters recipes given her by friends. They fill pages and pages of their little note-books (even depriving themselves of a half-ration of bread to "buy" a bit of a pencil). This little book of recipes is her wealth and fortune, and she would not consent to loan it to anyone.

The opulence of the recipes goes beyond the imagination. A good deal of emphasis is placed on fresh cream, butter, icecream, meat, and white cream sauce. The soup-spoon of Madeira wine that one generally adds to a sauce becomes three deciliters, a cupful. Other measures are correspondingly exaggerated. In my opinion, it is by means of an unconscious struggle, a manifestation of our "want to live" outlook, that we oppose the reality of the dearth and uniformity of the contents of our mess kits (rutabagas cooked in water) with a dream of abundance and rich food.

Every morning on our way to work, the Germans in the front ranks sang in cadence with the column's quick-step march while, in the rear, we would elaborate "the menu that we would offer our husbands if we were home." There's such a profusion of meats that the menus make one think of the Court of King Louis XIV. My male comrades confessed having the same magiromania. At the assembly camp in Gotenburg, Sweden, a Paris lawyer—to whom I had put the question: "Were you also interested in cooking recipes?"—replied: "We talked about them constantly!" He then gave an example of what happened to him: while out walking with another deportee, a former cavalry colonel, he repeated the recipe for a chocolate Yule log cake during a period of several hours; at the end of their walk, the colonel looked at him gravely and in all seriousness said: "Tell me again, you say the sugar has to be well beaten in with the eggs, etc."

As for myself, I remember having given several recipes for various kinds of French "pâtés," and outlining in detail my secrets on how to serve game and bake home-made pastries. I also remember a particular recipe for a "soufflé" prepared with cognac which greatly impressed me. However, I must admit that, in general, the quantity of the ingredients used in these diverse recipes seemed to be much greater than the food dishes called for.

— In our barracks,[1] there was a cute little blonde girl about 10 years old. Like us, she had to fall out for roll call...and partake of the infected soup we were served! She used to say: "When I'm grown up, I want to run a grocery store so I can eat lots of sugar." What became of her in this crazy homicidal world?

On October 29, 1942, Heinrich Müller, Chief of the Gestapo's Fourth Service, and Richard Glücks, Chief of the Services Group, received the following letter—signed by Heinrich Himmler:

— 1) As of this day,[2] I authorize the prisoners to receive food packages from their families.

1. Unpublished manuscript, Marcelle Constant. September 1970.
2. *Himmler aux cent visages* (already cited).

— 2) The number of packages that each prisoner may receive is not limited. However, the contents must be consumed on the day of their reception or on the following day. In the event that this will not be possible, the packages will be shared with the other prisoners.

— 3) This order applies not only to German prisoners but to all those who might have the possibility of having packages sent to them.

— 4) Any member of the S.S. who appropriates a prisoner's package will be punished by death.

— 5) Any prisoner who abuses this privilege by having messages, tools or other prohibited objects sent to her in packages will be immediately put to death. In addition, her barracks will not be able to receive packages for three months.

* * *

— Listen, Madame Audibert,[1] you shouldn't give your bread away to Mimi every day. You must eat.

General Audibert smiles at Madame Barreaud:

— Mimi's only 18 and I'm 70. She needs it more than I do.

— But what we receive is the strict minimum.

— I know. I know.

General Audibert died of hunger at Ravensbrück.

— We were a small group[2]: Simone, Suzanne, Annick (all from Brittany), Michou, a tiny woman from the North, and I. Poor Michou was only 18 years old: fragile as a rose, she could not swallow our "succulent" turnip soup so we looked for any potato peelings or similar debris swimming around in our mess kits to give her. One day we got hold of a dessert spoonful of marmalade and

1. Unpublished manuscript, E. Barreaud. May 1970.
2. Unpublished manuscript, Yvette Raymond. April 1970.

Simone asked me if I would like to give it to Michou, along with a little piece of bread—which I promptly did. The next day, after working at the factory, we squatted around on our straw mattresses, as was our habit, to gossip. Judge my surprise and emotion when I looked into Suzanne's "schüssel" (mess kit) and saw a cake— my birthday cake—because although I had forgotten my 20th anniversary, my comrades had not. Bread dunked in "coffee," topped with jam. It was a delightful moment, complete with tears of joy and expressions of sentiment. What I still feel today at the thought of that exceptional day is as indescribable as ever.

— You must eat! Eat your bread.
Pilouka, the young Spanish girl—a child of fifteen— continued to insist:
— No! I'm going to exchange this bread for two cigarettes.
The rest of the barracks:
— Enough!
— Are you going to shut up!
— If she wants to smoke, let her smoke!
But Brice Martinez, the Puss-in-Boots—she measures a bit over 4 foot six and, although she takes a size 36, received from somewhere a pair of old boots size 43— decided to save Pilouka. She insists:
— Listen, little girl, it's easy to understand; I knew dozens of girls like you who chose to smoke. Today, they're dead. We receive only one miserable ration here, just barely enough to survive...not even....
— Pilouka[1] had a fairly pretty voice and she liked to entertain us by singing during "breaks." I had nicknamed her "little black devil" because I don't think I had ever met anyone with eyes and hair as dark as hers. Striking. She slept on the very top bunk, just above me. I must have surprised her at least ten times in the process of

1.   Unpublished manuscript, Brice Martinez. April 1970.

exchanging her bread for cigarettes. It was up to me to defend her. By sheer force of patience and tenacity, Pilouka stopped smoking. It wasn't easy. I was a real cop about it. But I succeeded and Pilouka got back home. In 1945, her mother wanted me to come and see them....I stayed two days. It was wonderful to see Pilouka again.

I don't know if Pilouka knew the poem that Brice Martinez wrote on a piece of wrapping paper the night that she realized she had won her battle: that from now on the "black devil" would eat her bread.

> *To live for oneself is nothing*
> *One must live for others*
> *Who can I be useful and agreeable to today?*
> *That's what one must ask oneself each morning*
> *And at night when one can recover and think clearly*
> *Happy is she who, in her heart, can softly murmur*
> *Thanks to my care I saw on a human face*
> *A trace of pleasure or a momentary absence of agony.*
> *I did not lose that day.*

VERMIN

All measures of hygiene[1] seem to be taboo in our barracks. In our ward, there is no question of going over to the shower-room or putting our clothes in the drying-room—as is done in other barracks.

It wasn't long before we were invaded by vermin which spread at lightning speed. Our foreign companions certainly came from the lower ranks of common people in their respective countries; rare were those who bothered to delouse themselves—and when they did engage in this occupation in the dormitory or in the refectory, they just threw the living lice (which they had picked from their clothes) on the floor with disgust.

1. Maisie Renault: *La Grande Misère*. Chavane, 1948.

Very few had bought a change of clothes. In the Waschraum, a room set aside for washing (at least three of the ten sinks are plugged up), clothes were thrown all around and on top of each other.

Almost all of them had had their facetowels stolen; some had made one by cutting off a piece of their shirt, but many washed themselves with their hands and the piece of soap they were given on arrival had long since been used up; some exchanged bread for a tiny bar of soap, but the large majority did without.

And while some washed, others were content to delouse themselves; some ate the lice.

In this room where everyone pushed and shoved each other about and argued endlessly, where the dirty piled-up clothing created an indescribable aspect of filth, where nude, emaciated bodies shuffled about, punctured by louse bites and covered with sores caused by a vitamin deficiency, the women who had died in the barracks lay; until they were transferred to the morgue, they were unceasingly splashed with dirty water.

Suddenly, the ward women burst into the wash room and demanded its immediate evacuation. Clothes are hastily assembled because stragglers are chased away with large buckets of water.

And when the "waschraum" is finally evacuated and has a fairly presentable aspect to it, the Blockowa, carrying a pot of hot water and a superb bar of soap, tranquilly enters, locks the door and has a wash in peace.

Ah! This vermin,[1] I'll never get used to it, it crawls all over the place. I have lice, but that's not new; however, they are as enormous as a grain of wheat: it's true! and when they run down the length of my body, it gives me a very funny sensation; in addition to the "pleasure" of being tickled all day long, a person tends to shake and twist about so much that, to see us, one would think we

1.   Unpublished manuscript, J. Brun. Already cited.

were afflicted with Saint Vitus' Dance! The fleas, even though they bite, are nevertheless more discreet. The bugs pestered us from morning 'til night and we get to a point where we're so tired of squashing them that we just let them run all over. And the rats—some so large and robust that they steal chunks of bread from anyone who has left them lying about. How many times have we gone at them with galoshes, but these ugly rodents fight back without fear; and they attack without provocation. A proof is that, yesterday, a girl was bitten on the arm. Me, I'm all right, I'm not afraid of mice or rats; spiders are what veritably revolt me. I haven't seen any here yet. And I am forgetting the crabs, those charming little beasts that make you itch so frantically. When I think there is an adage which says that God was convinced of the utility of every living thing on earth! It's difficult to believe!

Black, with a white mark under his right eye. He has his habits and his friends. How can he be so thin when he spends most of his time foraging in the garbage cans outside the kitchens? Perhaps because the garbage cans are also thin and that "savages" are in competition with him for the scraps and peelings. He has ten names, maybe a hundred. He is the cat of the French, the Poles, the Germans, the Russians....

— For me and the Poles,[1] he is "Pubi." A tiny crumb of a cat that purrs; one can hear him far away. No one can pet him. Two sisters swore to catch him and pop him into a stew. They had already exchanged several hunks of bread for two onions and seven cloves, but "Pubi" senses danger, all dangers. Helena, the young notions peddler from Krakow, tamed him day after day. "Pubi" was seduced by the melody of her voice. To recompense Helena, every morning "Pubi" brought a still-warm magnificent rat to the foot of her bed. Despite my hunger and the long discussions on Chinese food recipes, I never

1.   Unpublished manuscript, Yanka Oulianova. April 1971.

tasted any of "Pubi's" gifts. The two sisters ate their onions with the third rat. They traded the cloves: "After all, we're not going to kill the goose that lays the golden egg."

One night, "Pubi" changed barracks:

— In barracks 15,[1] along with my mother and my sister, I also fed a famished cat. Every day it brought to the foot of our bed a rat it had killed during the night.

* * *

SEARCHES

— Achtung![2]

The order burst like a fire-cracker. It's the chief guard. Today she has come up with something new; she is going to make a search. We have to empty our sacks in front of her. Pitilessly she ransacks the objects which we have acquired at the price of a thousand sufferings. Quickly we throw all of our most precious possessions under the tables.

At last she decides to leave. Happily, we re-assemble the few things we have been able to save.

About ten minutes pass.

"Achtung!" She returns. The search begins again. Relieved by her departure, we had put back into the sacks everything we had managed to save.

The objects that had been spared a few moments earlier quickly disappeared; she took everything that looked as if it had value.

For more than an hour the game continued. She would go, then come back and start the search again. It was a tiring, depressing experience.

"Achtung!" Here she is back again; this time she's laughing.

1.   Unpublished manuscript, Antoinette Hugot. May 1970.
2.   Maisie Renault. Already cited.

Himmler inspecting the camp guards. The special-type functionaries are aided in their task of surveillance and repression by prisoners, often common-law criminals, who, like themselves, employ Gummi (clubs) to assert their power.
Bernadac Archives

An S.S. trooper passes in the alley on a bicycle. In a flash he takes in the scene and the hunted expression on the faces of the women. He cannot resist.

"Achtung!" The guttural voice makes us tremble. Abandoning the bike, he jumped on the table near the window and stood there—feet apart, immense and looking down at us cruelly.

Those who did not see him coming nervously turned around.

Encouraged by his presence "the Gracious One" begins to search even more furiously. Finding a little medal that I was keeping, she threw it on the floor and stomped on it.

Earlier she had stolen the little powder compact that my mother had given me for my birthday. It was a precious souvenir that I had spent a lot of time and taken trouble to keep.

At last she decided to leave with her male companion—both of them laughing as they went.

After their departure we gathered our belongings together. It didn't take long to make an inventory: we had almost nothing left: thread, needles, soap, change of linen, everything had disappeared.

Feeling completely desolate, we contemplated our little sacks made out of the piece of shirt—sacks that looked even more miserable now that they were empty!

In a corner sat an aging woman whom we called Mother Gueguen—relaxed and laughing to herself. During the entire search she sat with her hands crossed on her stomach and stared without blinking at the Aufseherin with her little cunning peasant eyes. A few things had been taken from her; but, at least, she had managed to keep, hidden in her belt, the thirty thousand francs and the two gold watches; with an ability acquired only after long practice, she hid them during all the searches which the guards, in the different prisons where she had been incarcerated, obliged her to undergo.

It must be said that I tried many times to point out how dangerous and useless it was to keep such valuable objects at Ravensbrück, but, like a landed proprietor, she insisted on carrying her nest-egg around with her.

And now she was thrilled to see that she had kept them from finding it again.

— There[1] was an elderly woman among us who came to Ravensbrück with some splendid rings, valued at 2 millions. Not wanting to have them found on her during a search session, she agreed to confide them to a Polish woman, through the intermediary of a young woman in the Transport Section—very pretty and, according to her, from the best of families but who, as we later learned, was found to be disposed to entertaining the soldiers of the Wehrmacht. Toward the month of June, the Polish woman came to return the jewels to their proprietor, saying that she no longer wanted to assume the responsibility of keeping them. After a few days, the aged lady had suspicions about the authenticity of her rings. She asked to see the camp commander; the rings were appraised and found to be false. One morning, a group of policewomen surrounded barracks 18 and all its occupants, valid or otherwise, were taken to the showers where, lined up ten by ten, they waited for two hours under a terribly hot June sun. I still have a vision of one of the sick inmates vomiting without stop into the camp commander's begonias; she was taken to the infirmary but died the next day. Finally, we were told to enter the shower room, five by five: undressing, search of clothing and search of the vagina without the slightest sanitary precaution being taken (as a result of which some fifty women contracted serious infections). The result was almost null: a few little objects of no importance.

Meanwhile, the policewomen emptied the barracks of all illicit contents: baskets full of linen, overflowing onto the ground, were taken to the camp commander. Afterwards, we were permitted to re-enter the barracks:

1.   Elizabeth Will. Already cited.

an indescribable mess, some twenty centimeters thick, covered the floor. Everything that had been in the clothes closets and in our sacks had been thrown on the floor and all the straw mattresses had been ripped open; the costumes for the next show (a recital featuring songs from the year 1900) had disappeared; the women in the next barracks told us they had seen a bevy of girls called the Red Armbands dancing like crazy women with feathered hats and Can-Can-like skirts. But the jewels were not found. In the afternoon, as everyone was trying to recuperate their lost belongings, the policewomen returned and took away the very pretty intermediary. The next day, a woman getting on in years—one whom it would have been ludicrous to suspect of anything—was arrested. She was taken away for X-rays: the rings were in her stomach. After "working her over," she was locked up with an "Aufseherin" who was specially trained to recover such treasures: there was no doubt, these were the authentic jewels. The "fence" (who had swallowed the rings during the search) went back to her place in the barracks as if nothing had happened. Her pretty friend went into "solitary." But the next day, everybody in barracks 13 came up before the military court. Although we were in bad all-around shape, about three-quarters of us were declared apt for work in a factory. During eight days, we had no knowledge of what our fate would be: the police demanded hard labor (transporting this and that) as a punishment; the camp commander and the medical corps wanted to put the barracks in quarantine. In the end, a compromise was reached: about 150 women, including almost all my friends, left for a so-called biscuit factory in Hanover. The others, including me, continued their existence as contaminated, contagious women. But just previous to this compromise, some 300 freshly arrived Belgian women joined us. At this moment, the Russian and Allied advances were making it necessary for the Germans to evacuate the camps in the East and the prisons in the West. All the women were pouring into Ravensbrück and this excess in the camp's population became absolutely unbearable. An example: while our matriculation number was 27,000, the latest arrivals neared the 43,000 mark. There was no longer any question of striped dresses: the new "residents" were outfitted with civilian dresses taken from the baggage of prisoners and marked—front and back—with an enormous, brightly colored cross. All jackets had been taken away but, even in summer, dawn was glacial and it became routine to see these wretched women running to roll call dressed in crêpe de Chine—arms tightly wrapped around the chest to keep warm.

12

The Parish Priest

— Have you seen the Parish Priest?
— The Parish Priest? Here?

— You are certainly the only one who doesn't know "the Parish Priest"; where are you from? "The Parish Priest" is Mama Cadennes...she organizes the sessions during which we recite the rosary and, on Sunday, she reads the Mass. I'd like to attend the Mass tomorrow....

— Me too! If you see the Parish Priest, speak to her about me as well.

* * *

The pickaxe!
The pickaxe!
We will form the pickaxe team.
We'll swing the pickaxe
And if anyone falters
We will give her courage.

(Official version)

And when the guards are off somewhere or do not understand French:

The pickaxe!
The pickaxe!
We will form the pickaxe team.
We'll swing the pickaxe.
And on the heads of the Krauts
We'll break the pickaxe.

13

Work

Work!
Like all the other concentration camps (and even those of extermination),[1] Ravensbrück had to participate in the Reich's war effort—notably by furnishing labor for the traditional work sites in and around these veritable cities, in perpetual expansion. In fact, the huge labor camps had been rapidly formed from small squads of workers performing useless tasks of "re-education." Some of these labor camps were so large that they were self-administrating or were attached to other "mother camps" located nearby.[2]

The chief of the labor service at Pflaum, near Ravensbrück, had a huge, almost inexhaustible supply of available workers. Pflaum was nicknamed the Merchant of Cows.

1. By the same author: *Naked Puppets—Auschwitz*.
2. The twenty most important Kommandos (labor camps) outside Ravensbrück will be presented under the title *Women's Kommandos* which will constitute the third and last volume of *Naked Puppets*.

— Small,[1] rotund, greasy spots on the lapels of his jacket, his pantlegs wrinkled up like an accordeon, he screams loud enough to break our eardrums. Our fate depends on his finger as it moves down his gigantic lists of names. Good or bad work camp. Survival or death. But he doesn't choose. He's a machine. No intentions. He has to have his quota. Much more dangerous is the presence of Binz next to him. She has no business being there, but she's there anyway. Binz has her blacklist of names, and Pflaum can't refuse her anything. Binz is by far the most famous personage in the camp— also the most diabolical.

I saw her this Sunday.[2] She was riding an awful black bicycle with large wheels. What a spectacle, girls! The female officer in all her splendor, with grades and hashmarks everywhere, booted, and buttoned up tightly in her impeccable uniform. When she got off her bike she let it flop contemptuously into the arms of a "bike maid" running behind her and, followed by an enormous Red-Stocking aide, she began her inspection. Cuddled in her arms was a horrible, hard-mouthed, stunted dog so small that it could fit into a person's pocket. I looked at her closely. She is pretty, with the beauty of marble; tall, blonde, but with a glacial, cruel look that destroys all. It makes one shudder; and the mouth! Lips so thin and pinched they are hardly visible.

Dorothea Binz was only an Oberaufseherin, "second chief": her superior, Klein-Plaubel, rarely left her office, where she was literally swamped by administrative tasks.

— Dorothea Binz[3] was born in 1920. When war was declared, she was nineteen and a half years old; she

1. Unpublished manuscript, Hélène Rabinatt. Already cited.
2. Unpublished manuscript, J. Brun. Already cited.
3. Lord Russell of Liverpool met Dorothea Binz in her Hanover prison. He attended her trial. *Sous le signe de la croix gammée,* Les Amis du Livre, Geneva 1956.

helped out in a kitchen but she grew tired of domestic chores and, through the good offices of one of her friends, she volunteered for the S.S. and was accepted on September 1, 1939; she was immediately sent to the Ravensbrück Concentration Camp, which had just opened. To her great chagrin, she was appointed to a post in the kitchen—undoubtedly because of her previous experience there.

— She quickly convinced her superiors that she was destined for finer things. Within a few months, she had been given the grade of Aufseherin and it was the crowning day of her life when she put on her feldgrau uniform and strutted about the camp in her black boots, whip in hand.

— From that day on, this brutal and sadistic creature became one of the cogs in the machine that shredded thousands of innocent women; under the circumstances, the women turned out to be more cruel than the men. She lashed out with her club, thumped prisoners with her feet and lashed them with her whip from morning 'til night; she assaulted all the inmates without exception— sometimes for insignificant infractions of discipline, and sometimes for no reason at all—just for the "Schadenfreude."[1] Sometimes she used a cudgel, often a whip, and at other times a belt or even the heavy hand-blotter on the desk in her office—anything that she laid her hands on. The camp trembled in terror when she arrived on the scene.

— Binz once beat a prisoner until she collapsed, then she stomped on her; another day, while inspecting a group of deportees working in the forest, she struck a woman with a pickaxe over and over until the poor woman, covered with blood, no longer showed any signs of life. Then Binz jumped on her bike and pedaled back to camp.

1.   This word, with no equivalent in French or in English, can be translated as "the joy which the suffering of others procures."

— She had the right to send concentration camp inmates before the disciplinary board for the least breach of discipline, when she wasn't thrashing the victim without any form of trial. She also carried out the punishments handed down by the camp commander who, on his own authority, would condemn prisoners to be lashed 25, 50 or 75 times.

— She beat all those who were late for roll call or left them standing at attention for hours; she slapped them—and a Binz slap is no joke: "It was as if a strong man hit me, because she had the technique down to a fine art; she hit so hard that one could hear the sound of the slap two rows back," one of her victims related.

— Binz is also responsible for the administration of "the showers." Stanislawa Szeweczkowa, who had been condemned by Ramdohr to nine showers because she had not shown enough docility during an interrogation session, told how Binz operated:

— "She took me to the shower room. In one of the corners was a shower with a vertical pipe from which water shot out with strong pressure from different height levels. After ten minutes of having the water streaming into all parts of my body, I collapsed and Binz brought me to with a pail of water on the face. Then she opened the door and whistled for her two dogs. One of them bit me on the hand. I fainted again. I suppose I was then dragged to my cell because, when I regained consciousness, I was covered with bruises and my clothes were scattered about the floor.... From that time on, Binz gave me a shower twice a week—every Tuesday and Friday. Each time I fainted."

— Binz had a favorite sport: ram her bicycle into a group of immobile women. They are so weak that, in general, they fall like a house made of playing cards and Binz rides back and forth over their stretched out, inert bodies, laughing all the while. She also amuses herself by sicking her dogs on the prisoners. One day when she was taking it out on a Russian woman, she excited the dog to much that he literally ripped off what little skin there was on her withered arm.

— One of Binz's great pleasures in life was to go over to barracks 10 to see the "nuts" guarded by Carmen Mory. They constituted a veritable attraction—they were put on exhibit like monsters in a circus—and Binz got a kick out of cursing and making fun of them.

— One can only outline the monstrosities committed by this girl at Ravensbrück, from the first day of the war 'til the last. She was at Belsen and she learned her lessons well under the famous Irma Grese. For more than five years she was the terror of thousands of unfortunate women who crossed her path: she was hanged at Hameln in 1947, but this form of death penalty was much too lenient for her.

— When she appeared anywhere,[1] one literally felt a wind of terror pass by. She would slowly walk between the ranks, her whip behind her back, looking with her small mean eyes for the weakest woman or the one who was most afraid so that she could beat her up. (Like almost all Germans, courage intimidated her.) I cannot cite all her exploits; they were daily; but one of them struck me as being particularly wanton and psychologically symptomatic. One of my friends, a woman with a lot of judgment and very moderate, who had been locked up for a long time in solitary, saw this act with her own eyes.

— The classic punishment at Ravensbrück was 25 strokes with a whip, sometimes 50, and sometimes 75; generally, they were applied during two or three sessions, but not always. When 50 strokes were given during one session, the victim more often than not died; she always died if 75 strokes were dealt out.

— After one of these floggings (I don't know the number of strokes involved), my friend took a chance

1. Germaine Tillion: *Cahiers du Rhône.* La Baconnière, Neuchâtel 1946.

after it was all over to see what she could see through the skylight window; the victim was half-nude, lying on the floor on her face, apparently unconscious and covered with blood from her ankles to her waist. Binz looked at her and, without saying a word, stepped forward and stood on the bloody calves of the woman's legs, the two heels digging into one calf and the points of her boots resting on the other. Then she began to rock back and forth on them, bringing the weight of her body to bear on the tips of her boots and then shifting it back to the heels. The woman was perhaps dead; in any case, she was solidly "out" because she did not react to this treatment. Shortly after, Binz left, the bottom part of her boots frothy with blood.[1]

THE COAL

Carefully guarded,[2] shovel on shoulder, our column painfully wound its way toward the Fürstenberg railroad station—painfully because we were screamed at and

1. Upon her arrival at Ravensbrück, a prisoner told this story about Binz. (Fanny Marette: *J'étais le numéro 47117,* Robert Laffont, 1954): "Our neighbor, a young Russian who slept near our straw mattress, went mad, too, but that's another story.... Maybe you noticed the Oberaufseherin, a young pretty blonde woman with a charming appearance, Binz; she's the mistress of the camp's vice-commandant. To please her lover, and to please herself as well, Binz had a prisoner (destined to be punished) forcibly clothed with a pair of soaking wet underpants, fitting tightly around the buttocks; another prisoner, the Russian in question, whose guileless expression clearly justified her nickname, "the Angel of Death," flagellated her comrade until she fell screaming to the floor; then, right beside this dying woman, the Commander, Binz and the "Angel of Death" let their affection for each other take full rein! One day, the Russian (the Angel of Death) fell into disgrace. Binz replaced her with a Polish girl. Our neighbor, deprived of her "varied exercises," went mad with rage and hurled herself at us, while making obscene gestures. Happily, she was taken away. She is now with the idiots.

2. Unpublished manuscript, Madame Bisserier. June 1970.

beaten along the way. Our galoshes clomped on the frozen ground. Escaping for a few hours from the atmosphere of the camp—with its smoke pouring from the crematoriums—and warmed by the walk, my morale nevertheless started to rise as we strode along the road like free people....

The heaps of coal which were waiting for us and which, for twelve hours and on an empty stomach, we had to fill and then push, cooled off my optimism. Of all the work, this was the job I hated the most. By teams of two, we loaded the little wagons that other prisoners would push...where?...This question has appeared to me to be superfluous for a long time now. My horizon, for the moment, is my heap of coal, my preoccupation: my shovel....

My teammate, a Yugoslav, manifestly used to doing forced labor of this type, manipulated her shovel with dexterity....My poor efforts remained in vain....Under the reproachful eye of my companion, I nevertheless applied myself to the job as courageously as I could. I plunged my shovel into the heap just like she did, but I ended up by putting only three or four pieces of coal into the waiting wagon. I was woeful.

The team that did the pushing silently watched my pitiful performance; but they also feared that our guardian, estimating that our rhythm was too slow, might stimulate our zeal with blows. A whispered conversation began among my three companions; I was undoubtedly the one they were talking about, but I would not have been able to understand what they were saying even if I could have heard them.

Vaguely worried, I tried my best to seize some word which would divulge what my fate was to be; the German guard was not far away and prisoners were denounced all the time; besides, I was the only Frenchwoman in the group—my attempt to escape from work having separated me from the French work details that we had tried to form.

Finally, one of the "wagon-pushers" grabbed the shovel out of my hands and pushed me towards the coal cart. It was heavy, and the road was bumpy, but I had avoided a rain of blows which undoubtedly would have been forthcoming from the guard to punish me for not being able to fill my quota of the wagon. Solidarity has no frontiers.

SHOVELING

— About a mile from camp,[1] we were told to stop. The guard dispersed us over a hilly and mountainous area of sand, right on the edge of the road. We were supposed to flatten the entire sector. This was called Planierung-machen. We were arranged in a line, placed just below each other according to the declivity of the terrain. Lying before each of us was a little heap of sand that we had to shovel down to our neighbor on the level immediately below, while our neighbor on the level above filled it up. The sand came from the shovel of the woman working at the very top of the line and, after many stages, ended up at the extremity of the line at the base of the hill. The woman located there scattered it about.

— This first vision remains unforgettable; it is certainly one of the most perfect images of prison work that one can imagine. We had to work without stop. The guard tramped about the terrain and distributed beatings. They also unleashed their dogs on prisoners who worked too slowly. The dogs bit our thighs and, as we were all in a general state of bad health, the bites festered. My immediate neighbors and I took the time to see just how long it was possible to raise one's head and remain inactive: we counted 1-2-3-4-5-6-7...then a guard would approach and scream out in a menacing tone: "Weitermachen!" (Continue!). We could never get

1.   Denise Dufournier. Already cited.

beyond the number 7 . . . from top to bottom and from left
to right the Weitermachen could be heard mixing with
the dry noise of shovels digging into the sand. We had
another little game which consisted of taking as little
sand on the shovel as possible. But if a guard surprised
someone engaged in this act of "sabotage," she administered a first rate thrashing to the guilty party. We tried to
talk among uś in a low voice, even though it was very
difficult.

— Finally, at noon, after this morning which seemed
to be interminable, we got back into ranks and headed
up the road to the camp. The heat was heavy and
oppressive. It was typical continental weather for the
beginning of spring—freezing cold mornings and sultry
afternoons. We arrived at the barracks around 12:15.
Soup, whose odor and aspect were equally revolting,
awaited us. At 12:30, the siren reminded us it was again
time to fall out for roll call; same ceremony as in the
morning, same ranks of women. At 12:45, we were back
at our sandpiles.

— It was difficult getting back to work again, particularly since we were already stiff. We tried to get some
amusement out of our labor by building little hillocks,
tunnels and fortified castles. But the Weitermachen came
at us from all directions. The dogs, tired of always being
on the watch, were lying down half asleep. The guards,
who were probably even more bored than we were,
snarled at us more than ever. We could no longer be
stingy with the sand. A mountain of it accumulated at
my feet. I dug into it vigorously with my shovel while
listening to my neighbor softly recite:

"There, all is only order and beauty,

"Luxury, peace and pleasure."

— The last hour of work was almost intolerable.
Finally, at six o'clock, a whistle blew! We were so tired
that we walked with difficulty. One could only hear
the clic-clac of our shoes scraping along the paved
road.

— Once back at camp, in impeccable ranks like experienced soldiers, one of our group began chanting *la Madelon*. Immediately we all pulled ourselves up straight and began to sing at the tops of our voices. It was the hour of daily "recreation," which lasted until 7:30. The other prisoners watched us go by with a dazed look of admiration. We heard them say: "Französinnen! (Frenchwomen!)" This incited us to sing even better and louder and we tapped our feet to keep time. After arriving at our barracks, we marched around the building just for fun— like we were in a parade; then we went inside. The Stubowa was stupefied at our discipline and a little taken aback to see that we had not the air of beaten dogs. But we were broken, shattered, and half-dead.

* * *

The Aufseherin responsible for keeping watch on the sand detail (she was reputed for her brutality) planted herself one morning in front of a solid prisoner from Toulouse:

— Hey, you, the shovel isn't to lean on....

The woman from Toulouse, who expected to be clubbed, dropped the handle and protected her head with her arms. The German roared with laughter:

— I'm not going to kill you. Where did you learn German?

— A little at school and a little in the camp.

— You don't do badly. None of your French comrades wants to learn German. That's why they don't understand the orders.

The Toulousian was stunned by the Aufseherin's "cordiality" and she muttered something along the lines of:

— I'll tell them to make an effort.

— Good, said the Aufseherin, I will too, how do you say "Schnell" in French?

— "Schnell"? It's very simple...you say...(she hesitated)...you say: "take it easy!".

On the work site, prisoners push small wagons full of sand. Absurd labor which extenuated them to the point of total exhaustion, when it did not completely destroy them, under the blows of guards and the menace of police dogs.
Tallandier Archives

That's why for the last month the Aufseherin in charge of the sand squad lashes out at the Frenchwomen, screaming: "Take it easy!...take it easy!..."

*   *   *

At the beginning[1] I worked hauling sand with the help of a little wagon—right next to the crematorium ovens. It was very hard. One day the wagon went off the rails; the Aufseherin was standing near me with her big wolfdog. I don't know whether she slightly unleashed the dog intentionally or not, but I do know the dog took a chunk out of me and ripped my dress (my beautiful patched-up dress) which, though it looked like any other striped prison garb, I had made to look presentable by tying a piece of string—which I had found in the camp—around my waist. The charming cow of a Kraut with the cute little dog, large as a beautiful calf and fat enough to go to the butcher, asked me to pull up my dress and show where the dog had bitten me on the buttock—my poor bony-looking buttock. She slapped me and told me I had to have my dress repaired in time to go to work the next morning. Happily, my little friend Odette was a seamstress. She got hold of a needle and thread for me and I sawed up my dress. The Kraut wasn't there the day after; she and her dog had been replaced by a superb Dane—very good-looking, very tall and very mean. What a beautiful animal; it's too bad that such animals are trained to do so much evil and wreak so much havoc. Once I saw one that had torn open the stomach of a poor woman who was the mother of 14 children. Her last infant had been born in a French prison and she did not know what the Kraut had done with it or whatever became of the unfortunate child. She was the wife of a coal-merchant and she ran a grocery store. The poor thing lay with her guts exposed to the wind for

1. Unpublished manuscript, Léone Bodin.

several days before she died; two days, if I remember
correctly.

Valere and I[1] had known each other more than a week.
We met at the quarry and I immediately took a liking to
this tall thin Russian.

Exchanged smiles, silence, work, slight coughs,
smiles....

In a low voice, I began to hum "Plain, my Plain"—just
to see....

The result was immediate. First this young Russian
sang "The Plain" along with me, then she sang "The
Partisans," "The Funeral March" and this chant of Soviet
youth from which the "Chant des Auberges" in France
was taken.

Sympathy, slow work, smiles, songs!

It's astonishing how one can get along and exchange
secrets in pig-Latin Russian, French, English, Esperanto
and German. Symphonic music greatly helped to bring
us together. With my mouth closed, I softly hummed a
few measures of the folk songs from the steppes of
Central Asia, or of the crowning of Boris Godounov....
Valere hummed also. She is the only Russian prisoner
with whom I could discuss Moussorgski, Borodin and
Rimsky-Korsakov.

Valere had studied in Rostov. She talked to me at
length of her native city which the Nazis had demolished.
She had had no word of her mother or brother in the last
two years. She is a Communist and firmly believes in
ultimate victory by the U.S.S.R.

Patience, calm...the Volga continues to flow. Let's let
the days flow along, too. The U.S.S.R. will win the war,
only the end is important...everything about her is
coolness, patience, immobility and certitude. When she
works, her gestures are slow, ample and sure.

She introduced me to her four friends:

1. Catherine Roux: *Triangle Rouge*. Editions France-Empire.

— This is Katiouchka!

Thus was formed the team that worked on our little wagon—which Valere had baptized Simon Kapo.

Who could Simon Kapo be?

Intimacy....

— Katiouchka?

— Yes, Valere?

— Are all the French Communists?

— No, Valere.

(Long pause to reflect.)

— Nevertheless, it's in your country that the Revolution of 1789 took place. And then you had the Commune. In Russia, we celebrate the anniversary of the Commune every year. Do you know the date?

— Uhhh....No, Valere!

— March 18. On the 18th of March everyone gets together at my house. We built a monument to the glory of Gavroche and we celebrate the Commune in front of the statue. Lenin is wrapped in the flag of the Commune of Paris....

— A prisoner[1] pushing a heavily loaded wheelbarrow falls to the ground—completely exhausted. The blows from the German guards' heavy belts are unable to get her back on her feet. A heavy wagon, drawn by two horses, is right behind her. The horses refused to pass over her body. Instead, they reared back and then went around her.

— We were on the way back[2] from our work detail. En route, we crossed a column of men. All of a sudden, just in front of me, a young girl broke ranks and, like a crazy person, ran toward the men. The guard grabbed her, dragged her by the hair, belted her with a bludgeon and threw her back in line; called before the camp comman-

1.   Unpublished manuscript, E. Barreaud. May 1970.
2.   Unpublished manuscript, Marcelle Constant. Already cited.

der, the young girl was asked to explain her behavior: "It was my father."

— The work[1] is very painful—particularly since the cold is almost upon us. I see comrades who, during the first days of winter, can simply not go on. With their tired arms and legs, they are extremely hardpressed to push their wheelbarrows full of earth. Dragging the roller is also very hard, so hard that, little by little, our ranks are thinning out and our friends are pouring into the infirmary—from which they will leave only once: to be transported to the crematorium.

— If the work was hard, I nevertheless stayed with it for several reasons. In the corner where we worked there is a little auxiliary kitchen and naturally we "sometimes" had the chance to unload vegetables. This was always a windfall because, although the sack which each of us carried was forbidden, we still carried it around with us to fill with cabbages and carrots, or potatoes. But when this good fortune failed to befall us, we had another source of food: the fertilizer heap. We watched for the moment when our comrades would throw out cabbage leaves and so forth and then hurry over to gather them up along with cabbage stumps which our friends back in the barracks greatly appreciated. It was one way among others to help the weak hold out—and hold out was the order of the day, every day.

* * *

The noise[2] made by the galoshes worn by the teams who worked at night (they had just left) had faded away. After twelve hours of hard work, interrupted by only a quarter hour rest—largely enough time to bolt down the meager soup which constituted our meal, I voraciously

1. Unpublished manuscript, H. Le Belzic.
2. Unpublished manuscript, Madame Bisserier. June 1970.

devoured my "dinner": the piece of bread that I had wisely kept on my person all day long, despite my throbbing hunger.

Harassed, seeking a little warmth under the thin blanket which the cold would quickly penetrate—it was always cold, every night, in our unheated barracks—most of the windows were either broken or missing—I tried to recuperate a little strength for my fight for life which would begin again tomorrow at dawn.

Curled up, my mess kit and my shoes under my head, so they would not be stolen during my sleep, because they would be impossible to replace, I was already dozing off—despite the hullabaloo in this overpopulated barracks.

Suddenly, not far from me, a voice rose. Progressively, complete silence fell. The "Song of Solveig," sung by a Belgian opera singer, filled the room—bringing with it a breath of purity and humanity, memories of an existence which we had known and which we had almost forgotten.

Life seemed to have stopped, hung for an instant on the almost unreal clear notes in this savage universe. All of us felt an emotion which we no longer believed we were capable of; when the last note died away, the silence persisted for several minutes—broken, to everyone's regret, by the whispering of several comrades; the whispering turned into the usual infernal roar to which we had become accustomed in this nightmarish world where, for a short moment, the magic of music had given birth to hope.

FREIGHT CARS

— Unloading freight cars[1] was one job we always tried to avoid because the S.S. trooper in charge was an

---

1. Unpublished manuscript, H. Le Belzic.

absolute brute who lashed out at everyone without reason. "Bekleidung" was the locale where these men brought the fully loaded trains; the freight cars contained everything that had been stolen in Poland, Czechoslovakia, etc.; the contents—which stretched for 200 meters (60 meters wide and 7 meters high)—ranged from linen and the most luxurious to the most decrepit type of clothing to gorgeous crystal, the most beautiful porcelain, though some of it was quite ordinary, to pots and pans, typewriters, pencils, thread and what have you. We called our little work site "the rummage gallery." From this tremendous heap of clothing, we took wearing apparel for our comrades. Sometimes we left our barracks wearing absolutely nothing under our coats. After the long roll call, we remained in this state of attire for almost the entire day; although we were chilled through to the bone by the cold, it was nevertheless prudent not to put on the clothes we were stealing for our friends back in the barracks until just before the work day ended. The most important thing was not to get searched. In general, there were two types of searches: the first took place as we left the work area, and the second when we arrived back at camp; sometimes there was a third search—more severe—which took place in the showers. Our comrades were filled with anxiety until our return to the barracks. One Sunday, when I had brought back a container of machine oil, some toothbrushes and nail brushes, one or two knives and some embroidery thread, it was announced that a close search would be made in the showers in the presence of the camp commander. There was no way to escape. We were a large column of 580 women, guarded by armed soldiers. However, I gave the high sign to the French "Lagerpolizei" and I managed to get everything through right under the nose of the Aufseherinnen. And the whole barracks celebrated that night.

Doctor Paulette Don Zimmet was lucky enough to discover a case of medical supplies in a freight car that had come from the Polish city of Pruskow.

— The case was immediately hidden;[1] later, some of my comrades sorted through the supplies and then buried them in the sand and in large sandstone jugs. This unhoped-for treasure provided us with 2,000 vials of cardiazol (containing 2 cubic centimeters each), some acetylsalicylic acid, a few boxes of "phosphotonine" (an injectable medicine containing phosphoric acid and a strychnine salt) and several boxes of vials made up of an hepatic extract. Each night these various medicines were distributed to a number of barracks by our comrades. We hid them in the rolls of our stocking tops in which we had sewn little compartments for the transport of the vials because we were searched every night at roll call (during which we were allowed to wear only the minimum of clothing): the S.S. were always searching us to see if we were stealing woolens—which we were all doing daily with perfect regularity—to take back to our comrades who, in the middle of winter, had only their dresses to wear. I was even lucky enough to find a phonendoscope which I brought back to camp and hid in my straw mattress, as well as a Recklinghausen machine (used for the study of pressures) but which, because of its size, I could not bring with me; I left it in the place where I worked. I administered the vials of cardiazol to my edematous comrades: to each I gave a vial of 2 cubic centimeters to swallow so they could fall out for the morning roll call; the medicine had a marvelous effect on them. I wonder how many of our edematous comrades—plus those suffering from pneumonia or convalescing from attacks of typhoid, and even dysentery—were able to hold up during the last months, thanks to this miraculous find of cardiazol vials which we distributed to the sick or to our fellow

1. Paulette Don Zimmet-Gazel. Already cited.

doctors who were absolutely without any type of heart stimulants.

— While unloading[1] the freight cars, I don't think I ever broke so many Bohemian glasses voluntarily. We had brought back to camp the entire contents of a freight car full of belly bands and woolen knee pads belonging to the Polish Army, as well as an enormous 100-liter drum containing a mixture of colza and whale oil. We tapped the cask and every night we filled up a tiny flask (also stolen). Our fatigued comrades drank this horrible mixture with relish. To make socks, we filched the most marvelous of materials... rabbit skins.

PAINT

An Aufseherin[2] gave an order in German. Violette immediately replied: "Ja, ja," and got me into the act as well.

I don't understand what's going on but it doesn't matter; I have confidence in my friend.

The Aufseherin led us into a small building where she ordered us to pick up some cans of paint, brushes and ladders; then she led us to another building and gave her instructions. "Ja, ja," replies Violette again! We are locked in the room and Violette explodes with laughter.

— I told her we were landscape painters, so now we have to paint the interior of this whole room. They're going to come and get us at noon; until then, nobody is going to be on our backs; it's the job I've dreamed of....

— Well, I'm going to make a mess of the job because I've never held a paint brush in my life.

— Don't worry about it, let's open the cans.

1. Unpublished manuscript.
2. Fanny Marette. Already cited.

As I crouched down to get them in the unlighted corner of the room where we had put them when we came in, I suddenly saw two nude bodies in the shadows....

— Violette, Look!

We both bent down...there were two dead women.

We called out for help and banged on the door but nobody answered...so, with what resignation we could muster, we set to work painting.

Violette could handle a paint brush pretty well but I got more of the stuff on my clothes than I did on the walls; I looked like a wild savage!

Despite the two cadavers, we engaged in small talk.... At noon, the Aufseherin came back and expressed satisfaction with our work.

Violette showed her the two bodies.

— It's nothing, just an oversight.

She pushed them aside with her foot and then held her nose; they were already decomposing!...

After lunch of soup, we came back to the room and sang as we painted, happy to have gotten out of other work details....

And the two dead women?...Taken away!...

Thanks to our artistic talents we continued painting the room for the next two days while our comrades continued to carry furniture around and spade the earth.

When we got to the barracks that night, we found our comrades very upset. Mania told us what happened: the wife of General L... was coming back to the camp at noon with the rest of the column: seeing a group of Frenchwomen leaving for some difficult transportation task and noticing how desperate some of them appeared to be, she cried out: "Have courage, it's soon finished, they've lost...." The Camp Commander, who was nearby, heard her: he grabbed her and ordered the Aufseherinnen to lock her in the Strafblock.

And the general's daughter had just arrived at the camp. Now she could not even see her mother.

— During this summer of 1944,[1] I made the acquaintance of the guard in charge of the paint squad. She was a "red" German who had been interned in the camp for the last three years. By profession, she was a draftswoman. She spoke very pure French. Her name was Helene. The reasons for her arrest were fairly mysterious, apparently resulting from active anti-Nazism. She had traveled a lot and had broad cultural knowledge. She was perhaps 35 years old.

— The fact is she was an adventuress, seductive in a way (her physical charm was indisputable) that tempered a very Germanic uncouthness, coupled with a fairly violent and capricious character and an exaggerated penchant for admiring the impeccable parades around the camp which work details were ordered to put on....

— What exactly was her role in the camp? A lot of rumors, both false and true, circulated about her. One day, one of our comrades was, by chance, inserted into her work squad. It was both an innovation and a revolution because the paint gang, the Malerkolonne (which usually consisted of twenty Stücke), had been reserved for "black" Germans, or the Bellpolitik, up 'til now. Inasmuch as the work was considered to be Schwerarbeit (hard work), prisoners who appeared to be solid and robust were recruited. These Germans were veritable monsters, with enormous builds; and they swore like sailors. Therefore, when they saw that a Frenchwoman had been inserted into "their" column, they welcomed her by giving her the cold shoulder. On the other hand, the column chief immediately appreciated this new recruit, the first normal prisoner that she had ever had under her orders. The two rapidly became fast friends, to the daily, increasing anger of the other painters.

— This work column was not made up of little innocent women: traditionally, they all ended, one day or

1.   Denise Dufournier. Already cited.

another, in the Strafblock—either because they had caused some scandal in their encounters with male prisoners, or because they had been caught red-handed in the act of stealing, or because their Lesbian-like advances had become a little too ostentatious.

— The work was quite varied: during the good weather they painted the exterior of the barracks, the "green," as they said, or else the interior of the barracks, the kitchens, the showers, and particularly the barracks housing the sick—whose number was always increasing; sometimes they had more "delicate" work to do—like painting the operating rooms, S.S. apartments, etc.; some had less comfortable projects—like whitewashing the stables or cellars. At other times, they would be put on work details responsible for transporting heavy objects or doing some similar hard work: helping the camp carpenter or the masons, whose workshops were next to the paint shop. A Meister supervised the technical work ordered by the "Chief of the Camp's work projects." The work squad even had an automobile at its disposal. The principal advantage of being on this work detail was that, if the project to be completed was within the confines of the camp, no guard was present. The overseer was the only one responsible, but she usually stayed in the shop and only came to the work site from time to time—thus giving us a fair amount of liberty; abuses and accompanying periods of punishment inevitably resulted from such comparative liberty. The second advantage in being on the paint squad was that, in order to avoid any eventual intoxication caused by paint fumes, each Stück was given a liter of milk daily. They couldn't have shown more concern for our personal welfare....

— As soon as our comrade Suzanne had been accepted, Helene, despite the internal difficulties which cropped up for her, had only one idea: recruit other Frenchwomen.

— At the end of September, she proposed to take me in with the other workers—which could only be done clandestinely because the Work Bureau had it in for her and opposed any new non-German recruit.

— The life of an "all-around worker" became more and more hazardous; and the transportation of any and all objects doubled in size and difficulty. In addition, the seasonal work which I was doing was entering the dead season. If, on the one hand, I had less liberty, on the other hand I was going to benefit from the inactivity which the days of bad weather ahead and the grade of being a fixed laborer would bring me. There were only 13 Stücke left on the paint squad (from time to time, several Bellpolitik were sent home). Finally, the only beneficiaries of this work were the prisoners, whose barracks—thanks to our whitewashing efforts—would be a little less sordid.

— Helene secretly inscribed me at the Work Office. I put on a pair of overalls, a large apron made of canvas, got hold of a bucket and a brush and entered the ranks of the paint squad.

— We were in the month of September. The Germans, my future comrades, gave me a very cold welcome and put into operation a plan to expel me immediately. They plotted all day long; they pretended that my inscription was illegal and they threatened to denounce me; and the word Strafblock periodically came into their conversation—an obvious effort to intimidate me. During the work period, they either ostracized me completely, under the pretense that I was incapable, or else they used tactics which imperiled my health, if not my life. For example, a beam would suddenly fall on my head, a firmly-fixed scaffolding would brutally collapse, or a ladder would suddenly lose its rungs...but the god who watches over the innocent was protecting me. I always managed to grab hold of something to keep from falling, or just stepped out of the way in the nick of time (as if by miracle) to escape being hit by a pail that someone had "accidently" knocked over.

— I began my career in the toilets and in the washrooms of the Betrieb. Naturally, I was given the most fastidious work: I did all the "leftovers." For long periods of time the Germans were either absent or just stood immobile on their ladders, leaving their brushes in the paint cans. If I tried to rest for a few minutes, they started threatening and tongue-lashing me. They really couldn't see me at all. I had the impression I was in the presence of ferocious animals devoid of all reasoning. When I got exasperated with their yelling and screaming, I bellowed louder than they did and, even though I was only a lone voice among them, they calmed down for a while.

— The head of the paint gang was called Erna, a real bandit. It was impossible not to imagine that, sometime in the past, she had killed her father and mother. When not in prison she had worked as a farmer. A roadhouse servant named Hilda never stopped talking about her licentious adventures, with accompanying gestures. A future prostitute, Lisbeth, 18 years old, had the stigmas of all known vices etched on her face. She was constantly humming languorous tunes. She was Erna's adjutant and did a lot of the stealing and beating-up for her boss. Another brute, Lotte, hated me in particular; she had a baleful, bestial appearance which was accentuated by a voice that uttered raucous and inarticulate sounds.

— The spoiled child of the column was Francisca whose love affair with a toothless "Butch" lesbian was closely followed by her comrades. (The "Butch" had the "cross of cows" engraved on her forehead with a knife, which was supposed to attest to the "butch's" fidelity.) Not a day went by that Francisca did not reveal the latest news about her sentimental entanglement. Of all the painters, she was certainly the most civilized and wittiest. Perched up on her ladder, Francisca would act out some comedy, using her paint brush as a partner. Then there was big Hilda, whom I baptized "Hilda the Terror." She was dirty, brutal and a thief, but in the tragic circumstances prevailing at the end of the war, she gave proof of a certain measure of understanding. These were the co-workers whom I remember best, for one reason or another.

— After the first Frenchwoman (Suzanne Legrand) had been put on the paint squad, Helene managed to bring in Christiane de Cuvervilley. We were now three. When we had the chance to work on the same site, we didn't give a hang for the hateful remarks made by our German co-workers. We sang and jabbered; the curious human animals who worked alongside us were the object of interminable psychological discussions. It must be said that, even in the corridors of the Palace of Justice in Paris, where some of the lowest elements of society can be found pacing up and down, I have never met anyone comparable. The three of us clung together. We worked better than they did. The Meister completely adopted us.

THE FACTORY

A camp within the camp.[1] Nothing lives, except for the women transformed into machines. The wooden barracks, the cement-lined workshops, the cement walls as well, the earth covered with gravel and sand: not a plant, not a tree, not a bird—except these enormous grey and black ravens which crow unceasingly. Beyond, behind the cement walls, a few scruffy pine trees—constantly tormented by the brisk winds. The only thing that we often had the time to admire was the beauty of the sky; the sunrises and the sunsets were the only superb things in the region.

In this "Industriehof" camp, there were five barracks. Barracks Nos. 1, 2, 3 and 5 were reserved for workers; No. 4 housed the "Kolonnenaufseherinnen" (the heads of each workshop), as well as the work team chiefs. Each barracks was separated into five rooms; each had 120 to

1. Unpublished manuscript, Madeleine Perrin. June 1970.

140 women, two or three stools and a table for decoration. Our life was as follows: stand-up roll call, work, sitting or standing—depending on the task at hand; the rest of the time, on all fours—like the "ancestors from whom Darwin said we evolved"; then to our straw mats—on or under which we dressed, ate, slept, and kept our shoes and clothes, etc. Everything had to disappear from sight if we had the right to sleep during the day because, if there was an official visit by some "tinhorn," everything had to be in its place (there was always this concern for how the barracks looked). Our dear room chief, "Marichou," amiably said to us: "Ladies, take down everything that's hanging" when our coats were hanging on a nail; the Russians and Germans, however, were permitted to leave their togs hanging up.

The work hours remained the same until January 1945. I must give you an idea of what my work entailed in 1943 when I was put in the dressmaking shop. I was assigned to workshop No. 2 where I stayed until March 1945. I was told to operate an electric sewing machine (which I had never seen before) and, under the threat of being beaten up, I forced myself to succeed in turning out the work required of me. I had to sew cuffs on the shirts of male prisoners—240 sleeves, either at night or during the day; almost every month the quantity increased. In October, 1943, I put pockets on white capes to be worn by the Wehrmacht soldiers fighting on the Russian front. I had to do 120 pockets, each with two flaps, out of an artificial silk material. As of December, 1943, I was shown how to put sleeves on dresses and jackets for prisoners, the famous striped uniforms. During the first two months, I had to put on 150 sleeves, night or day, and again the quantity required rose each month. In July, 1944, I had to sew on 460 sleeves, always either at night or by day; in October, 1944, the number dropped to 440—which turns out that I must have sewn some 150,000 sleeves during the time of my incarceration. If we did not meet our work quota, for example, if a

machine broke down or something else happened, the
entire team (the gang, as we used to say) was punished:
this is how one could get in trouble with the other
prisoners, that is to say, if one prisoner worked slower
than the others (all punishment was always collective);
the first beating was given by the workshop Aufseherin,
then by the S.S. on duty; another form of punishment
was to take away our "breaks," or have us stand in ranks
for an hour or two by the workshop door—instead of
going to the barracks to sleep. If a quota was far from
being reached, due to, for example, a piece of the
machine breaking by accident, it was considered to be a
clear case of sabotage—as was the theft of a piece of
material or thread. "Corrective measures" were meted out
by the workshop boss, by this savage called "Binder," or
by another brute called "Roslow"; then a report was
made to the camp commander: punishment was usually
two or three months in the "Strafblock."

Since the middle of 1944, we received a food supplement composed of a piece of buttered bread and a little
slice of sausage, or a substitute for pâté, which was
normally distributed during work hours—either at noon
or at midnight—on condition that our work quota had
been met by that time; if not, we didn't get the bread
until the end of the day, or the night; and if we still
hadn't reached our quota at the end of the work period,
the food ration was either abolished or given to another
team.

Our comrades working in the shops that made the S.S.
uniforms were worse off than we were; the shop bosses
were even more fussy about the military uniforms than
those destined to be worn by prisoners, and the work
that went into making the former was a lot more difficult
to sew than for the latter.

I saw women struck by men in the most barbaric
manner—kicked with boots—hit by fists and even stools,
and smacked across the face with everything from a pair
of shorts to a jacket. At all costs one had to avoid falling

down. The Frenchwomen had by far the most guts among the prisoners when these dirty Krauts began their beatings. The Frenchwomen did not cry, even if they were suffering under the blows raining down upon them; they paled with rage and pain, but tightened their jaws and fists instead of crying.

I once saw the furious "Roslow" strike a Polish girl in the workshop; he made her come forward because she was not putting the pockets on the prisoners' pants correctly; he struck her square in the face, so hard that she had a nasal hemorrhage; one would have thought her dress had been dyed red. She lost consciousness and collapsed; he thought she was just putting on an act and he grabbed her by the arm and pulled her up. She collapsed again. He had someone go get a pail of cold water. The guard on duty hesitated to douse her. So he took the bucket and poured it on the Polish girl. She came to and then he left, white with rage. The work chief had her taken to the infirmary where they wrapped a bandage around her head. It was about 4:30 in the afternoon. She went back to her barracks. The next morning, she showed up for work. Roslow arrived very early and went directly up to her machine to inspect her work. He reproached her for having herself bandaged up "...when a person works as badly as you do...."; then he slapped her across the face several times. The hemorrhage began again but he forbade her to go wash....

Workshop No. 1 was still worse. A minimum of 700 women were employed there—most of them making S.S. military equipment: trousers, jackets, coats, gloves and camouflage-colored jackets and pants. Two permanent workshop chiefs and some auxiliary members of the S.S. were responsable for two teams each—in addition to the Aufseherinnen who had the right to walk into any workshop. They walked in and hit anyone they felt like. For a certain period of time, we led a life of fright from morning 'til night.

— At the beginning of summer,[1] I was put on the "Betrieb"—thus escaping the "Sandpile" squad.... For me it was a minimum of vital space; at last I would be able to eat in relative peace and be relieved of the anxiety that I would suddenly be called to join the work detail transporting heavy objects. My new "profession" obliged me to work with rags: I cut up military clothes that were dirty, dusty, bloody and verminous; some of the material was so thin and frail that it could be seen through. And there was worse.[2] I was seated at a table full of Germans, and I had to put up with the dust and their equally filthy conversation. Two tables away worked Geneviève de Gaulle—as courageous and "chic" as ever. Speaking of her, a touching story comes to my mind: working with us was a brave woman from Lorraine, around 60 years old. She often abused French grammar, but she had the heart of a patriot. Learning that this small, pale and frail worker was the niece of the great de Gaulle, the woman came up to her and spontaneously offered her soup. This naïve but generous gesture can well be appreciated by those who know the value of a bowl of soup in a concentration camp. Geneviève was very touched, but she did not accept it.

1. Marie-José Zillhard: *Témoignages strasbourgeois.* Already cited.
2. Unpublished testimony of Madeleine Perrin: "From the Russian front arrived trucks loaded with pants, jackets, and large hooded overcoats that were badly in need of disinfection; they were matted with blood, lice, mud and other clotted stains which one would expect to find on the clothes of a wounded or dead soldier being returned from the battlefields. It was our job to unstitch all this material and cut out the parts of the cloth that could be re-used—along with the buttons, etc. When we entered the workshop—from which no light emerged in case of an air raid—an odor of decomposing cadavers almost immediately wafted up into our nostrils and stayed there the whole night; even our dresses reeked of the smell. We had to unstitch 15 jackets or trousers per night. The S.S. trooper called Wim knocked around all those who failed to make this quota.... This calvary went on until March 20, 1945."

Binder, who ran the most important workshop, was a former tailor who had joined the S.S. in 1933. He was the typical example of an S.S. trooper: crazy, brutal and sadistic.

— Binder was rough and brutal[1] toward the women in the workshop. He beat us every day and didn't seem to calm down until he saw blood run. One day he beat a Polish girl so badly that she had to be taken directly to the hospital. She never came back to the workshop and rumor has it that she died. When we didn't do the required amount of work, he took away our little pieces of bread—the only food we had for 11 work-hours—and he made us sew standing up for hours at a time.

— Sometimes he would swing a stool at the women, and I've seen him drag them around by the hair before beating them up. When he noticed a woman with her head inclined—we were so underfed and tired that this often happened—he banged her forehead on a table. He also took away our clothes and even obliged us to stand nude, pretending that he had to make sure that we were not hiding any pieces of material in our clothing; at that time, we had practically nothing to put on our backs.

— Another young Polish girl in Binder's workshop had an open sore on her arm—from a lack of vitamins. Binder refused to let her go to the hospital and said, as he ripped off her bandage: "You're not at all sick."

— The girl collapsed; when she finally rose, he summed up all his strength and smashed her face with his fist. She dropped to the floor with the blow and he stomped all over her body with his feet.

— Binder used to strike women with a pair of scissors or lacerate their faces with the metal buttons on tunics. He was responsible for the death of an incalculable number of prisoners by obliging them to work when they

1.   Testimony of a deported Dutch girl, recorded by Lord Russell of Liverpool.

had no strength left or by leaving them outside under a belting rain—nude and often for more than an hour.

One night,[1] when we were desperately trying to turn out the quota of work demanded of us, Binder, his eyes looking like they had been injected with blood, pounced on an elderly Polish woman and beat her savagely, undoubtedly because he was not happy with her work. Having worked in this "Betrieb" for only a few days, I wasn't yet accustomed to the sight of such treatment; seeing this young brute using his fists and feet on this poor sprawled-out woman profoundly shook and revolted me. We were not permitted to stop work or to stop our machines, and we knew that our production was unceasingly controlled. However, before such cruelty, we gave full and open vent to how we felt and each of us expressed the revolt within our hearts.

"Vreselijk!" murmured Rika, the young Dutch girl.

"Bastard! Abject fleahead!", chorused Titine, and a whole range of epithets emanating from her rich vocabulary of slang from the North tumbled out without stopping.

Vida, the sweet Yugoslav girl, hid her eyes behind her hands and emotionally murmured to me: "Es könnte meine Mutter sein."

And the limpid look of Wanda, my complaisant Polish friend, had become hard and fierce; she whispered to me: "Kommt anders, wird aufgehängt!"

Yvonne de Charleroi cried softly.

Tamara, the Ukrainian, put her hand on my arm and said: "Weina conchista, tsepajede da moi."

We were both stupefied and frozen with horror. Was such brutality possible—such violence heaped upon this aged white-haired woman whose blood ran over the cement floor. After Binder had finally left, we placed the

---

1. Testimony of Lily Unden: *Livre du Souvenir*. Bourge-Bourger, Printers. Luxembourg 1965.

unconscious woman on a pile of uniforms. Unfortunately, this was all we could do!

A German woman, who had been arrested many months ago for her political opinions, was assigned to the distribution of material. She was distinguished, cultivated, and loved music and the arts; during our short "breaks" we enjoyed listening to her recite a poem.

Going up to her for more supplies of cloth, I asked her: "War das nicht furchtbar? ("Wasn't it awful?")—Dieser junge Kerl, der diese alte Dame so misshandelte!" ("This kid hitting that old woman.") The German woman looked at me strangely and replied: "Nehmen Sie das nicht so; sehen Sie; ich hatte einen sehr guten Mann, aber er hat mich auch manchmal geschlagen!" ("Don't worry about it; I had an excellent husband but he used to push me around, too.")

At noon I went over to barracks 14 where the Polish women lived; there I saw a group of them kneeling before the dead woman, they were reciting the "De Profundis" loud and clear.

Convicted as a war criminal, Binder was hanged.

14

The Phlegmon

— I was working[1] in the forest on a sand-digging detail. We dug enormous holes in the hard and icy snow. When those overseeing the work felt the hole was big enough, we filled it in! We were cold, very cold. We were hungry. We were always afraid—of everything: beatings, tortures, dogs, humiliations, deprivations. Fear was always with us, underneath everything.

— In the forest, as elsewhere, each group had its surveillant to whom we attributed nicknames: there was "The Beast," "The Cow," "The Chink" (who was our guardian). These latter two cordially hated each other, and it was this hate which certainly saved my life. One day, I was suffering from an enormous phlegmon located in my throat; I was so afraid of being sent to the infirmary that I continued to fall out for work in the morning. Suddenly I had a fainting spell and I collapsed on my pickaxe. As I fell, I saw "The Cow" striding toward me like a hurricane, swinging her club; the enormous,

1. Unpublished manuscript, Françoise Archippe. June 1970.

terrifying dog that was with her suddenly sank his fangs
into the calf of my leg. More out of fear than any
suffering I was undergoing, I experienced a tremendous
hiccup...and I spit an awful packet of blood and pus
into the snow. "The Chink," furious that another guard
would dare horn in on her sector, drove the woman and
her dog away. I found myself, still terrorized, with a
lovely bite wound...but my phlegmon was healed!

15

Bluette the Clandestine Goldbricker

On arriving at Ravensbrück, Bluette Morat remembered the advice which the resistance movement in France gave to young people called up for the Forced Labor Service:

— When you receive your convocation to go for a medical check-up, by no means should you go!

Bluette Morat scrupulously conformed to this rule, thus escaping being sent from Ravensbrück to the war factories;

— Upon my arrival at camp,[1] I became recalcitrant about doing any work. Once all the names on the roll call list had been verified, the convict guard of the day knew she had all the women from the barracks at her mercy. Then it was very simple to form the column for the medical visit. My name was called, as was that of my comrade Mona—my accomplice in refusing to work. We didn't move. We took the precaution of easing away from

1. Testimony of Bluette Morat, dated February 20, 1946, and published in December, 1946, in *Les Cahiers du Rhône.* La Baconnière, Neuchâtel.

the other French prisoners because their collective attitude of impatience and anxiety might have revealed our
presence, involuntary as it would have been on their part.
Immersed in a mass of sleepy Polish women, we waited
for this roll call slave to get tired calling out names. It is a
known fact: these powerful and well-organized people
could not succeed in "smoking out," from among several
hundred women, two measly, missing prisoners.

— Upon their return from the infirmary, our comrades
told us that the doctor had violently called out our names
over and over. "We shall see what we shall see," we
said. But nothing happened.

— A few days later the same comedy took place: roll
call and a column formed to go to the infirmary. Again
our names were screamed out. The brutes in the barracks, primitive Polacks, hardly even recognized them.
After the tenth time, they gave up. The third séance was
almost fatal for us. This time they called us by the
numbers inscribed on our sleeves, and in all the languages used in the barracks. Our hiding place in the
middle of all these Polish women no longer served our
purpose. We must get out of the ranks and enter the
column going to the infirmary; off we went, five by five,
just as a magnificent sunrise appeared on the horizon. We
were comforted, however, by the fact that, if and when
our presence was detected, we could always leave it.
"Even from the train, one must always try to flee." This was
repeatedly told to the "recruits" back home. Why not?
We then decided to leave the column. There are so many
women up front and behind, poor, worn-out souls incapable of any reaction, that no one noticed anything. And
inasmuch as no one expects anyone to escape from the
infirmary, the Lagerpolizei were not paying attention either.

— But what is going to happen at the end of the
morning? Our presence back in the barracks cannot be
justified—all the French, about 60 of them, have been
called out on work details. So we went to barracks 31
where we found Camille, the farsighted upholder of our

spirit of resistance. She approves and reassures us: in the confusion of their overpopulated camp, they will never notice our absence. Then she gave us some technical advice: itineraries to take, barracks to avoid, replies to give. And we began our life of "goldbricking" at the back of the camp.

— Result: when the first transfer of prisoners was made, our names were not on the list that had been made up from those women who had had "medical" visits. And they were not on the lists for any of the convoys that followed.

— Thus, we had won the first round by adhering to set rules.

— For the entire camp there were two roundups, organized daily: these were the work calls.

— When the signal was given for the morning roll call, we had to "lose" our comrades from the barracks by running to the column headed for the infirmary and slipping into its ranks—or into the column made up of seamstresses. These were the good times when we found the other "goldbricks" in the camp: Camille, her friend Jeanne, General Ely, and Suzy, the Dutch girl, arrived from 31; Violette Maurice from 32; Andrée, Jacqueline Lelong, and Jenny from 28; Pierrot, Marie-Louise, Renée from 15—to cite only the "regulars." It was Violette's song which best expressed the atmosphere in which this daily adventure took place—sport at sunrise, very hygienic for the souls awakened from the gloomy torpor in which 5 hours of Zählappell had plunged them.

> *Since the day I became a Verfügbar*[1]
> *At Ravensbrück, life is beautiful,*
> *Since the day I became a Verfügbar*
> *I hardly ever hesitate to hide.*
> *Every morning I join the seamstresses*

1. Verfügbar: available ("idle") person who is not assigned to a work squad, workshop, or mobile work detail and can, at any time, be called upon to perform tasks or beef up a work group.

And I take my time getting there.
Posing languorously
The back hunched, the head doddering.
With my stool under my arm } *repeat*
Again we're going to get them.

If by chance there is a "control"
At Ravensbrück, life is beautiful,
If by chance there is a "control"
I'll be forced to change my role.
Toward the infirmary with a tragic air,
Wrapped up in my rags and tatters,
Like authentic sick persons
Every woman for herself, we're getting out
The camp commander reviews the ranks, } *repeat*
Once again we got them.

When we're liberated
At Ravensbrück life is beautiful
When we're liberated
We will no longer be able to be "Verfügbar."
Oh, how grey our existence will be,
And it will be considered bad taste
To be able to cheat at will
Without fear of blows from clubs.
This is why we want to remain } *repeat*
"Verfügbar" forever.
　　　　(Melody: *"Depuis que je suis louveteau"*)

— When the "work selection" process took place
between two barracks, the situation was much more
difficult. The general roll call was for those living in 24,
next to 23—which was unused and locked up. A few
moments before the Arbeitsappell siren, the policewomen, "the officerine,"[1] an ignoble group of Polish

---

1. In reality, Aufseherin (supervisor wearing the S.S. uniform);
but the French found it more convenient to call them Officerine.

servicewomen, the "Zimmerdienst"[1] of the dormitory
(with the help of their "Butches," this was the only work
they did all day long), made a chain at the ends of the
barracks where prisoners went in or out; thus, all the
women found themselves encircled between the two
buildings and the two groups of convict guards. The
game consisted of trying to guess, on the basis of what
information we could gather, just what these women
were preparing to do with us and then, as fast as we
could run, escape their surveillance long enough to get
ourselves lost in the mob that inhabited the neighboring
barracks; we ran the risk of falling into the hands of the
"attendants" in that barracks, but it was easier to get
away from them since we were not known to them. The
technique we used took time to perfect. If we were
cornered in the rectangle, it took all the keen attention
and sturdy obstinacy within us to keep from being
hunted down like some prey—at least for the first thirty
or forty minutes.

— No sooner did the "Zimmerdienst" in charge of the
"toilets" turn her head than we would jump through the
window of this delightful hellhole—even at the risk of
falling into a disgusting mixture of mud and excrement;
then we would hide behind a rickety door and wait there
with our fingers holding our nose; three out of four times
we would see some uniformed authority surging toward
us to yank us out of our hiding place, give us a good
drubbing and, with her "gentle" hands, shove us into the
work column. After this "emotional" welcome, we would
take advantage of say, a fracas or fight among prisoners
to discreetly leave the column in order to slip in among
the elderly women, a small group apart. This was a
delicate operation because these elderly foreigners were
minutely lined up in rows of five—and a sixth person
risked compromising the security of the whole line. In
addition, they "welcomed" us frigidly because our "sport"

1.   Zimmerdienst: a deportee assigned to clean the barracks.

prolonged the operations and delayed the moment when these sad creatures could go back to their barracks. Dislodged from there by the outcries of one of the old women, or chased away by a Zimmerdienst wielding a heavy stick, we next tried to hide among the sick; but there were not very many of them. Even so, we could not sneak into their ranks except at the very end of the "roundup" operations—otherwise, we would find ourselves back in the labor column. This time, however, there was no hope of escaping from in front of the barracks. Therefore, we left with the column, resigned to our fate; but we had not given up hope. We met other prisoners from other barracks, coming back from the "Lager," and, after a little pushing and shoving here and there, we slipped into the herd bound for camp. Saved! Another method of clandestine goldbricking that worked well (if we had managed to avoid being rounded-up for a work detail) was to sneak into the "Waschraum" or the toilets in Barracks 14 and 15, which were open, and wait until the column was far away.

— The roundup operations were generally simple to avoid at the beginning of the afternoon. The "roundup women" had quickly formed their columns from all those lured by the "soulag." The seamstresses stayed around for a long time in front of their barracks; we only had to go and squat down between a couple of stools in front of number 31. The only risk we ran was just one more smash across the choppers from the ineffable Gerda.

— Certain barracks, like 26, did not show up for this call; this was the moment when Violette and I went to visit dear friends housed there. We were greeted with the soft and serene smile of General Allard's wife and the optimistic pep-talk given by a brave butcher-woman from Brittany. On the third floor we found a magnificent team of patriots; along with Odette, the little English parachutist, there was Marguerite M. and Madame Gaby, who had such a marvelous past, Madame Jeanne, who embroidered the flags for the 11th of November,

Madame and Mademoiselle Leminor, Madame Parisot
and still others—all of them work objectors.

— We often forewent this call-up to walk between the
barracks. One could breathe, talk and laugh. It was the
hour of the day that was least cold. Pierrette and I had
chosen this moment to stroll about as the best opportunity for me to teach her Greek. Instead of putting on
the work harness and suffering a rain of blows, we chose
to study the language of Plato and evoke the summit that
man had attained—even though we were wallowing in
the depths of savageness; we could not have invented
anything more impertinent to do, and it put us in a
delightful mood. Pierrette had learned the word for
"liberty"; she was up to the second declension. Then our
lessons stopped because my barracks, No. 27, was put
under quarantine because of an outbreak of typhus.
When I could get out again, Pierrette had been hanged.

— Identity at Ravensbrück was no longer by name,
true or false, but by a printed number on white calico and
placed in a ridiculous manner on our sleeves. This was
the only sign of individuality which we were accorded
and the only thing that showed we participated in some
type of order in the camp—just as in the rest of the world
where the identity card gave one an official standing
(obligatory in time of war). In renouncing any real
identity, one escaped from Vichy and its aura of armistice
in order to consecrate one's self (in this clandestine
adventure) to serving one's country in time of conflict.

— At camp we had two ways by which we could
persevere in this direction: the reserve of false numbers,
and the rejection of all numbers. We tried to get hold of
false numbers and keep them for the time when we
would be "rounded up" and taken somewhere; such
"roundups" could take place in any camp "street"; our
numbers would be taken down and we would be sent
back to the barracks to await the hour of departure. This
could always happen if we were picked up in the "soup-
line," which formed several hours before any food

distribution was made in front of the kitchens. We were at the mercy of some "roundup cowhand" on the lookout for work recruits.

— One of our group did even better: having come to the camp under a false name, she managed to live there from October 17 to April 3 without any number. Then came the ultimate in clandestineness. Having avoided being picked up in the "roundup" that took place in her barracks, No. 24, she was trapped in the one held in barracks No. 21. She escaped four times from their column, and was recaptured four times by force: fists, feet and clubs. When she arrived at the "Lagerstrasse," some 100 meters from the camp's gate, an unhoped-for occasion presented itself.

A fight started somewhere and the convict-guards ran to break it up. No one of any official authority saw her go. But a "political" German prisoner like her, also a victim of the Nazis and caught in the same way for the same act, decided to run after her and bring her back into the ranks—not acting out of obligation or for any profit, but out of a stupid instinct of passive obedience to everything. The woman being chased would certainly have been lost if she had not suddenly remembered a rule which stipulated that one could not leave camp without a number. She furtively tore hers off—and the trick worked. At the camp's last control check-point, she was sent back to the barracks to sew another number on her sleeve. One can easily imagine the column guard's anger; after all, she had put her back into the column five straight times, and she knew what the prisoner was trying to pull off. But she could not get the guard at the camp gate to believe the story! As for the "Kraut" prisoner, she ended up holding an empty bag!

— It was a good method to use for the purpose of getting out of a work detail. Of course, it was a grave offense to walk around without a number, but the gravity of the risk involved taking extreme precautions not to get caught.

— It did not suffice that a small number of resistants, who had shown up late at the camp, refused all work. Many more of our comrades had to be convinced to do the same. We first ran up against the skepticism of the "oldtimers" who had known the camp when there were less "inhabitants" and when discipline was ineluctable. However, it was easy to point out to them that one could attempt, in September 1944, what was impossible when the "27,000" first arrived. In any case, many of them had, little by little, left their fixed work squad or their Betriebe to become simple Verfügbar. The real ace in getting out of these work columns was Violette M., from Barracks 32. She was thrown off more work details than she can remember because she always managed to discourage the column chiefs with her incredible unwillingness to work; so, having grown tired of hitting her, she was "fired."

— To those who were arriving, it was explained that, though they were still suffocating from the horror felt by their first contact with Ravensbrück, working in a factory would not necessarily ameliorate their situation. Toward this end, we cornered the women returning from the transport squads, and then went from barracks to barracks relating the ill-treatment they had undergone.

— To tell the truth, the discussions were multiple, eternal and lancinating. Despite our motto—"Do Nothing But Listen," which Miarka had thought up—we could not continually keep from answering our censors. They confronted us with "realistic" considerations: What did this attempt at opposition signify? Wouldn't the same work be accomplished in the end, anyhow? We should renounce all these great pretensions and look at the situation as it really was—in other words, resign in order to survive. Nothing irritated us more than this type of argument because nothing was more contrary to the spirit of June 18—the spirit that inspired our attitude. If, in 1940, we must subordinate our efforts to their immediate efficacy, we might as well

Inspection in a workshop. The women, transformed into machines, "meeting their quota." Nevertheless, at the "Siemens" and "Massa" factories, some women are carrying out acts of sabotage to show that the Resistance Movement goes on—thus underlining their their refusal to participate in the war effort.
Bernadac Archives

follow Vichy. But my friends and I were more Gaullist than ever. We were as much so as were the early Gaullists—having the same intimate fervor and exercising it in an irrevocable manner. During the four years in the Resistance, we were absorbed in the needs of each day; through the sacrifice we made of not living a normal life, and during the actions in which we took part, we had held out hope. But in the camp, we had time to think about what our faith meant and evaluate the meaning of June 18—and to feel its virtue. On the eve of my arrival, in the macabre vision of that first night in the "showers," after having seen the lines of prisoners returning from their abominable labors, after having every object, every souvenir, every bit of rag or clothing or banal reminder of the outside world taken from me—absolutely every-thing, except my Cross of Lorraine—I heard within me, like an obsession, like a faraway echo, the first word of the Resistance: "Hope." It was the power to remain faithful to the country at war, to remain, wherever possible, the enemy of its enemies and not just their victim. The first results showed that it was as possible as it was necessary.

— "It's sheer folly, children," said the cool-thinking "seamstresses and knitting-women" affectionately. "It's difficult enough already. Don't increase the risks unneces-sarily." Good-sense reasoning for a world of good sense. But good sense here means the ability to understand, once and for all, that we're living outside the world of good sense. Undoubtedly, we were doing everything possible to warrant being sent to the Strafblock, but we were not going there for nothing. In any case, we could only keep up our courage by not losing our head.

— Another argument went as follows: was it not silly to get out of work that we could sabotage so well and abandon our posts to the Polacks, those zealous slaves of production? Rather than invoke the "realism" aspect of Vichy's political reasoning, we should, instead, face up to one simple reality: our finite numbers, in comparison

to the mobs of foreigners. Our attempts at sabotage
would not change the enemy's production statistics. This
was only the second line of combat, which our personal
honor required us to hold; after all, we could not defend
the first line: that of absolute refusal.

— Finally, the last assault: it would be better "to figure
it out for oneself" and enter a column—with the express
intention of doing no work to help the war effort—rather
than to expose oneself, like a Verfügbar, to the risk of
being suddenly seized on the corner of a camp street and
sent to a factory like Siemens. Naturally, this entailed the
risk that one would be making powder for having refused
to shovel sand. Nevertheless, this argument, despite its
sentimental impact, never completely enthused me. The
reason was because, beyond this war of machines and
powder, there was Nazism's horrible combat against the
human person. And we saw with our eyes, we went
through the experience with our flesh, the degree of
bestiality which these monstrous enemies reached as
they ravished their slaves. Therefore, one can consider
that the slightest solicitation, necessarily transmitted by
some faceless Pole, holder of a small parcel of their
strength and thus an accomplice to their crime, would be
contrary to the demands of human dignity. It is better to
stay among the most humble Stücke, always "available"
for a worse fate, than to owe anything to an iniquitous
organization that, for the honor of France, comprised not
one Frenchwoman.

— Be that as it may, other religions opposed the one
that was exclusive in France. The Catholics and the
Communists had often been among those most unwilling
to work, and they were both good propagandists for this
conception of war. But on the whole, they usually had a
more important worry: that of how to help their comrades. We had no objection to this laudable expression of
solidarity. However, we were tortured by the thought
that we could never do anything for the others: never
bring them a potato or scarf; never be able to follow a tired

comrade leaving for work; never be able to continue holding up someone standing in line when the work call siren sounded; there, within ourselves, was the true debate, the painful debate.

— From one group to another, there was solidarity—both moral and practical. Without the woolen articles from Monique, from Claire, and from Lucienne, and without the "fresh garbage" from Ariane, I would never have had the strength to keep one step ahead of the "roundup women." And in this moral desolation, any unselfish gesture or motive, that went against the Nazi desire to render us even more dull and stupid, was a form of resistance. Therefore, there was no point in hashing the whole thing over with the faithful of other religions; we understood their attitude, and we asked them to understand ours as well: that is, the proof of liberty that would not capitulate, and the absolute will to hold on until the very end in a combat for "Our Mother, France."

— A Verfügbar who absolutely refused all work could not re-enter the barracks after roll call—particularly numbers 23, 24, and 27, temporary-quarters barracks, which guards were liable to enter in search of supplementary work columns; "Arbeit," "Arbeit," they would scream. It was thus wiser to seek refuge in the barracks which housed "fixed work teams" because there was little risk of a "work roundup" after the roll call. Thus it was that, in October and November, Mona and I roamed from the corridors of 31 to those of 26, from the Waschraum in 30 to the one in 28. In addition to being on the look-out for any signs that we were considered foreigners in the barracks, we would hide among the elderly women squatting in the shadows of the doors; a curious look from one of these hags was enough to send us on our way. It must be said that these extenuated women, pitiful bags of greasy rags covered with stinking vermin, remained inert. We mixed among them because our security was more important than any sensation of repugnance. When the call went out that food was

en route, like the "Brot holen," or when the soup arrived
the scene changed: after somnolent inertia, they came
alive like animals in a jungle. They grabbed their mess
kits, which they usually turned upside down to have
something to sit on, and held them out—gesticulating
aggressively in their atrocious avidity. And us? We ran to
our barracks to see if the soup had been served there—
barracks far from those where it was already being
swilled down.

— In the Waschraum, the strategy was to strip down
naked. But one could not stay many hours shivering in
the cold air drafts or just standing around the faucets
which were always so avidly fought over.

— The two big difficulties in this errant life were not to
miss out on the soup ration served in the barracks,
despite continued absence, and to find a way to "delouse"
one's self when one was never sure of having five
minutes of peace in a hiding-place.

— In February, my life-style changed. At the very end
of Barracks 27, I delightfully stretched out on my back, a
dream that had obsessed me during the autumn when,
from 3 o'clock in the morning, when we got up, until
nightfall, we could never sit down. Now it was bed all
day long, on and under! No more fatigue, of course, but,
alas! no more air either, no more real light, and almost no
more contact with comrades in the other barracks. The
Zählappell was not even held regularly anymore and we
hardly ever went to the work call; but almost every day,
we heard the sinister cry: "Alles raus!" The "merchant of
cows" was coming to round up" a work detail, undoubtedly accompanied, when the "roundup" was for the
purpose of transferring prisoners, by the doctor from
Auschwitz who made his "on-the-spot selection." The
sick would be sent to Barracks 22 where the "gas truck"
would come to pick them up. As soon as I heard the
"Alles raus," I raced downstairs from the second floor. I
looked around to make sure nobody saw me and then
slipped under the bed, where I was soon joined by the

General and Jacqueline Lelong, Mona and Madame Tiran. We banged our heads on cans containing a dubious liquid, and we crawled as best we could through filthy pieces of rags and paper, trash and rubbish from our lousy hole. The straw from the beds fell over our faces. Arms, heads and legs got all tangled up. At last we got settled; we could breathe, if that is the word, in a shelter that protected us from the "operations" taking place outside—without thinking too much about what would happen if we were denounced and caught. It would have been a flogging to the death. I went through the experience on one of the last Sundays in March. Just at the moment when I was beginning to lose consciousness, thanks to the beating I was receiving from the "officerine," she was called away, by miracle, for something; otherwise she would have beaten me to the very end.

— We got out from underneath there more Schmuckstück[1] than ever, but joyous, for an instant, at having succeeded. Then came the infernal nightmare: the counting of those who had been caught outside; once, the "seamstresses" left, without any cause for fear, to answer a morning roll call; they did not come back; another time, the sick disappeared. Had the "roundup" been an important one? We hid until the return of the work force; it was only then that we could circulate about in safety.

— One day, however, the work force did not return. Silence in front of the barracks. Silence inside. We took the risk of creeping up to the window: barbed wire separated the barracks located in the back from all the rest of the camp. Our comrades "camouflaged" in the attic came down to join us. Council meeting. Why was no one around? Did they have the intention of tearing down our barracks, one of the most verminous? Was this

1. Schmutzstück: garbage, designating the most miserable of deportees. Comparable to the "mummy" in the men's camps. Out of derision, Schmutzstück was transformed into Schmuckstück: jewel.

the beginning of a total evacuation? One of our comrades finally found the Blockowa and brought back the details: the barracks was definitely emptied of all its morning occupants. Thus, our comrades who had gone out on a work detail would find none of their poor personal belongings when they returned; in addition, at least that night, they would have to fight with unknown women for some tiny part of a straw mattress in a new barracks.

— We could still join the work columns recruited in the afternoon. Could we stay? The Blockowa was going to get in a batch of Hungarian Jews and some Gipsies during the night. The Blockowa accepted our clandestine presence, but could not guarantee that we would be fed regularly. Now that we were no longer being counted among the inmates of the camp, we would always have to hide and depend on what food our comrades could procure for us in other barracks. All of us accepted this situation, exultant with joy and liberty—the liberty of being able to be one's self for a few moments, despite the barbed wire. There, with the other habituées from underneath the bed, were Jacqueline d'Alincourt, Rosine Déréan, Annie Renaud, Noélla Peaudeau, Sylvie Girard and three Dutch comrades. True, our liberty was only a symbol, and practically a deliberate choice to eat even less. But surrounding us were women of ingenuity. Kettles of supplementary soup rations arrived. The number of prisoners eligible for a piece of bread underwent "mysterious changes," enabling us to have almost a regular ration of this staff of life. Sometimes it was brought to us at night, when we were already asleep: it was awfully good, this bread for the "insubordinates"! The other Frenchwomen in camp had baptized us "the outlaws of 27." This was the origin of the cry from Kiki, our good-natured Stubowa: "Soup's on, outlaws!"

— Unfortunately, those wonderful days during which we reveled in being outlaws did not last. We had to leave the end of the filthy, but safe, dormitory for exposure on the third floor of the Tagesraum—which constituted the "frontline" in case of a brusque "roundup." Along with such splendid Frenchwomen as Madame Michel, Madame Suzanne, and Madame Noguès, we found some others (whose names I have forgotten) and a Russian from Paris, Ina; there were also some girls there, whose nationality we did not know, who had also managed to keep away from work columns from the very beginning— but they did so because they found out that many of them were simply disguises for the transfer of prisoners to God-knows-where. Also among us were some incorrigible thieves, as well as some prostitutes—of whom at least one was of German origin, a girl who had worked with the Gestapo and was then arrested in Paris. Hunger and our abnormal situation, abnormal even for the camp, developed the worst instincts; we saw women, still "valid," snitch the last piece of sugar from a dying old woman; gangs of looters formed and then, as soon as their orgy of plundering was over, broke up—out of fear of being denounced. Girls from the coffee houses of Brussels, from Bucharest or from Afghanistan rivaled each other in voracity, the use of their fists and their penchant for revelry under the alternate invectives and cries of encouragement shouted at them by Nadia and Lydia, the two star performers in the everlasting fights that regularly took place.

— Shelter, in case of Alles raus, was, therefore, the attic: up we went at the slightest menace and there we stayed for hours—trying to keep our balance on beams that were only 15 centimeters wide, while holding our breath and contracting our muscles. Sometimes we would be as many as thirty up there; some of the girls were dangerous because we always felt they would start a scene or begin denouncing one another. We put up with them because they were hard-rock accomplices in our "resistance movement."

— Finally, we were again counted among the inhabitants of the barracks (a new contingent of recent arrivals was simply "enlarged"). A large number of undesirable inmates left soon after in a column, and I was able to return to the dormitory.

— This perpetual hiding and camouflaging was, without doubt, a nerve-wrecking experience, and this daily fear of being caught for the first time became a hallucinating obsession. But, just as in all religions there is a Providence, chance would have it, happily so, that I always got out of any really bad situation. Luck increased the efforts made through strong will power, impotent as it might seem under the circumstances—but strengthened, nevertheless, by a clear, imperative need, that of honor and human dignity, that can be found through the observance of freedom. That was the whole mystic significance of June 18. And that was how I managed to hold out, without working, until the very end....

16

Bastille Day
in Barracks 21

They arrived June 15, 1944....They were appalled
when they saw the Ravensbrück camp....

— ...Then it was the infernal barracks[1]...number
21....The communal hall had been built for 200. Some
600 were packed into it; 200 of us were French. One
stool for four....One table, seating eight, for 32....There
were women everywhere (phantom-like women!), on
the tables, and under the tables. The tiniest space was
fought over—sometimes savagely. The first few days
were an ear-shattering din. The most valiant among us
just shut up—facial muscles contracted and teeth
clenched. One morning, Lise Ricol-London came up to
me. Together we looked about the room, at the poor
faces of our companions. The oldest among them already
had that "resigned" look, and we realized many would
never "rise to the surface again." "If this goes on, we'll
soon be mad, all of us." So, with a few friends, we
decided to hold a series of conferences, group discus-

1. Unpublished manuscript, Lise Lesèvre. July 1970.

sions and travel talks—as we had done in Saarbrücken
(Neuenbremm). But how could we keep the Russians,
Poles and other foreigners quiet during such sessions?
They would have no interest in such activities. Well,
then, we'll sing!...These morning songfests were quickly
organized (we were in quarantine and thus exempt from
work). There were all types of songs and singers—choral
groups from France, Russia and Poland. The Germans
who were interned asked to participate in these "con-
certs," then became vexed when we would not let them
be the first to sing.

— All of a sudden the Fourteenth of July "arrived" at
Ravensbrück! A big artistic event was scheduled for the
morning. Rehearsals were going full blast in the "Waschraum" (washroom) during the hours of the day when it
was closed—thanks to the complicity of our Blockowa,
Hilda Sinkova, a Czech whose husband had been shot.
She bent over backwards to help us put on our little
show, and closed her eyes to many infractions of camp
rules. Denise Morin-Pons was in charge of the dancing
and singing. Juliette Duboc (our Yvette) was the orchestra leader. You should have seen the radiant expressions
on the faces of our young women as they came out of
rehearsals!...

— Morning of the national holiday: it was decided
that the roll call would take place in complete silence—
something which our most severe guardians could never
get us to do. Our impeccable decorum and dignified
manner had impressed our foreign comrades: they, in
turn, maintained complete silence. This extraordinary
"roll call" reminded us of home....The sky was not so
overcast....There were no more ravens....We heard the
sound of our own bugles, and of our own cannons....The
bugles and cannons that signified festive days for us—
and days of liberty and freedom!

— During the roll call, "Radio Gossip" functioned.
Who could have heard it? It doesn't matter because it
was heard....Listen! "Paris has been liberated....Seven

divisions entered the capital this morning.... General Leclerc is at the head of his troops.... The Normandie-Niemen squadron is in the sky over Paris.... De Gaulle is at Notre-Dame!"

— "Radio Gossip" had not lied...it had just anticipated the events a little—only a month or so.

— Tables were pushed to the back of the communal hall to form a stage. The orchestra pit was on the side. The ground-floor seats were really on the ground, and there was such a pile-up of bodies that you could not imagine such a scene unless you had been there: the prisoners sat with their knees apart so that others could do the same and increase "the attendance." Pitiful links in a chain of misery that we were going to forget for a few hours. Stools were the "best seats in the house"; "second-best" were the tables. The lounges were located between the partition wall and the backs of the spectators seated in the last row—and the show began:

— Guittou recited a poem written by one of our group, entitled "Ravensbrück." It said, in splendid and orderly verse, what we all felt at the bottom of our hearts: misery, hunger, death, horror.... But it also expressed hope for the resurrection of our country! Then it was time for the parade of the "French Provinces," with their costumes, their customs, their dances, their songs.... Oh! Those costumes, how magnificent they looked (our Blockowa had contributed much material). The blue, the white, the red in our flag were almost constantly prominent on the stage. Louise, a solid girl from the North, sang "Le P'tit Quinquin." Jacqueline Rigaud (Jacotte) and her mother sang a duet ("Le temps des cerises"); their voices harmonized well together, as fresh as a brook. "Le Cabanon de Marseille," by our little Dedou—the voice full of sunshine, like the girls in the French South. I have forgotten your names, and I've forgotten your faces. Dear friends who sang "Ma Normandie"; I only remember the apple blossoms in bloom, a sweet mirage that masked the scene for me while you were singing. Roberte, you

sang "La Morvandelle" so well.... And you, the little
waves of women who sang and swayed to "Les Marins
de Groix." And you, frail grape pickers with your baskets
and pruning-knives made out of cardboard.... Where did
you find the cardboard for "Les Vendanges"? And you,
charming companions who danced "La Bourrée." Are
you not a little grateful to the Grand Reich that was
generous enough to provide you with an important part
of your costume? The clogs!... And you, Denise, Régine,
Yvettou, Josy, the beautiful tricolored "Fandango" that
you danced for us! "La Bourguignonne," sung and
danced by four young women.... And how pretty was
our little bride in "La Noce berrichonne," Francine
Bonnet. And how her mother devoured her with her
eyes, perhaps feeling that this was one of the last visions
she would have of her little girl (poor mommy, why do
you have white hair; you know the S.S. does not like
white hair?). Bisi, the bagpiper, and Denise, as the old
father in this wedding, were given long but muted
applause while, at the windows, a few comrades kept a
close look-out. Then, we had: "Les Quatre Filles de La
Rochelle."

— Suddenly, a girl in blue, one in white, and one in
red appeared on the stage, and our "Marseillaise" began.
We all sang its refrains—not at full voice, but with all our
hearts. It was a magnificent spectacle that you cannot
imagine, you who did not see it! I sincerely believe that
you could even regret not having seen it... this spectacle,
I mean (I won't insist, you should have seen the other
"spectacles" in the camp).

17

The Undesirables

Ramdohr, chief of the political section at Ravensbrück, is an official in the judiciary police force. Responsible for interrogations, he handles and investigates all "cases"; even the S.S. does not intervene or dispute his decisions. It is true that Ramdohr is a superior member of the hierarchy who had perfectly assimilated the concentration camp system. Since he was put in his job in 1942, he had, by the time the camp was liberated, tortured nearly 1,500 women. Only two ever defeated him.

Stanislawa Szeweczkova had founded a clandestine resistance group composed of around ten young Polish girls who met once a week. Denounced by a compatriot, Stanislawa was shackled, dragged into the office of the political section and stretched on a table, with her head hanging down over the end. Ramdohr placed a large pail of water on a chair and then slipped it under Stanislawa's head. Question. No answer. The head is plunged into the pail.

— The name of your friends?

Ten times, fifty times the same question. Ten times, fifty times the same torment in the "mini-model bathtub." When she fainted, blows from a Schlague brought her to. Ramdohr is obstinate but he is in the habit of taking his time. He condemned Stanislawa to 12 days in the disciplinary section—"without food or blankets."

The thirteenth day: table, pail, question, questions. Still no answer. It is winter; Ramdohr had still never experimented with "the jet" in below-zero weather. When he leaves his office, he simply says: "six showers."

The treatment is simple: the nude prisoner is attached to a pole outside; for a quarter of an hour a high pressure fire hose "washes her down." At the end of the séance, she is left to "cool off" for an hour. If the inmate has not spoken...it's because she is dead. Stanislawa went through one séance....Three days later, she got a second treatment. This punishment was prolonged for three weeks, "two showers" a week. Again the table, the pail, and the questions.

— We'll see you again in two months. Two months in the disciplinary section with hot soup...served every four days....

The entire Polish colony was solidly behind her, and they literally gorged her with food to such a point that, when she came up before Ramdohr at the end of her period of punishment, she was in great form. An hour later, the Polish girl's body was just one big wound. She did not speak. Ramdohr, thinking she was dead, had her carried to the infirmary. A month later, Stanislawa was on her feet. Ramdohr preferred to abandon and forget the whole affair.

*   *

— The Red Army prisoners do not want to work.
— It's not my problem!
— They say they are prisoners of war and they should be treated as prisoners of war.

— See the camp commander.

As Ramdohr said during the trial of war criminals in Hamburg in 1947, "It was too big a mouthful to chew."

— There, for the first time, I felt I should not put my nose in this affair. It was just too big a piece for me to bite off. Later on, I was obliged to hear out certain "soldates" who had refused to work in a factory. I merely took note of their disposition.

Everything had begun at the beginning of 1943. 53 "soldates," considered undesirable at Maidanek, were expedited to Ravensbrück.

We underwent a medical visit.[1] Again this humiliating wait—nude, in the corridor, the doctor's examination....

After a new verification, we learned that we are not to be recognized as prisoners of war. We are given the same numbers handed out to Russian civilians. We refuse to sew the Russian "Winkel" (a red triangle with the letter R) on our clothes because prisoners of war do not wear them. Everything was fine in the quarantine barracks, but when the quarantine ended, we went up before the Arbeitseinsatz (office of work distribution) and that was a whole new ball game.

— Your triangle?

— Prisoners of war.

— From where?

— From Lublin.

— We don't recognize you as war prisoners; it was not us who took off your uniforms. Come back in a half-hour with your triangles.

Thirty minutes later we were back again.

— Well, your triangles?

— We are prisoners of war, nobody wears them in our camp.

1. Testimony of Antonia Nikifovora: *Plus Jamais.* Moscow Publishers, 1958.

— You will come back tomorrow morning at seven a.m. with your Winkels. Go, Raus!

We were obstinate, and we felt we must fight. We might die, but we would not surrender.

The next day we came back without the triangles. We were led out onto the square of the chancellery. We waited. We were sent to the Bunker, the prison. We were afraid. The Bunker? The "25 lashes"? After the quarantine, the fresh air made us weave with weakness. Among us were two elderly sick women and Lisa, a recent arrival, who was pregnant. They would not be able to stand 25 lashes.... What were we to do? They lined us up by fives in front of the prison, to punish us. We relaxed a bit. Was this our only punishment?

We laughed.

The inmates were looking at us through the bars of the prison. Many wore the German uniform. That consoled us: The presence of so many German military personnel confirmed to us that fascism was coming apart at the seams. It's not that easy to stand up. Two, three, five hours passed. It's the hour for the soup ration. Then the roll call. We are still standing up. It's hot. Our legs and kidneys hurt. Chourka-the-Torturer passes on her way to the administration building. We shudder and quiver. Has she come to get us? She reassures us.

— Have no fear, we beat our own, the Russians, less than the others.

— You may be Russian, but you're not one of us, you bitch, cried out one of us!

— Shut up, have you forgotten that Lisa and the sick are with us?

We clenched our teeth and waited. It happens that Chourka-the-Torturer had not come for us. We asked the Aufseherin to take us to the toilet. She led us by groups to barracks 12 where there were prisoners of war. We received a friendly welcome from our comrades. We talked with the Aufseherin while something to drink and a little soup were brought to us. Those few spoonfuls of

Wooden chair used for floggings. The "Schlague," administered on the slightest pretext, and following an established technique, was officially limited to 25 lashes or blows. Too often, however, the punishment was dealt out until the victim fainted or died.

Bernadac Archives

spinach soup were delicious! Just the time to take a breather before we found ourselves in front of the Bunker.

It began to rain, buckets of water fell from the roofs. The Aufseherin went into her lodging. We're still there. Some of us washed our hands or our head; others washed their handkerchiefs—and still others just tried to get their tired backs to stand up straight. The rain became torrential. Our thin clothes became heavy: water trickled down our neck. Our faces were livid and our lips were blue with cold....

The siren. Some prisoners were coming back from work detail, and to eat; others were leaving with the work squads that labored at night. We are still standing there....

The rain stopped, the wind dried our dresses. The body is broken with fatigue. We look over at the door of the administration building. When is it going to end? The Aufseherinnen have gone in. Are we going to stay out here all night? The siren sounds the call to go to bed. We are allowed to go, but the same penance is promised for tomorrow. You would think we would fly to the barracks, but our legs are like lead and refuse to obey.

In the barracks we're welcomed like heroines; we are given wooden stools and something to eat.... Now, there is no longer any difference: Poles, Russians, Germans or Danes. The important thing is that 53 women resisted. The Lagerpolizei Turi, who gets along well with the deportees, is asked to straighten out the mess we are in. We call for witnesses from Lublin, and all the prisoners of war, the veterans and the new ones, receive a Winkel "S.U."—Soviet Union.

A bad moment has passed. Another one arrives. A number of us are to be sent to the factories in Leipzig. All our group, or almost, are involved—as well as our three girls: Vera, Lida and Zina.

I will never forget that dawn, the black earth, the green barracks and the three silhouettes wrapped in small white shawls: they make a little sign at us with their hands and go off to new dangers and misfortunes. We wipe away our tears.

Barracks 21 is evacuated to make room for a new convoy, and we go into others.

There are about 500 of us in the small barracks No. 12, which was destined to house war prisoners. We all have our own closet and bunk. Order and cleanliness reign. When the day team leaves, the night team arrives. The bunks are occupied all the time; it's a perpetual rotation of night teams and day teams, but each one's tranquility and interests are respected.

It's silence. No sooner does someone raise her voice than one hears: "Quiet, the night team is sleeping." We scrupulously share our rations of bread and margarine. If someone momentarily turns aside, someone else will ask: "Whose is this?" There is never any question of theft.

*　*
*

Lioubov Semionovna Konnikova refuses all work.

On the morning of January 16.[1] I was again shut up in the Bunker—a sort of cell about four feet long and a foot and a half wide, with no air and no light. I was sitting on the little bench nailed to the wall. I couldn't sleep; I was very cold in my dress. I distinguished night from day by the noise of the day and night teams going to and from work. I was given nothing to drink or eat. A wretched stench rose from the body of a woman lying nearby; she was quickly decomposing. The second day, I heard keys rattle, the cell door opened, and I was blinded by a lamp.

It was the Camp Chief. He had brought me some bread and water. I wasn't hungry: the muscles in my face hurt me, as did my teeth; they had been chattering all night

1. *Plus Jamais.* Already cited.

because of the cold. Bronning, the Ravensbrück Camp Commander, arrived on January 22. He began his interrogation by grabbing me by the collar and smothering me.

— So, you don't want to work, you dirty Russian. We'll teach you to work! It's not like it was up on the front lines when you fired on our soldiers! He pushed me away so violently that I banged up against the other wall. You will work, or you will die; understood! I'll give you 24 hours to think it over, he added.

— I'm a Soviet doctor. I will not prepare arms destined to assassinate my brothers and my sisters.

I was again shut up in the Bunker. Twenty-four hours later, the Aufseherin took me out and spoke to me more humanely: I must work, I was young, I would get nothing out of not working, the only thing that would be waiting for me would be death by hanging.

— I don't fear death, I replied. Death was walking on my heels when I was on the front lines, and we're almost relatives now. How can you dare send prisoners, your number one enemies, to the factories of war? Don't you have anyone else left to work there?

The Aufseherin knocked me down with several blows.

The next day, I was sent to the factory. I told the workshop Aufseherin, a vulgar, stupid woman, that I was a prisoner of war and would not make rifle shells. She made me wash the toilet bowls. I washed them all day long. At night, the chief Aufseherin, learning of my refusal, began beating me; the following day, she came to the workshop to verify what I was doing. The forewoman grabbed me and stood me in front of a machine. I had never cried, but the sight of those shells (masses of them) on the assembly line brought tears to my eyes; I could not hold them back.

I was given nothing to eat because I did not work. In the evening, I returned to camp alone, behind the column, escorted by an S.S. trooper and a dog (undoubtedly out of fear that I would escape).

For a week, I was obliged to keep changing work-shops—where they kept trying to make me work. The Aufseherin in each workshop took in "The Ugly One" and beat me in their fashion. I didn't move a muscle.

On the night of February 7, I was told that the Camp Commander had called me to Ravensbrück. I knew they must have had a good reason for this convocation and I was ready for anything and everything.

I was awakened at three o'clock in the morning, and, as it was so early, the Aufseherin brought me into her room. There was a radio on the table. I paid no attention to it, so engrossed was I in my return to camp and in my thoughts of friends and our next meeting....

My thoughts were suddenly interrupted by familiar music.... I thought I was having hallucinations when I suddenly heard a feminine voice saying: "This is Moscow. It is 6 a.m. Here is the latest news." What a peaceful voice! And just like two and a half years before, as if nothing had happened to me, the announcer (Lévitan) said: "From the Office of Soviet Informa-tion...." He reported the capture of certain localities, as well as the city of Rovno; then the Aufseherin turned the radio off. I cannot describe what took place inside me.... During the entire trip to Ravensbrück I kept hearing that male voice: "From the Office of Soviet Information...."

I arrived at the camp at noon. I thought I would be put in the Bunker, but I was sent to my barracks. The inmates, not knowing why I had come back, asked what had become of me—and looked at me curiously. It was only when I was in the barracks that I learned that, during my absence, the "Himmel-Transport," the "Convoy to the Sky," had taken place and that all the prisoners, including the women in good health, had been taken away to be gassed.

I didn't understand: on the one hand, there was that familiar voice of Lévitan, and on the other, the extermination of these unfortunate, innocent women who had no defense.

Each day, I waited for something to happen—but it didn't. On March 10, after roll call, I was taken behind the camp to a large building with an incalculable number of rooms. The Chief of the local Gestapo, Ramdohr-the-Torturer, was in charge of the interrogation. An Aufseherin secretary-typist and an S.S. interpreter wrote everything down. Here is how the interrogation went.

Ramdohr: So, you don't want to work in Germany?

Answer: I worked every day at the camp; but I refuse to work in a war factory.

Ramdohr: We'll force you to. Perhaps you think we're going to take your crap. We should have exterminated you a long time ago—all of you. And you, what are you doing with our soldiers, with your prisoners?

Answer: I'd like to be in the shoes of the German prisoners in the U.S.S.R.

Ramdohr: May be you offer them apples?

Answer: Maybe not apples, but certainly not rutabagas; and we don't make them work in war factories.

I had no sooner finished my sentence than Ramdohr came up to me. He struck me in the face and on the head. Had I not been leaning against a wall, I would have fallen.

Ramdohr: I don't know why prisoners of war are in the camp. I regret that you are still here.

I was given the confession to sign. I refused, demanding a Russian translation.

Ramdohr: You don't want to sign, you don't believe a German officer?

Answer: I demand a Russian translation.

I was pushed out of the room and sent back to the camp. I couldn't calm down. My face and head hurt. The next day, I was again called up before Ramdohr. A woman, with a poor command of Polish, translated for me. I could hardly understand her, but I was in such a state that I signed.

On the morning of March 16, I was sent to the disciplinary barracks. It was a building of small dimensions surrounded by a picket-fence. There were mostly prostitutes there. The doors opened, and the Aufseherin pushed me in. I didn't even have time to see where I was when a hand grabbed me. It was the Aufseherin. She asked my name and why I was there. I wanted to explain, but she screamed at me.

— Ah! From the Genthin factory, I know.

A young Soviet, Zoïa Savelieva, was also there—and had been for two weeks. She had escaped from the "Himmel-Transport." Before that, she had spent a month and a half in the Bunker. Now we were two. We were not permitted to work outside the camp. At four o'clock, we had to fall out for roll call—after which everyone went to unload the vegetable barges on the lake side, or dig up the earth. Those who remained behind cleaned the barracks. We almost had fist-fights to get this job because the lucky ones who got it received a supplementary ladle of soup.

If it was raining or cold, I froze outside; if the weather was nice, I was locked in the washrooms. Then I was permitted to go back to the barracks where the day-long "Schweigestunden" (hours of silence) had begun. I had no little corner to myself: The Germans were on top of the situation here. They spied on all my moves, to provoke me and "turn me in."

I could not sit down or write; I couldn't even have a pencil. It was forbidden to turn around—the silence might be broken. It was necessary to keep clean, but it was forbidden to wash. We could only go to the toilet at fixed hours. The Blockälteste, the Aufseherinnen, and the Stubendienste took turns beating us up. In fact, any inmate could beat us. Filth, syphilis and scabies. It was the inmates who served the food. They could give us our whole ration, or half, or nothing at all. I did not sleep the first night because the lice were swarming all over—and then there were those screams, those thefts, those fights....

For three and a half months I did not say a word to anyone: it was too dangerous to talk to the Russians; a person was "turned in" on the slightest suspicion. I didn't know German, and anyway, what was I to say to these women? They behaved here as they did elsewhere. There was no end to the punishments, and then there was the "Ohne Fressen" (nothing to eat). Often, as a punishment, the entire barracks was deprived of food for the day—sometimes for several days.

When we were sent out to work, the Stubendienst beat us, as well as the Blockälteste and the Aufseherin; the Aufseherinnen escorted the work commando details, accompanied by dogs. They were aided by the S.S. We were sent out to work without distinction. The sick, who stayed in the rear of the column, risked being torn apart by the dogs. And often they were taken to the toilets where they committed suicide; or else their death was hastened by a washdown with icy water. It was a very widespread method.

The physical pain was horrible, but the moral pain was even worse. On any and all occasions we were offended and humiliated.

Conversations with deportees in the regular barracks were rigorously forbidden. The women in the work details had to sing German songs; those who did not sing were punished.

On June 16, at roll call, I was sent to the Schreibstube, the administration, to receive twenty-five blows with a club; but I did not receive them. This happened every Tuesday and Friday.

On July 4, I was taken to the basement of the Bunker. A little table was in the middle of the room. The inmate was put on her stomach, knees resting on a stool, the arms stretched forward, with the feet and hands tied and the chest lashed down. The head was wrapped in a blanket. It was impossible to breath; if I'm not mistaken, the club was made out of bone; one end was covered with leather, the other with rubber. After this "manipulation," the doctor verified the "prescription" to see if it had been properly filled out.

The Camp Commander, Aufseherin Klein, and Doctor Treite witnessed my flogging. Therefore, I cannot say how I felt. I only thought of one thing: don't scream. I don't think I did scream.

A letter from my comrades made its way to me—along with a little poem written by an inmate. I was all stooped over and could not walk, but my soul was injured even more: I no longer wanted to live. I had such awful moments of despair that it was necessary to assemble all my moral strength in order to reject the idea of suicide.

* * *

— When, in 1947,[1] the War Crimes Tribunal of Hamburg condemned Ramdohr to be hanged by the neck until dead, it happens that many of his relatives and friends wrote to the authorities to say that "dear Ludwig would never harm a fly"; that this comrade "breathed happiness itself"; that he was the "protector of the poor and the unfortunate"; that "while walking in the countryside, he would jump to the side in order not to step on a snail or a lizard"; and that when he interred his mother-in-law's canary, he "tenderly placed the little bird in a box and covered it with a rose before burying it under a rose shrub." It is difficult to superimpose the brutal Ramdohr of Ravensbrück, the terror of the entire camp, on "this dear, brave Ludwig."

1.   Lord Russell of Liverpool. Already cited.

18

Ravensbrück Christmases

Ravensbrück, December 24, 1944.[1] At the camp, each of us thought about past Christmases, Christmases of liberty. For each of us, believer or not, Christmas is joy and love. Here, at camp, these words seem to belong to the vocabulary of years gone by, of time gone by, so far away, when we still knew how to cry. A time when we were free.... When we thought of those whom we love so much; all of us, without exception, had a tightening in the throat.... How far it is, how it hurts, souvenirs!...

That night, Annick Pizigot, a Breton from Locminé, and I were next to each other in the "Revier," barracks 10; we were both contagious. One had tuberculosis and dysentery, and the other one had typhus. We united our microbes and our thoughts. This Christmas Eve, we were just two twenty-year-old kids, two N.N. who had heavy hearts. We knew that we had little, very little, chance of getting well.

1. Unpublished manuscript, Monique Barbier.

Just before the hour that soup was to be served, several of our camp companions came to sing us a few Christmas carols. It was the only gift they could give us. The graciousness of this gesture made us feel bad and good at the same time because, in this place, it is painful to think of joys gone by—and to think of joys of the future.... We did not dare think of them. It was in this state of mind that, as the soup was being distributed, we had the surprise of being given some pickles. Yes, that's right, some pickles!

Annick said to me: "In our state, if we eat them, it's certain death." For a few minutes we remained silent, looking at the pickles in the bottom of our mess kit. Which one of us expressed our common thought? "In any case, we're not going to get well. We might as well die on Christmas Day."

For one, as for the other, it seemed that it would be a very particular type of death to die on that day.

Therefore, we decided to eat what was supposed to put us "six feet under." Before going to sleep forever, we said a very sincere prayer... proof that we had found joy and confidence; our "good-night" was a smiling "good-bye."

Even today I still find it extraordinary that we both had the profound, absolute, indisputable conviction that we would go to Paradise: straight up there, and nowhere else.... Comforted by this certitude, I fell asleep.

I was truly in Paradise because I was bathing in a debauchery of resplendent colors, colors that had never been seen before. I was entirely and fully happy. It was in the midst of this newly found joy that I heard a voice cry: "Aufstehen!... Roll call!"

In a fraction of a second, an immense anger invaded me; I was seized with rage and submerged by indignation and, insulting God himself, I screamed to myself:

— Oh, no!... Not here, too!...

Imagine the effect on someone finding a Ravensbrück in Paradise.... It would be the height of all horror, no?

Howling my indignation, I was awakened by the sound of my own voice. I again saw the barracks, the straw mattresses, my companions and...Annick. Annick, who seemed to be touching her body, had her incredulous eyes fixed on me. I was feeling myself too. Yes, we were alive. We were not in Paradise...we were still in camp!

This was the only night when both of us slept profoundly, the only night of real refreshing sleep.

Is that the miracle of Christmas? Be that as it may, I sometimes have the impression that, because of my anger, I lost my Paradise.

What would you have done in my place?

. * .

CHRISTMAS LETTER

My dear little ones,[1]

You must[2] have been very sad that beautiful morning in May (May was such a lovely month!) when you saw your father and mother leave.

But you kept up your hopes of seeing them soon. Your good and gentle aunts watched over you, and protected

1. Naturally, this letter was never mailed. I wrote it with hopes an "occasion" would present itself for it to be sent; the moment never came. I found it by chance in the cover of a little prayer book which I had confided to a Belgian worker just before our departure, at the end of February. After the Armistice, this Belgian, whom I did not know, was kind enough to send my little book to me with 3 knives made at the factory—and a notebook of cooking recipes.

2. This letter "opens" a long unpublished manuscript of several hundred pages written for the intention of Jean, Catherine, Marie-Claire and Pierre-Marie, the children of G...H..., arrested May 13, 1944, for resistance activities and deported to Ravensbrück. Madame G...H... wants her name to be anonymous. This "history of their mother" is, I think, the most beautiful poem of love ever written by a mother for her children.

you; serious events have come up which have held your attention and prevented you from thinking too much about the absence of your parents. Your father's return must have brought you great joy, but he returned alone and your mother's absence was perhaps even more noticed.

What became of her? Where was she? You will soon know; but from today on, which is Christmas (because I spent it peeling vegetables, it is just another day for me), I am going to begin telling you the story of my absence—even though you are never absent from my thoughts, especially at Christmas; in addition, I want to tell you of my desire to live for you.

When it is written down, it will stay with you; all of you; even Pierric, who is so little, will have it to read and, as the years go on, you will all understand it better. You will not forget it.

I do not want to inculcate you with sentiments of vengeance, hate, and even rancor, which I never felt here for one minute; but it would be good for French children to understand and to remember.

I also hope that, in reading the story of your mother, you will have greater confidence in her and that you will confide in her (your small and your great problems and worries) as she is going to confide in you.

You will see to what degree she has been protected and miraculously supported, step by step, during this common ordeal, wanted by the Good Lord, for the good of us all; Marie-Claire must not imagine that her mother is "in prison" for having done something bad. No, from the point of view of humaneness, and even from the point of view of the Germans, I did not deserve this punishment.[1] I feel that all the events that led me here

1. Punishment equivalent to a death sentence because, since we had to work and sleep in the aircraft factories, we did not go down to the air-raid shelters at night—even during the most dangerous alerts; while admitting that we survived the bombing attacks, it was only afterwards that we learned how fortunate we

occurred through the grace of God, and I accept his wish as such. I feel this internal peace that flows over me more today than ever before—despite my deep sorrow.

I know that the ordeal of captivity, even though it is accepted in a Christian manner, is a powerful method of sanctification and a source of grace; but I would never have imagined that it could give such plentiful and supernatural joy.

Today, Christmas Day, I can say that I am "happier" than I have ever been; I worry about nothing; I am like a baby in the hands of the Divine Providence. I feel as though I have been pardoned and that I am almost in the heavens; and I would like these minutes to endure forever.... I could never thank the Good Lord enough for this grace—whose price I know because it is the greatest thing He could give me.... I will reveal all my thoughts to you—not so that you can judge me (one must never judge one's parents), but so that you will pardon me for the pain that I have involuntarily caused you all.

I have already been reproached, and I will be reproached again, for not having always recognized my obligations as the mother of a family, and for having followed a visionary, fanciful and secondary road, instead of ful- filling my duty to the state. A voluntary worker, who, in fact, knew nothing about the resistance movement and nothing about what we did, said to us, without beating around the bush: "After all, we don't pity you that much; you would have been better off home darning your husband's socks!"; my excuse is that I thought I could conciliate the two: patriotism should not diminish with the number of children one has.

On the contrary, the more one has, the more it seems necessary they should be given a sense of love for their country.

---

were because no political prisoner got out of the concentration camps alive.

I was not out searching for adventure; at first, I steadfastly refused to enter a resistance movement. They had to ask me four times before I accepted to render the services demanded of me, and I truly hoped that the modest "aid to the enemy" that I made would never be divulged. I only did what I considered to be my humble duty—as a Frenchwoman—in a tiny sphere of the provinces.

If, while in a cell at A....I had any remorse, any scruples, if I had a tortured conscience, I no longer have it now. I met mothers of families with eight and nine children; one, arrested as a hostage for her son, had eleven. I knew women who had the responsibility of aged or infirm parents; they were indispensable to their homes. I know that, among the men, there are priests in charge of a great many souls; their departure was heavily felt. None permitted themselves to be arrested out of any strict duty of the state—so why would I? And, of course, there were many other women there—ignorant, innocent and completely baffled by their misfortune. Wasn't it better to be with them? No, I must say, I regret nothing; in fact, I could even have done more. My only regret is having pressured P... of having gotten him to consent and go along with me. He is now free, thank God, and I am sure that he has forgiven me those weeks in A...; he was even happy, I think, to share them with me; if I do not come back, he will be alone with the children; their life will be a gloomy one and I will be the cause.

Therein lies my only chagrin—was lying, I mean to say—because now, by the Grace of God, I see farther ahead, and I see better. I understand now that all this ensemble of circumstances was wanted by God. He does everything well. He decided to put my daughter, as well as myself, through this ordeal—and I thank him for it.

And since he has given me this peace and this calm, he would not have refused it to my loved ones. I am certain of it. I feel today that all of us can sing with the same deeply-united heart: "Gloria In Excelsis Deo Et In Terra Pax Hominibus Bonae Voluntatis."

19

Old Maria

I met old Maria one afternoon at the Ravensbrück camp.[1] To get out of a work detail, I had hidden in a barracks full of Slavs. Seated on the ground at the feet of the women (from Dniepropetrovsk) sewing away, I vaguely looked at their ashen faces framed by dirty kerchiefs. Once in a while, one of them would intone a prayer; the others joined in, almost in a whisper—abandoning their needles and thread to look out beyond the low barracks at the pale sky and the black heads of the fir trees.

I first set foot in the camp one wintry night some two months ago, and I was struck by the barren and miserable land surrounding it. Since then, what discoveries I have made in this inhuman world, particularly on the faces that I come across every day; the expressions cannot disguise a dead or dying soul.

Souls are not killed with a single blow. They vacillate a long time before dying. Despite all the belligerence

1. Geneviève de Gaulle: *Les Cahiers du Rhône,* December 1946. La Baconnière, Neuchâtel.

and violence, a breath of pestilence sometimes slips within one: concessions to the tough-minded that can no longer go on, revolt-fatigue, and sinking will-power.

Is it this crematorium chimney, with its reddish, greyish smoke, a dirty mixture against the Baltic sky, that frees one?

Old Maria came to sit next to me. Very ugly, large and heavy features, the face marked with pimples. As she speaks, she passes her thin fingers through her balding grey hair.

Maria is German and Catholic. She was a professor in a Berlin highschool. In order to continue struggling against Nazism, she inscribed herself in the Communist Party after the Catholic Center had betrayed its members. Then she spent 10 years in prison. "Even the Nazis could not have thought up anything worse, Maria told me, than to separate me from men and the world. Two years in secret confinement—without a human face, without even a book. But me, whom they thought they could shut away from the living, I've had my revenge here." And she pointed out the elderly Russians with the clear eyes. "Women arrive in this camp every day in long convoys. They come from all over Europe with their tight little bundles of clothes, or their suitcases. Now, tell me about France."

Leaning up against the partition-wall, Maria closes her eyes. Does she hear beyond the walls the distant murmur of people liberating themselves?

I told her of our refusal, in June 1940, to be reduced to bondage, and of our fight for liberty. Maria listened with all ears, and even asked questions. After the struggle, she predicted there would be various exchanges between peoples, constructive steps towards peace— in which the Church would play a role. She cited Saint Thomas, or talked of her combat experience at the heart of the Communist Party. Maria was a liberty militant.

* * *

Hours passed. Evening fell. A "barracks chief" came and roughly shook the elderly Russians and told them to go get some heavy tubs of soup. I felt comforted and serene in the shadow of Maria. But in a few minutes I would have to go back to my sordid shanty of a barracks and face again the howls of a shrew and the indifference or brutality of the other prisoners.

Maria, Maria, where will I find joy?

* * *

Maria took my hand and we went out together and walked in the "streets" of the camp. Women were coming back from work—tired, used up, with grey faces.

"How beautiful the sky is," said Maria. "It's like an immense fire glowing above the walls. Had I gone to work in the swamps today, I would have seen this astonishing purple light reflecting on the lake. Tomorrow there will be mist and the seagulls will fly back to the sand dunes; and perhaps I will hear the siren of a boat looking for its way through the fog, en route to the Baltic."

"And the day after tomorrow is Sunday. In the morning, if I can get out of work, I will go and pray in barracks 15 where the French read the Mass. In the afternoon, the Polish sisters sing Vespers. And in the evening, I'll meet with the Russian soldiers. I already know Polish and I have learned enough Russian to understand. One of them recounts the battle of Stalingrad. She is the wife of a colonel. She improvises poems. You should come with me Sunday; will you?"

* * *

Old Maria left me on the doorstep of my barracks. She died a month after our meeting. Of misery, of being worn out, of everything. A comrade brought her flowers on one of the last days of her life. Maria, our old Maria, What a human woman!

20

The Tent

It was from barracks 31[1] that we watched the construction of the tent. No barracks had ever been built on the
vacant site situated between barracks 24 and 26 because,
it seems, the earth was not stable and would not
withstand the weight of any solid construction. Inasmuch as the Zugegangenen[2] were arriving at a more
and more accelerated rate, and inasmuch as there was
no longer any room in front of the showers to contain
them, they massed behind the small Kammer, the
Revier and Work Office buildings. There, French, Dutch,
Yugoslav and Polish women often spent several days
without receiving any food other than a few large cans
of coffee.

— That's when the tent went up.

— For flooring, bricks were put on the ground. Then
pickets were planted and a large canvas was stretched
over them. It looked like an immense exposition hall. It

1. Denise Dufournier. Already cited.
2. New arrivals.

was called barracks 25 and destined to shelter temporarily the Zugegangenen before they went to the showers.

— About three weeks after our arrival at barracks 31, Frau Louisa called us over to barracks 26. Without hesitation, we hefted our bundles of belongings on our shoulders and returned to our former "domicile." We were right in the middle of August. We could easily observe all those entering and leaving the tent, which was always full. The heat was torrid. The first prisoners to occupy the tent were Poles from Warsaw. They were very elegant and very astonished to find themselves there. They had been caught in a trap when the Russians were about to enter Warsaw.

— The Germans had encouraged the Polish population to put itself under the protection of the Third Reich. In addition, they all but ordered them to gather up all their most precious possessions. With one swoop of the net, they picked up all the people and their prized belongings. They got this huge herd out on the road and, without any explanation, took them to Ravensbrück. There they were stacked up under the tent. It was forbidden to go outside. As there were not enough mess kits to go round, empty food cans were distributed when the soup was served. And as no sanitary installation had been provided, huge cans were placed in the street and around the tent—to be used as toilets. Among these people that were being "protected" by the Reich were entire congregations of religious women. Armed soldiers, accompanied by dogs, stood guard night and day.

— The approaches to this sinister site were carefully defended. But as soon as the prisoners had undergone the formality of the showers and had had all their riches taken from them, the guards became less severe; however, the prisoners were to remain under the tent for an indeterminate time—until they could be lodged in the barracks. We could go up and talk to them, and they even had permission now to leave the tent. But their poor treasures, saved with great effort and lugged on their frail backs, despite their intense fatigue, had been taken from them. Once again this instinct for theft and highway robbery, which we had observed during our entire stay, reared its vicious head—particularly where our guards were concerned. The surest and quickest method of getting rid of these "supplementary inhabitants" was, obviously, to transport them elsewhere. The arrival and departures multiplied. The convoys crossed each other on the roads.

— The eight days spent[1] in the tent were days of misery. It was the beginning of February, and the weather was cold and humid. Most of those among us had dysentery; having to sleep on a floor of damp bricks aggravated it. At night our situation became horrible, unimaginable; here was this long tent with only one little entrance, a tent that sheltered several hundred poor women, most of them sick with dysentery—a humiliating and irritating illness; at least once during the night, all the women were obliged to go outside—without the slightest light by which to find their way. Many times I was awakened by women walking on me as they tried to find the door, and I know that I did the same thing to others when I had to go out. I scrambled over bodies, feeling around with my hand for a place to put my foot; sometimes I lost my balance and fell on someone's stomach or face. I excused myself, although I was sobbing. If I walked on someone who knew me or recognized my voice, she accepted my excuses; but if it was an unknown person, I was hit and pushed—and I usually fell on someone else. It was a nightmare. By "holding themselves in" in an extraordinary manner, the women were generally able to get to the door before it was too late, but, once outside, nothing counted any-

1. Virginia d'Albert-Lake: *Comité d'Histoire de la Deuxième Guerre mondiale—Tragédie de la Déportation.* Hachette, 1954.

more. The space between the barracks was in an indescribable state every morning. Prisoners were designated
to clean it. In the daytime, the lines of women waiting to
go to the "toilets" were so long and slow-moving that
many of them could not "control" themselves until their
turn came. So, the Germans had holes dug, about three
feet in diameter—at regular intervals between the barracks. There, without any shelter, one would always find
at least two or three women squatting down around the
same hole.

— Having to live in such unsanitary conditions, and
without any medicaments of any sort, our state of health
continued to worsen. Our morale fell lower and lower.
Some women even gave up trying to leave the tent
when it was necessary for them to do so, and it became
intolerable to have to sleep there. Others were so weak
that they could not move, but, being exempt from the roll
call, they were not eligible to go to the infirmary. Women
died day and night, but their bodies were not taken away
until several hours after their death. "Neighbors" covered
them with whatever they had at hand. I saw all my
friends getting weaker and weaker, and I felt that I was
following suit.

— From the tent[1] came noises and screams. We asked
ourselves what was going on. This time, we went into
the tent. How can I describe the sight we saw? Words do
not have enough force to tell of the horror. Can you
imagine this "barracks" of canvas, of enormous dimensions, which the wind, rain and cold penetrated? The
bare ground is covered with mud... and on this ground,
prostate with fatigue, were 2,000 to 2,200 women—lying
down, here and there and on and under each other.... An
awful odor wafted up into our nostrils, a mixture of
human clothing and...toilets, which were improvised in
the most rudimentary fashion: simple, open buckets

1.   Unpublished manuscript, H. Le Belzic.

located in the most narrow part of the back of the tent.
We are there, thirty-five Frenchwomen. We look at this
spectacle with eyes that do not dare believe what they
see. These women lying there, are they really human
beings? We spoke to some of them: they are Hungarian,
Slovak, and Gipsies. There is also a group of Austrians
from Graz. One of them, with whom we spoke at length,
is on a stretcher. As a result of being beaten up by the
Gestapo, she is paralyzed. She was part of a group of
patriots. There was a revolt in Graz and they were
arrested. Their crime was "monumental": they were Jews
and almost all of them belonged to "high society." The
others belonged to inferior races that must be destroyed.
It's terribly edifying. With two of my companions, we
spend the night pacing back and forth. We are very weary
and hungry. We arrived too late to get the slightest parcel
of food; we must wait until tomorrow![1]

1. During February 1945 (the Russians were advancing stead-
ily), the tent disappeared. Testimony of Denise Dufournier: "The
tent was completely emptied. The prisoners who lived in it
(among them were our compatriots who had come back from
the "Petit Koenigsberg") had either been sent "elsewhere" or had
been dispersed throughout the other barracks. Just as we had
witnessed its construction, a symbol of so much immeasurable
evil, we were able to witness its destruction. Once the canvas
and the huge tent pegs had been taken away, there was nothing
left except a heap of ruins—in the middle of which decomposing
bodies had been buried. One would have said that a bad
bombing attack or huge conflagration had taken place here.
Within 48 hours, the area was clean as a whistle. The terrain had
been leveled. Thus, there was no trace or sign that could feed
anyone's suspicions that, on these few square meters, thousands
of human beings had suffered—suffered as no human imagination could conceive."

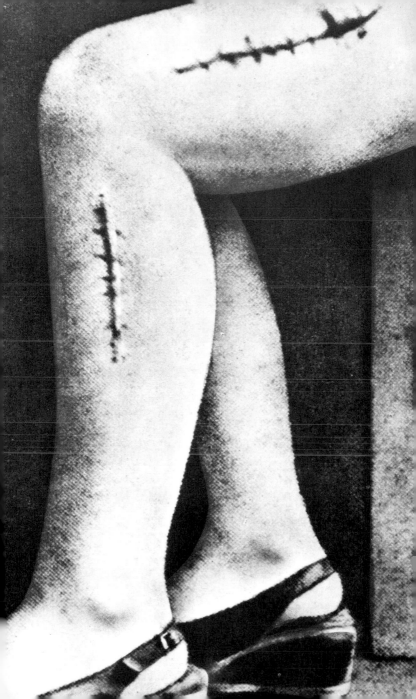

Woman with a mutilated leg. Those inmates to be used as guinea pigs were placed in the hands of the doctors of death. Their multiple experiments had but one goal! to determine the most rapid biological methods of extermination.
Tallandier Archives

21

Ravensbrück, Extermination Camp

As in all the other concentration camps, German doctors in Ravensbrück carried out medical experiences on the "human material" so graciously put at their disposal by Himmler. Close by these criminal doctors were a number of deported physicians who performed veritable "medical miracles" (often under the same roof of the same infirmary where the Germans were "operating"). Without the help of any medicine or even surgical instruments, and dependent only on their willpower and their courage, they saved hundreds and even thousands of inmates. As in all the concentration camps, children lived and died at Ravensbrück. And, like the women's camp of Auschwitz, women who were well along in their pregnancy gave birth at Ravensbrück. I think it is unnecessary, in this book, to go back over the crimes of Professor Gebhart, to speak again of the suffering undergone by these 74 Polish students who were sacrificed or mutilated by the experimenters, and to discuss once again these "antechambers of death" which were derisively called infirmaries. And inasmuch as several chapters of *Devil's Doctors* and *Doctors of Mercy*[1] have been devoted to the unbelievable "survival stories" of Guy Poirot, Sylvie Aylmar and Jean-Claude Passerat (these three French nationals, born at Ravensbrück, were the only survivors of all the forgotten children assassinated there), I see no reason to cover that ground. But perhaps, while we are speaking of the children of Ravensbrück—the most atrocious crime, even if it is true that there is no hierarchy in crime, it is necessary to present a new testimony, a last unpublished document.

— I gave birth[2] on January 25, 1945, to a girl, whom I named Chantal, at the Ravensbrück camp. Ten hours later, we were sent to the N.N. barracks (32) until March 13, at which time we left for Bergen-Belsen. At the beginning, I breastfed my daughter, but at the end of a month I had no more milk. I had to give her a bottle. After having been given their bottles, all the children in the camp had to be put at the entrance of the building— lined up on an inclined plank which was covered with a straw mat, dirty, of course. Mothers were forbidden to take them on work details; there was no heat but plenty of broken window panes here and there. So, I went to get my girl every chance I got, and I slept with her to

1. By the same author and publisher.
2. Unpublished manuscript, Marie-Louise Ozon, née Gigleux. January 1972.
   Another deportee, Jeanne Barsacq, called my attention to the birth of Chantal (unpublished manuscript, May 1970): "Among my comrades in the convoy that arrived at Ravensbrück on September 1, 1944, was a very young woman named Marie-Louise Gigleux. This patriot, born in Strasbourg on April 25, 1925, spoke fluent German and the purest of French. During her internment and captivity, she obstinately refused to speak the language of her torturers, but she understood absolutely everything within earshot. She refused all work assignments—in the infirmary, the kitchen, the sewing-shop and administrative offices. She was expecting a baby. During one interminable roll call, she squatted down and gave birth to Chantal."

warm her up a bit. I had only one fear: that she would cry. It only happened once; fortunately, there was no surveillant around at that time. We were lucky! I had to swap a piece of bread to get clothes for my daughter. Washing them out was a major project; particularly since I had no soap and the clothes wouldn't dry. I hung them on the wooden frame of my bunk, just above my head. To get them really dry, I ended up sleeping on them; it was the only way I could change her.

— On the night of March 13, I embarked for a trip of a day and a half: only one baby bottle and water that came from the locomotive. During the voyage, the son of a Belgian died. The guard had him put in a little tool chest. Just at that moment, the train made a violent jerk. The baby's arms moved. The German said to her: "You dirty Frenchwoman, your child isn't dead (alas! The child was dead): and I suppose now you're going to tell everyone we killed him." When we arrived at our destination on the evening of March 15, my comrade had to pick up her dead son in her arms. After we had gone through the shower, I never saw her again.

— I found myself in a building where, naturally, no provision of any kind had been made for babies. We even had to sleep on the floor. During that night, my daughter died in my arms. I felt the life leaving her little body. I was full of despair but I didn't want anyone to notice I wanted to keep her. But toward noon, I had to take her to the morgue. I cut off a lock of her hair (I still have it, along with a few of her poor clothes) and I put her down gently. I waited in the vicinity, hiding myself.

— I watched as they placed her on a large shovel and threw her into the crematorium oven. And I was left alone with my sorrow—and my twenty years of age.

THE MAD

I remember Mama Deshaies.[1] We all knew that, after the last good-byes she had with her husband and son at Romainville, she would never see them again. We had learned that the father had been gassed upon arrival and that the son died several weeks later in the Auschwitz camp. I admired her courage and the hope she held out to see them again after victory, but, alas, she died among the mad. Dysentery made us more or less sick. She had lost her reason and was taken from our barracks and put with mad women.

Parked in a naked room without food or water, matted with all sorts of befouled matter and with only one window—grilled—these mad women screamed without stop. They were guarded night and day by an Aufseherin who, with the help of her club, prevented anyone from approaching the room, threatening to lock up all those who insisted. Every time we passed in front of the barracks, we heard plaintive cries from the dying and howls that had nothing in common with a woman's voice. Once, taking advantage of the guardian's short absence, I ran to the room to see if I could catch a glimpse of Mama Deshaies. I was struck with horror. Nothing one can imagine could compare or even slightly resemble the spectacle of this inhuman dungeon soiled from top to bottom: nude bodies tangled up in poses that approaching death had distorted, arms and legs that agitated, haggard eyes that looked right through me and moans and groans that suddenly became screams of terror. Nothing was human about it! I was simply floored....So much so that I turned and ran away. How could anyone be found in the middle of these specters whose eyes, postures and screams were all the same. The memory of that scene haunts me even today. Why were these women being treated in this manner? Why were they not

1. Unpublished manuscript, Simone Lampe. June 1970.

given food and drink? The answer is simple; the object of their torturers was: death for all.

EXECUTIONS

The execution of women took place,[1] as far as I know, on three occasions. Naturally, these massacres remained secret; they were spoken about only at the risk of one's life; we learned about them only after the deed had been done (their clothes came back to the disinfection service).

A few weeks after our arrival, we were told about one such execution (the terrorizing effect upon us was complete). It seems that one night, around five o'clock, some Poles were shot in a building at the entrance to the camp, a hundred meters from us; we heard the shots... behind us.

At the beginning of January 1945, two Czechs, three Russians and a Pole were put to death: Zofia Lipinska was executed one morning at dawn. She was one of the prettiest women in Warsaw, a distinguished lawyer, a woman with a kind heart, a pleasing personality and a great friend of France. She was a Stubowa in Barracks 26, where she worked like no one else to care for our sick. Oh, she was not one of those who collaborated with the enemy. As a journalist, she had taken an active part in the rebellion; the Krauts knew this, and Zofia never left Ravensbrück! Nothing frightened her; still, she nevertheless had the impression that life was soon to end. She dominated her suffering and her fears in order to comfort those around her; she was bold and daring and it was through her that we occasionally heard bits of "magnificent" news—this word was familiar to her and she pronounced it with emphasis in a half-voice—from a contact which we supposed she had found "on the

1.   Rosane: *Terre des Cendres*. Already cited.

outside." In October 1944, Zofia was called to the political office; the Commander had already signed her death warrant; she was to remain at his disposal and not leave the barracks. Months passed before, in January, she was taken to the Bunker; Zofia kept her sweet smile, Germany would be defeated. At night, in "the building of the patriots," women undressed before the firing squad.

Fifteen days later, January 18, 1945, the French barracks was in mourning. As of the dawn roll call, Pierrette Salinat and Marie-Louise Cloarec, our two parachutists, and Suzy and Jenny, their radio operators (as liaison officers, they had—while on a mission not far from Paris—been arrested and incarcerated at Fresnes, then deported to Germany), were warned, according to a set formula, that they were at the disposal of the Camp Commander and were formally forbidden to leave their barracks until the appointed hour—4:30 p.m.

Few of us were aware of the news; we didn't dare envisage the drama (it is prudent to keep quiet, for the little ones and for ourselves). I spent the day with them. Pierrette and Marie-Louise are children. Pierrette, 22, earned her stripes in London; she loves Africa where she prepared the American landing. Marie-Louise is a valiant Breton, aged 24, who has been to war; and Suzy, from Metz, is the mother of a six-year-old girl. Jenny adores taking risks. All four fell into German hands in April 1944. Will they be treated as soldiers?

Then the fatal blow came. Although no one was better informed than we were, the effect filled us with stupor. That night, we waited for them to return to the barracks— without hope. Marie-Louise had imagined a thousand possibilities; full of illusions as always, she had taken along several addresses. Pierrette didn't say a word, she was thinking. Nevertheless, they were shot. Night came, the barracks was closed; the little ones would not sleep there. The next day, we made a tooth-comb search. On the register, next to the four matriculated numbers, was the vague and classic notation: "Transport," destination unknown. How strange; between her teeth a woman murmured: "This is how they indicate people have been shot." Later, our Czech friends were able to find the clothes, which had been sent back to the drying room. Our search went on. At six o'clock, they had left the Bunker; they were seen passing by. A column outside had seen the road barricaded at a particular spot, and in the woods, near a lonely building, the S.S. fidgeted. Even the shots had been heard. A truck went off in the direction of the crematorium. That's all the sure information we could find out; we badly disguised our sorrow.

THE YOUTH CAMP

A simple circular,[1] which announced without commentary that the mortality rate was too low, arrived in the office during the second half of 1944 (but I cannot furnish the precise date because, at the time, I did not give the matter the attention it deserved). Nevertheless, the rate was much higher when we first came—mainly as a result of the Hungarian Jews that had arrived and the evacuation of camps and prisons in the East, which had brought to the camp convoys of women in a state of misery never seen before. The secretary who had seen this letter drew no conclusion. I had no knowledge of more detailed instructions on the subject. Perhaps the commander had received them directly. The secretary added that it was the first time she had seen this type of memo, and that her superior was upset she had seen it too.

One night, a little later, Schwester Martha came to visit the sick in barracks 10; she offered sleeping pills to those who slept badly. Several dozen women asked for them; the majority did not wake up the next day. The others became sick, but survived. (It is hardly necessary to say

1.   Germaine Tillion: *Cahiers du Rhône.* Already cited.

that no one in the camp suffered from insomnia.) The S.S. doctor Treite said that it was a prescription "error"— but it set us thinking.

Along about this time, all the old, sick and tired women were "invited" to a convalescent camp called Jugendlager, several hundred meters from ours. Despite the cruel experience they had already had with the Germans, many of them accepted the "invitations."

Still later (end of December, beginning of January), a second crematorium oven was built and, from then on, both operated without interruption, 24 hours out of 24; still, they were not able to burn all the cadavers; the camp officials raised their temperatures to increase cremations—but this resulted in the explosion of one oven in mid-February.

However, only six months earlier, when Ravensbrück was just a camp for simple work projects, a lone oven, lighted only twice a week, and then for hardly more than a few hours, sufficed. The population of the camp had considerably diminished since then (August 1944–January 1945), but even taking into account the misery, which was much greater, a single oven burning for two half-days a week would have been ample to handle a normal mortality rate.

The gas chamber began functioning in December.

The camouflaging of these assassinations was probably, at least within the general framework of the German camps, the only real novelty about Ravensbrück. (There was no point in taking the risk of provoking panic that would paralyze a model industrial group!) Therefore, when the moment came to create Jugendlager, precautions were taken to give confidence to the sick and weak women who were sent there. In particular, the camp was blessed with an infirmary which was supposed to be run by a French doctor-prisoner who was perfectly honorable and known as such (5-10 December, 1944). Naturally, the comedy did not last long; we almost immediately realized that the infirmary in question had no medicine, no heat, and not even any straw mats; we also learned that the sick arriving at the camp were promptly stripped of their coats and woolen garments and obliged to stand out in the snow for entire days—almost without food, a practice found in many extermination camps; there was no real reason for it because those who were most ill were precisely the ones gassed every night. This additional suffering was therefore unnecessary; and it did not even save gas....

Only a few days passed before the doctors and nurses were called back to their old camp; but the unbelievable fact about the infirmary was that theoretically, it was maintained by S.S. medical personnel, called Sanitäts-dienst; their names were Rose and X... (their exclusive role was to brain the sick who refused to swallow the poison) and a prisoner called Vera Salveguart, a veritable monster who was in charge of poisoning. When a contingent of women arrived at Jugendlager, they were put in a barracks and then subjected to intense cold and hunger. A small number of them, rigorously chosen at random, were reserved for the so-called infirmary—where they died either of misery or of poisoning. This was the case of one of my comrades, a young, reserved and exquisite woman of letters who was highly cultured and serious-minded; she was bashed to death for having refused to swallow her dose of poison.

In my opinion, the only plausible explanation for such incoherence and apparent intricacy was, that it was an attempt to apportion the mortality rate—an idea which I presume was the invention of Commander Suhren.

On the camp register, women sent to the gas chamber came under the column "dispatched to Camp Mittwerda," or "sanatorium"; in other words, Jugendlager was, at least on paper, an extraordinary camp where one almost never died. On the other hand, the women who were beaten to death or poisoned in the infirmary were listed as having died a natural death on the register—and naturally, there had to be a few live inmates around, if

only for the sake of credibility. But who were they trying to impress, and who were they trying to fool? The
prisoners, perhaps? Hardly. They wanted nothing more
than to believe in the story about Mittwerda—caring
nothing about statistics; they ran a much greater risk of
being struck by the horrors that took place in this phoney
hospital than by any trumped-up set of figures—which
they fortunately did not know existed. Was it some kind
of administrative fetishism? Perhaps. The commander
undoubtedly dreamed of the total extermination of witnesses, a clean-up operation through death, and of a
completely empty camp—impeccably swept up by the
last prisoner; he could show his superiors some lovely
statistics, proving that fewer women died in his camp
than in others and that everything was "perfectly correct."

But even from this Jugendlager, which was the antechamber of death, there were women who came back.
There were even survivors of Jugendlager's infirmary.
One, in particular, was very handy with a needle; she had
begun some kind of sweater or embroidery work for the
feared Vera Salveguart. Every night Vera demanded that
the work be finished by the next day, but every morning
she invented a new flower or festoon of flowers and, in
the meantime, she was fed and able to gather her
strength.

* * *

I never worked at Ravensbrück[1] because I had a "pink
card," given to all prisoners who were not capable of
doing any hard work around the camp because of age or
infirmities.

At the end of January, 1945, "selections" were made
among the pink-card holders; they were then sent to
Jugendlager (translation: Youth Camp), a former disciplinary camp for young Germans. On February 2, it was

1.   Unpublished manuscript, Irène Bloncourt-Ottelard.

my turn to leave; I was relatively happy about going there because we had been assured living conditions in this camp would be better for us, the old and the infirm, than at Ravensbrück. All those, who, like me, could not walk, were placed on a large mobile platform. It was drawn by about twenty prisoners whom the Aufseherinnen whipped to make it go faster. These poor women had a very difficult time pulling this makeshift vehicle, heavily loaded, on the roads filled with potholes made by the rain. In some places they had water up to their knees, and the wheels kept bogging down in the mud. I'll never forget that trip; it seems it lasted for an eternity—even though the distance we had to travel was short: three kilometers.

Finally we arrived at Jugendlager.

At first sight, it looked better than Ravensbrück. The barracks had been built in the pines; through the barbed wire we could see fields and woods. It would be a change from the eternal grey wall of the camp. But almost immediately we became disenchanted. We were ordered into a barracks where there were no lights; we had to install ourselves on infected straw mats, without blankets. There was no wash basin and no toilets in the barracks; in the middle of the night we would have to go outdoors, four or five barracks further away to find a large ditch bordered on each side with planks on which we could not sit because they were so filthy dirty. It is difficult to imagine the place without having seen it. The next morning, around 3:30 a.m., they came to get us up for roll call; this greatly surprised us because we had been told this terrible obligation did not exist in this new camp.

I stayed about ten days in this barracks and, while there, I saw some 25 of my companions die under horrible conditions. Exhausted by hunger and dysentery, they could not move and just simply lay there when they had to relieve themselves—at least those who did not even have the strength to do so in their mess kits. The atmosphere was one of pestilence because, as it was so cold, the windows were never opened.

But I was to see even worse in barracks 6, where I was later sent with around five or six hundred women.

It was an immense room with violent drafts because many windows had no panes; the straw mats on the ground were so close together that it was impossible to move around without walking on one another. At night, we could not sleep because of the continuous going-and-coming of women getting up to go out; most of the time, they didn't make it, collapsing in the obscurity of their neighbors and soiling them as they did so. This provoked vicious exchanges between the prisoners; above all this noise were the threats and screams of abuse from the Lagerpolizei (camp police) or from the S.S. Many prisoners solved this problem by relieving themselves on their mat or in their mess kit, which they either emptied out of the windows or stuck underneath their mat until the next day.

All day long, those who were able to stand had to fall out for interminable and murderous roll calls; then they spent long hours waiting to receive some thin rutabaga soup and some bread.

The only thing we had to drink was a quarter cup of substitute coffee at night, and, naturally, we had to stand in line to get it. There was no water in the barracks with which to wash and clean our mess kits. Vermin was everywhere: on the floor, on the straw mats and all over our clothes—which also swarmed with lice, literally.

In this room, there was a corner where prisoners who could not move any longer were put to die; they finished their time on earth without anyone giving a hoot; and morning and night the "dead detail" came to take them away.

During the roll calls, the S.S. picked out women at random. Their pitiful baggage was taken from them, a number was inscribed on their arm with an indelible pencil and, with appropriate kicks and curses, they were piled into trucks—which came back empty about ten minutes later.

Afterwards I learned these unfortunate women had been taken to the gas chamber. These "trips" took place daily. Once, an Aufseherin, tired of seeing certain women—those who could not walk—lying around on their litter of straw, instead of falling out for roll call with the others, ordered them sent to the infirmary. I was among them; one of my comrades came to warn me that, in the infirmary, they executed the sick by giving them shots. She pleaded with me to answer the roll call signal so that I would not be sent there. But it was absolutely impossible for me, despite all my willpower, to drag myself outside the barracks; besides, it mattered little if they put me to death with a syringe. I preferred that to the gas chamber.

Then it was that I saw, for the first time, Vera Salveguart—Schwester Vera, as we more commonly called her. She was the nurse in charge of the barracks. She made the selections among the sick sent to her; she put us in several little rooms, which made up the infirmary. It appeared to be relatively clean and well-equipped; at first, that is. Certainly better than the infested barracks I had just left. I even caught sight of two beautiful wash basins and two toilets—in white ceramic. At last I was going to be able to wash a little. The barracks was divided into small rooms containing seven or eight tiers of bunks—with about thirty women in each room. They were always closed and it was forbidden to go into anyone else's room. Along with a comrade, Madame Gaby Hamouy, I was put in room number 4, and told to sleep with a little German. As it was the only free bottom bunk, and as I could not climb to the one above, I was forced to separate from my friend—with whom I would have preferred to share a bed. It was not very agreeable sleeping with a stranger—particularly since mine was going through the last stages of tuberculosis and kept spitting blood into a basin placed next to her. In addition, she was covered with putrid wounds over which crawled all sorts of vermin. I cannot forget the nightmarish hours that I spent feeling lice moving from her body to mine. I was so revolted that, the next day, I made superhuman efforts to get up to where Madame Gaby slept—preferring to fall and break every bone in my body than spend another night with my contagious companion. The straw mat I occupied with my friend had just as much vermin, but at least Madame Gaby did not resemble a repulsive consumptive who had reached the end of her life and was now just rotting on her bunk.

The food in this infirmary was reduced to the strict minimum: a half-liter of hot water, in which a few round slices of carrots and rutabagas swam, a slice of bread weighing fifty grams, and, at night, a small amount of ersatz coffee—the commander having decreed that we were "material for the crematorium."

It was Vera who transmitted this information to us. I was already thin, but now I was turning into a skeleton; often I had dizzy spells caused by hunger that ate at my innards.

The whole day was like that—collapsed on our bed, my friend and I sometimes didn't have even the strength to talk to each other. However, I heard the Germans and other foreigners speaking in nearby beds; they fearfully spoke of the "Spritze" (hypodermic injection). Up to that moment, I had not noticed anything unusual about our room—we were left in comparative peace; but, as I dragged myself to the bathroom every night, I was surprised to find four or five nude women lying on the tiles, moaning, groaning and visibly in their last death throes. I realized these women had certainly been given "hypo" shots. In fact, through the glass door of our room, I saw Schwester Vera going along the corridor one night on her way to the Waschraum (bathroom) carrying a syringe and tourniquet; I heard screams, and then there was silence and the nurse came out. A few minutes later, I went to the Waschraum and found a woman's body. This scene took place almost daily, and I saw that the women Vera was putting to death with her syringe came from a room situated at the back of the infirmary where it was forbidden to go and which we knew only as the Tagesraum. Serious cases of typhus were sent there, and the only time the inmates came out was to go and die on the Waschraum floor. I also learned that, when prisoners were designated to go to this room, they were stripped nude and the little baggage which they might still have was taken from them.

One day, Schwester Vera came into our room and told Madame Gaby and me to get ready to go to the Tagesraum. We were stunned, but I had the courage to go and find Vera and ask why she was sending us into this awful room inasmuch as we did not have typhus. She replied that, in the small room where we were, only those with tuberculosis could stay; and besides, the Tagesraum had been cleaned and disinfected and we would be much better off there because there was no more contagious bacteria crawling about. I then asked why all our belongings were taken from us, and I insisted that she authorize us to keep them. Confronted with my obstinacy, she consented and we went into the Tagesraum where some twenty-odd women, who had been evacuated, like us, from the other little rooms, had gathered. But they had had their packages taken from them; and when some of them protested that we had been allowed to keep our belongings, Schwester Vera explained that we were being sent elsewhere, my comrade and I, the next morning. This news thrilled me because, at last, the moment had come to leave this horrible Jugendlager.

That night, Schwester Vera came into the Tagesraum holding a package in one hand and a spoon in the other; she was followed by an orderly carrying a bottle which, I presume, was filled with water.

"A number of you are leaving to go elsewhere," she told us, "and I am going to give you a medicine to give you strength to make the trip."

She began giving certain women a spoonful of white powder. As she came up to me, I opened my mouth to take what I believed was some magic medication but, to my great astonishment, she said:

"No, no, not you, you're not going yet; I received the list from the Ravensbrück doctor and you're not on it— but your friend is going...."

Madame Gaby swallowed the powder, which she said had a very disagreeable taste. A dozen other women— Jews, Poles, Russians, Germans, Rumanians, Yugoslavs—also took the powder, making a face of disgust as they did so. My friend said she asked herself if, by any chance, the medicine just administered to her was poison.

I was a little perplexed but I told her that, in my opinion, if the Schwester had wanted to get rid of these women, she would have given them shots—like she did others before. One thing upset me though: why was I not leaving with the others? Would I never get out of this camp of horror? Soon, all the prisoners fell into a deep sleep. In the morning, when I woke up, they were still sleeping. This prolonged slumber which seemed a little strange to me, persisted throughout the morning. Along toward three or four o'clock in the afternoon, the snoring stopped, one by one; I looked at my friend closely and saw that she was no longer sleeping; she was dead. In horror I realized that this "medicine" was actually a powerful narcotic which killed all the weakened organisms. The few women, who, like me, had not taken the powder, looked at the rigid bodies with fear and fright. Soon after, the "dead detail" came to take away the cadavers. I will not try to describe the state of mind into which I had been plunged by the sight of those nude, frayed skeletons being tossed about by their laughing "pall bearers." The "dead detail" finished their macabre duty with sinister nonchalance—manipulating the corpses like common packages.

Once the room was emptied and cleaned, other prisoners came to the Tagesraum to take the place of those who had just been executed, and, that night, Schwester Vera began again to distribute her moral "medicine." I lived in this atmosphere of crime for more than a month. Every day, prisoners arrived; the next day, their bodies were taken to join the others at the crematorium.

One day, a Frenchwoman, Madame Ridondelli, was brought to the Tagesraum. I had not seen a compatriot for some time so, immediately after her arrival we began to chat—even though the poor woman was in a lamentable state. She told me she had been evacuated from Koenigsberg, that she had walked fifty kilometers in the snow with other comrades, and that, inasmuch as she was afflicted with phlebitis and terrible dysentery—hardly able to stand—she had been sent to the infirmary. For the last few days, the Tagesraum had been supplied with several beds on which the sick slept, two or three together. Madame Ridondelli was given room on one of them, but the orderly warned her that, if she soiled the straw mattress, she would be given a "shot." The poor woman knew what that meant because, throughout the Jugendlager, it was common knowledge that "shots" were given in the infirmary. Despite this threat, she could not help from dirtying her bed. When the orderly found what she had done, she ordered her to get up and go to the Waschraum to get a pail of water and something with which to clean her "Schweinerei." She could not comply because she had no strength and was unable to walk. Paula, the orderly, lashed out at her with a leather whip and called her "Schwein." I stood by powerless and watched this dreadful scene. The Schwester appeared and Paula told her what had happened.

"All right," said Vera, "we'll put her in the Kammer (small room, next to the Tagesraum, where cadavers waiting to be sent to the crematorium were placed); and tonight I'll give her a shot."

Paula brutally pushed the poor woman, who resisted and begged for mercy in this antechamber of death. That night, I saw Schwester Vera pass by, with her syringe and tourniquet. She went into the Kammer. I heard a series of heart-rending screams from Madame Ridondelli:

"No, no, I don't want it.... No shot.... Have pity...." Then she howled: "Irène, Irène.... They've killed me."

On her way out of the Kammer, Vera said to me:

"It's just as well she dies like that...she was a goner in any case."

That was the excuse she gave for her deed of the day. And I could do nothing nor say anything. I was waiting to undergo the same treatment, one day or another. Up until then, she spared us, a few prisoners and me, because we were useful to her. Some women, who were seamstresses by profession, were obliged to make dresses or even lingerie for her out of material that she stole from the camp stores; and me...she had me sing, because she liked my voice....

The executions went on at an accelerated cadence and hundreds of women perished in this manner. Vera, armed with a pair of pliers, removed the gold crowns from the cadavers' teeth. On April 5, the order finally arrived to evacuate the Jugendlager and to take the few remaining survivors to Ravensbrück.

I would never have thought or believed that I could feel such joy at seeing this camp again—which I had left, full of hope, for a better one.

When I found myself in the infirmary, in the hands of a French doctor, it seemed to be Paradise.[1]

---

1. Another survivor, Emilie Fournial, wrote a long manuscript on her stay at the Jugendlager. This document perfectly blends in with Irène Bloncourt-Ottelard's story.

22

The Morgue

An underground shelter,[1] built with reinforced concrete; a few steps down to an open door from which seeps an odor of disinfectant, mixed with that of rotting cadavers.

A nightmarish sight....

An ossuary without name, nude bodies or, more truthfully, skeletons, veritable mummies without wrappings, the color of yellow parchment paper, or violet and blue, often spotted already with green...swollen stomachs, the bones around the pelvic region so apparent and protruding that they pierce the hips...

1. This chapter is an extract from Denise Leboucher's notebook on deportations. Her husband, Doctor Marcel Leboucher, gave it to me in January 1968, (see *Les Médecins Maudits* and *Les Médecins de l'Impossible*). Doctor Leboucher, who was deported to Oranienburg, saved several hundred of his companions— including my father, Robert Bernadac. As for Marcelle Leboucher, arrested on November 4, 1942 and nicknamed "Red-Cross" at Ravensbrück, she was, as Simone Saint-Clair wrote (*Ravensbrück, l'Enfer des femmes*. Tallandier, 1946), "a constant example of abnegation and devotion."

an arm cut off, a bloody leg, like meat in a butcher's shop.

On the autopsy table, an open cadaver...not even bleeding...a female doctor, if she could be called that...cutting, tearing and extirpating the arm, liver, stomach, lungs, heart, all these tired organs, exposed in the fetid air in order...to see what was in the corpse; then, with the inspection over, everything was thrown back into the poor victim's gaping stomach; this piece of human "meat" was then hurriedly sewn up.

The awful grins, the wide-open eyes, the tight little expressions on the faces, the exposed teeth that looked like they had been chewing the earth (the bodies had been thrown about here and there, pell-mell, and in any old fashion).

Women who had died giving birth, with the baby still attached to them by the umbilical cord, the little body sitting up between his mother's legs like a doll—and with his eyes wide open.

All this was heaped up in several piles, the feet of one in the mouth of the other, twisted hands, legs sticking up in the air, or doubled underneath, all with the awful expression of suffering and nameless distress.

The faces, all too often very young, sometimes seemed to be almost smiling; and on all their chests was a number written in ink—the only name which these poor women were permitted to have as a means of identity.

We were nothing but a piece..."ein Stück," as the S.S. called us. This indescribable spectacle was truly a vision of hell.

After this, one could not be afraid of anything; all sensitiveness seemed to be annihilated: it took little effort to recall the vast charnel-houses which existed in barbarous days gone by. We already felt insignificant in this horrid camp; but, in the underground morgue, illuminated by an electric light which cast its cold luminosity on these innumerable skeletons, one had no sensation whatsoever. This macabre display evoked the idea of nothingness within us.

When the morgue was too full—and that happened often in this winter of 1944 during which 150 women died daily—the dead were simply left outside. At first, the bodies were carried on stretchers; but later, the number of stretchers became insufficient and trucks did the job.

I remember those days in January 1945 when a long column of stretchers, coming from various barracks, had to be placed on the snow.

Nothing was sadder than the sight of these mortal remains—as some of them had just expired, their bodies were still tepid—resting on the ground in the cold snow....

I cannot express all my sentiments of repulsion. It seemed to me that I myself felt the contact of the frozen ground on the still-warm flesh of my poor dead. But, alas! it was no longer important because they had been freed from all pain and suffering. And, in any case, I had little to give my companions to show them my respect! Nevertheless, I would have liked to show my care and concern....

It became my pious duty to close their eyes—eyes that would never again see their beautiful country of France.

I also wanted them to know that, right to the end, I would be with them and do everything to care for them so that their departure would be a little less sad.

When I saw the acrid, black smoke escaping from the chimney of the crematorium, I knew what it meant, I often murmured a fervent prayer for the liberated soul which was now flying to eternity.

With the aid of a pickaxe, I sometimes had to pry away the dead who had been frozen into the snow—which had covered them during the night with the only white shroud which they would be permitted to have.

The ice had frozen them stiff.

The sad cracking noise that I made as I tried to wrench the corpses free was very painful for me. I felt that I was making them suffer even more.

When those in their last agony in the infirmary did not die fast enough, the orderlies didn't always wait for them to draw their last gasp; often, alas! some women, in the dying moments of their life, were placed with the group of cadavers piled up in the Waschraum.

One day a horrible thing happened:

When the official undertakers came into the room one morning with new "clients," a screaming woman, mad and nude, escaped from this sordid retreat and ran out into the snow—where she collapsed. She had spent the night under a heap of cadavers. She had awakened to find herself among these cold bodies, as cold as hers was with horror. Atrocious fear seized her and, crazy with terror, she sought refuge in front of the door. But when it opened, she fell to the floor. She was hastily taken to the hospital. News of this incident must not get around.

The poor woman lived another three days before dying for real.

The Germans performed another awful stunt. As soon as the carts had delivered their loads of bodies, the undertakers began tearing out all the gold teeth they could find in an inconceivable, brutal manner; when they had finished, they stomped on the stomachs of their victims and cursed them: "Bitches, Schweinerei (vile pigwash)...."—a funeral sermon as unexpected as it was sinister and uncalled for.

The poor dead departed without anyone shedding tears....

But our dead did not depart without prayers, thanks to an admirable Mother Superior in our barracks.

There were prayers for the dying, and a small flower was placed in the hands of the dead. But when their bodies were taken away, we weren't even allowed to place their hands on their breasts. What would be the use....

The expressions on the faces of the dying, coupled with their last words, were extremely sad and poignant.

They often became delirious.

They said such things as: "I'm hungry...." "Will you give me a nice fat chicken," "Mother," or the name of a husband or some other dear one.... Often I answered them...letting them think that this or that person, whom they were calling for, was standing next to them. Sometimes these little white lies succeeded in lighting up a poor, pain-stricken face, which only clamored for a tender word or a soft caress....

The sadness of such agonies, the indefinable anxiety of being unable to heal.... There was only one way left: try to console them, smile to the very end in order that the small light of hope burns eternally....

When, although in great pain, they were able to articulate something like: "Red-Cross, do you think I'll get back home?—But of course.... You'll get back and you'll see your beautiful France and your dear little ones again.... And you will have good white bread...."

It was then that they smiled, although their smile was more like a grimace.... A hand that tried to press mine a little to tell me that they had heard and understood.... The heart seemed to rekindle itself. A feeble indication of life in bodies that were already cold....

How painful all these hours were for me—and, at the same time, how sweet and precious.

I realized that a drop of this balm which I had just poured over them had an immediate, calming effect. But I also knew that they would never again see our beloved France...the ultimate thought that obsessed us all!

Their loved ones...and their country.

"Those who have reverently died for their country deserve the right to have a crowd come and pray beside their coffin."

Alas!...No shroud, no coffin, no tomb, no flowers, and no cross....

The oven....

A little smoke....

Those who have been through this must not forget. One must recount....One must recall....[1]

---

1. Antoinette Hugot, deported with her mother and her sister, went twice to the morgue, "clandestinely"; the first time was to take the body of her mother, "who died of cold" during the roll call; the second time was to find the body of her dead sister in the infirmary. During the second visit, she was horrified by "a large cubic meter" of baby bodies. Her testimony in February 1950, before the tribunal of Rastatt, upset that of Commander Suhren, who had always denied having killed newborn infants.

*Phantom-like women: the conditions of internment were
such that the mortality rate increased daily. To hunger,
cold and vermin were added the suffering, that went
with so much promiscuity, and the anxiety experienced
by women who feared they would give way to feelings
of hatred.*
Bernadac Archives

23

I'll have to remember

I'll have to remember[1]
Later, this horrible period,
Coldly, seriously, without hate,
But, nevertheless, candidly.

This sad and ugly countryside
The incessant flight of ravens
The long barracks on this swamp
Cold and black like tombs.

These muffled women
Old papers and rags,
These poor frozen legs
That dance in the too-long roll call.

Battles with such arms as manure-shovels,
Buckets, and fists

1. Micheline Maurel: *La Passion selon Ravensbrück*. Les Editions de Minuit, 1965.

Tight little mouths
When the soup did not arrive.

These "guilty ones" that were plunged
Into tubs of slimy water
These yellow arms and legs that sported
Large patches of ulcers.

This cough which made one breathless,
This desperate look,
Turned toward the faraway land,
Oh, my God, get us home!...

I'll have to remember....

24

The Clock

— **W**hy are they always talking about a clock?
— I don't know. They've been talking about it for a long time. Probably since their arrival at Ravensbrück.

The violet triangle (followers of the Bible) were in the habit of putting curses on things, or translating their thoughts and teachings into parables and, as regularly as possible, making predictions. As of 1940, the camp clung to the first "prophesy" revealed by this sect:

— When a clock chimes the hours in the camp, Hitler will die and the war will be over.

But Ravensbrück thrived on such sounds as sirens, roll calls, loud-speakers, and whistles. A clock! A watch tower! It's ridiculous!

— How could such a prediction come true?[1] How many others had been announced, had given us fugitive hope—and then never come true! The shooting star that appeared in the West on August 13, 1944—did it not forecast our liberation in the near future?

1. Suzanne Busson. Already cited.

— This prediction, like so many others, will perhaps be one more disillusion, just another disenchantment succeeding a short hope!

— But the Bibelforscherinnen with the violet triangle were all very happy when, in 1944, a square tower rose above the kitchens: on one of its sides was a dial. The Ravensbrück clock was born; at last it appeared in the grey sky above the camp!

— For many months it had no hands, and probably no functioning mechanism, either; in any case, it didn't chime.

— In July, 1944, exactly two days before the attempt on Hitler's life, the clock began to work—but it stopped the same day the assassination attempt misfired.

— Part of the prediction had come true, however.

— Months, long months passed; a year had begun; part of the prisoners in the camp had left. They had gone off on different work projects; some were sent to reinforce Berlin's defense infrastructure, while others dug trenches and ditches or worked in factories; still others were sent to Mauthausen to be exterminated; and the clock still did not work.

— Nevertheless, the Russians were approaching. The sound of cannons and bombings assured us that liberation was certainly near—but we also had an awful fear of total extermination.

— And on the 23rd of April, 1945, the clock began to run, to tick off the hours of hope—so precious for those who, during long months survived an hallucinating nightmare. The S.S. fled, the Russians arrived. Ravensbrück now opened its doors.

— The clock tolled the hours of joy!

— The prediction had come true![1]

1. The different "liberations" of the deportees at Ravensbrück, and of its work parties, the escapes of the "Steps of Death," and the exchanges and "removals" made by the Swiss and Swedish Red Cross organizations will be discussed in the last volume of of this series, which has covered women's concentration camps.

25

Janine

Janine Lejart died at Ravensbrück, the last to die there—just a few hours before the camp was liberated.

Janine Lejart was 17 years old. Seventeen years is also the time her parents in Dijon had to wait to "know" exactly—and totally. In December 1962, they received a letter from Belgium:[1]

Dear Madam,

...May your heart find peace and suffer no longer. This is how I came to know your daughter. In March 1945, I was in the infirmary; on my left slept Hélène Reuderer from Charenay, and Paulette Mulsade from Flers was on my right. The next bed was occupied by two other French girls—one of whom was very young, with very black hair; she seemed to be in bad shape: it was Janine. Her bunkmate cared for her, even pampered her, and foresaw her needs; she covered her up as best she could.

1. This letter was sent to me by Ginette Vincent, deported to Ravensbrück in the same convoy as Janine Lejart (unpublished).

I noticed that every day true comrades, who took the risk of coming into the infirmary (it was forbidden to enter), brought Janine a little stolen food (it must have been stolen because the items did not resemble anything that appeared on our "menus"). One day, there was suddenly an awful lot of hullabaloo: the Swedes (in the name of the Red Cross) had come back for the second time—April 25, 1945—and for the second time, some Frenchwomen were able to leave Ravensbrück. With great effort, the least sick were taken away. Poor Janine was in such a state of despair that I told Paulette and Hélène that, from now on, I would share Janine's bed with her. Completely unconsolable, Janine did not look at me or speak to me. That night, she needed my help; suddenly, she asked me, with her still-fresh young voice, who I was. Seeing she had regained some bit of hope, I answered:

— A mother.

— But that's not what I asked you. Who are you and what country do you come from?

— Belgium, I said.

— I don't want a Belgian, I want a Frenchwoman.

And the big tears began to flow again. When she was all cried out, I took her in my arms and softly said:

— Sleep, my little one, I kiss you for your mother.

She slept the entire night. For the next several days, she let herself be cared for and washed. She accepted some food and a glass of water. The food went down with difficulty. Brusquely she asked me:

— Are you a member of the Party?

— No, I said.

— Well then, why are you taking care of me? Why do you show such affection for me?

— First of all, because you are my sister. Like me, you were created; and secondly, because I have children— and their absence has made my heart lonely and empty.

Then she told me she lived in Dijon. She spoke to me of you, of her father, of the surroundings in which you lived and of her membership in the Party. That evening, a friend brought her a little rice and a pretty little teaspoon to eat it with. After tasting some of it, she asked me if she were really sick. I told her that she was simply all tired out.

— Well then, prove to me that I am not sick and eat after me.

So we ate together. She ate half the rice on the spoon, and I had the rest. She was in ecstasy. It was her last meal.

The next day, she breathed with great difficulty and was suffocating without end. Because of the bed above us, there was no room to sit properly; so I had to crouch as I held her on my knees. That night, she fell asleep talking to me about her home and about my children— because, slowly but surely, she had identified herself with my children.

The following day, Sunday, she was having even more difficulty breathing; she swelled up rapidly. Once again I managed to sit her on my knees. She wrapped both arms around me. The poor child was smothering, and gasping for air. Suddenly, she clasped me with all her strength and, with her eyes full of anxiety, she said:

— I am not going to die.

— Of course not, my little one, a child does not die on its mother's knees.

She pressed her head against my neck. Then she tightened her fingers and began sucking my neck (I still carry the marks) as if my life could pass into her body. In vain I tried not to cry. But my tears ran down into her hair—her beautiful hair—and onto her neck. And then it was the end. That night, two comrades appeared; one was Marie-Claude Vaillant-Couturier.[1] They decided to leave the body next to me, thus hiding the dead girl so that she would not be thrown on a heap of corpses.

1. Who refused to leave Ravensbrück with the Swedish Red Cross convoy in order to stay and care for the sick.

Alone, I spent the night against her little body, which suddenly swelled—becoming almost like marble. And I prayed for her because she was my child of suffering.

Dear Madame, my letter will be terrible for you to read. It is horrible for me to write. I will not read it....I will leave the erasures as they are...that's all for today....

26

Will it be true?

Will it be true that one day soon I will come back[1]
To you, to us, to these well-known roads,
That simultaneously, I will fervently remember
And hear again the sound of our Angelus?

My steps will take me straight to the familiar entrance,
My trembling hand will recognize the latch, and,
Heart beating with love, will I hear my mother,
My son or my sister cry out with joy?

Is it possible for human joy to be so great?
Is my heart large enough to hold it all?
I must get used to my dream and
Calmly wait, minute by minute, for the moment of return.

1. Last poem written at Ravensbrück by Françoise Babillot.
Unpublished.

27

Work Details

Another story. Practically unknown. Have you heard anyone talk about Abteroda? Holleischen? Ludwigs-feld? Beendorf? Rechlin? Gartenfeld? Other Ravens-brücks. Ten, twenty, fifty, sixty-three—at least—"other Ravensbrücks." The Ravensbrück of the mine, of the assembly line, of the work site, of the factory. Ravens-brück would not exist without such subsidiaries. Yes, other Ravensbrücks of work, of hunger, of cold, of total exhaustion, of extermination. Forgotten women, forgot-ten camps. Work details that are more savage and cruel than the mother-camp.

Ravensbrück, for all those survivors who only lived through periods of initiation and quarantine—and for only several days or weeks in the "Big Camp"—is, above all, the "elsewhere" of the work details. Their real concentration camp is not the gigantic one at Ravensbrück but the work detail to which they belong "on the outside." On a work detail, everything is so strangely similar, but yet so different also!

But with time, the shades of similarity and difference tend to reflect one's caste and class:

— Oh, yes, I know Hélène....She is a former inmate of Ravensbrück.

— And Martha?

— Martha is a friend, a Torgau sister.

"A former inmate," of Ravensbrück, "my sister" on a work detail.

It is impossible, within the framework of this study, to present all the testimony gathered on the work details. The pages which will follow, consecrated to Schoenfeld, are, I think, the best conclusion for this book. This world of "forced labor" in the twenty principal camps outside Ravensbrück will be found in a new volume which will appear under the title: *Female Work Details*.

28

Schoenfeld

THE YEAR THAT WAS TOO LONG[1]

I will not tell you about our miserable life in the
Ravensbrück camp: I will simply limit myself to the
last two days we spent there, July 18 and 19, 1944;
for hours and hours they consisted of medical visits
during which we were left standing nude in front of each
other in a courtyard in whose center there was a small
square of grass around which we took turns walking in
order to show the German officers present our teeth and
hands. That's all they looked at; then we entered a little
gynecological room where we underwent a swab test.
Was it a doctor or a doctoress that saw us? I don't know
because, before us, was a disagreeable hybrid of a
person with very short hair who spoke a little French, in a

1. *The Year that was Too Long* ("La Trop Longue Année") is an
unpublished manuscript by Juliette Colliet (in the Resistance),
Janine Dennery today. The subtitle is: "History of detention in
Germany, Liberation by the Soviet Army, and Return with the
American Army."

deep and raucous voice, and who tongue-lashed us if our uncomfortable position was not convenient.

Her gestures were brusque, and she (it turned out she was a female) hurt us—which seemed to give her real pleasure.

Several comrades were crying after the examination and others were pale or scandalized or revolted. This was the case of one of my friends who, about to reach fifty, had nevertheless kept her virginity; she was just before me, and this is what I heard:

"Say, you..." asked the monster, "how old are you?"

"Almost fifty."

"What, at your age! It's a disgrace, ridiculous and grotesque!" And with a brutal gesture....

Afterwards came the showers, a delousing operation and finally a change of clothes; we handed in our wooden shoes, skirt and blouse (on which large crosses were painted) for a dress that we were to wear until we were liberated. The dress was made out of a grey canvas-like material with three black buttons. We were also given a dark blue shirt with grey stripes and a pair of large bloomers which reached to our knees. Later, we changed these clothes with our friends for dresses and such which fitted us a little better because, when they were distributed, no sizes or shapes were taken into consideration. Finally, we were given shoes with wooden soles; the top was made out of a military sheet and we were barely given enough time to try just one of them on. After we had been outfitted, we were left to stand in ranks for about four hours in the torrid sun....

We were also given the red triangle, distributed to political prisoners, to sew on our left sleeve; on the triangle was the first letter of our nationality and a white rectangle on which our matriculation number was inscribed.

We were lined up in a column for the departure; naturally, mothers were separated from their daughters, and even sisters were sometimes separated; in many cases, those who stayed in camp, because they were to leave later in another convoy, saw, alas! their dear ones for the last time.

Toward four o'clock in the afternoon, we left by truck for the south. We were some eighty kilometers from the German capital. We rapidly crossed Berlin, where there were still a few vestiges left of the city; but a numerous population seemed to be leading a relatively normal life. We drove on for another fifteen kilometers before arriving at a sinister airfield framed by a dozen buildings called "Hall" which were to be our only horizon for nine months.... The truck stopped in front of the lone hall surrounded by electrified barbed wire; its appearance could not be more sinister.

It was hall seven of the Heinkel factories in Schoenfeld. This hall was specialized in the manufacture of the Messerschmitt 109's left wing.

LIFE AT SCHOENFELD

Hall seven was a long building, like those generally seen on airfields. The assembly line for the wings was on rails, in the center; behind the rails was the soldering workshop and the machines. On the left was a dormitory, next to which was a room for mending garments, and then the office of the S.S. Commander, the two-room infirmary and, finally, a sort of laundry-room. On the right was a special room reserved for German workers, and then several other rooms for the factory's engineers. Then there was the kitchen, consisting of several rooms, the toilets and, lastly, the tool shops. In the basement were hermetically sealed shelters and a refectory with room for six hundred; they had been made out of two large rooms which were lighted and aired by ventilators—as were other underground areas. On the mezzanine there were three dormitories on the left; and on the right were the storerooms, which were not open at night. We numbered 150 Frenchwomen, but we were surprised to find, already installed in this hall, 200 Russians, a hundred or so Poles and 150 Gypsies—as well as about fifty Yugoslavs or Italians; this brought the total number of women to 650.

The dormitories, four of them, ran along the length of the factory. When we arrived, three were already occupied—so, we were given the fourth. It was number 2—located on the first and only floor, between dormitory 1 and dormitory 3. It was a former refectory that had been transformed for such use and which consequently had neither running water nor toilets; this obliged us to go to either "Schlafsaal eins" or to the "drei" to wash and clean up (these two dormitories were well equipped, having a wash basin along the length of the room next to which was a smaller room where there were six showers and two toilets. Evidently, however, dormitory two was sufficient enough for us—the Frenchwomen.

Although we had the possibility of going to the other dormitories to wash and so forth (the term "wash" is completely relative because, during the first three months, we were only given a minuscule little piece of bad-smelling soap), our dormitory was locked with a key as soon as we were in our bunks, and the S.S. put only two or three hygienic buckets at our disposal; but what were three hygienic buckets for 150 women—particularly since their food consisted uniquely of clear soup?

When the Aufseherinnen opened the doors to get us up, it was, of course, an inevitable and disastrous mess—which gave them immense pleasure to kick and thump us with their feet, when they were not hitting us over the head; and the overflowing buckets were also all-too-often a pretext to let us stand without moving for two more hours at roll call.

I think all my comrades will remember the famous day when the Aufseherinnen, having knocked over makeshift latrines that were full to the brim, obliged all the girls in this dormitory to roll about on the floor in the excrement;

some of these guards even took advantage of this scandalous persecution to push the faces of many unfortunate prisoners into these stinking impurities.

If there was anything agreeable about this dormitory, it was the light streaming through the windows. I was on the top bunk and from my perch I could see, beyond the barbed-wire fence, a huge pile of black boxes painted with white numbers; I never did know what they contained. Then a little farther away was a railroad track on which a little train, carrying the "Meister," ran up and down several times a day. We waited for the sound of its bell, the only outside distraction we had during these long months—with the exception of a little white milk cart drawn by a brown horse.

About 500 meters away, we could see another hall; it was terribly sinister-looking. I think French war prisoners worked there. A little to the right was an airfield with a few planes taking off and landing; that was all.

In summer, we could see a little greenery way off in the distance, very far away; but in winter, the place was horribly sad and lugubrious.

The refectory was in the basement, or cellar, and when we rushed down there at soup-time, we had the impression of leaving the factory and its infernal noise to enter a somber cell.

This refectory contained 24 long and narrow tables and some benches. We were twelve at each table—provided we all squeezed together.

The underground shelters were a continuation of the refectory. Some of them had emergency exits, but most had only one door. After being in there a few hours, air became scarce (there were quite a lot of us—650 women sitting almost on top of each other). From January on, there were continual alerts, lasting 4, 5 and even 6 hours.

Being down in these shelters was a very trying experience; we were dropping with fatigue but it was impossible to sleep. It was forbidden to use the toilets down there and, as soon as the alert was over, we still had to

No provision had been made for the children born in the camp—unless it was drowning and gas. Some escaped, hidden in a mattress or transported from one barracks to the other. 850 children were born at Ravensbrück; a few survived, but they were spared no suffering.
Tallandier Archives

wait for more than half an hour before we could enter the few "leisure areas" which we had been allotted. Their walls were covered with inscriptions; here is an example:

"When I come in this place, in this charming place
Whether to dream, or for something more urgent,
And I see on these painted walls all these commas,
I think of your moustache, O! ridiculous one!
And when my rear end is seated on this chair
I find your face has much less character
And instead of a hat on your silly head,
Your face would be better off, Adolf, in the seat of a pair
*   of pants."*

A few of my comrades and myself ended up refusing (and energetically so) to go down into these shelters— but it would be difficult for anyone to imagine the frightening moments we endured because we were more afraid of the commander's "schlague" and the blows of the sentinels' rifle butts than of all the bombs, luminous rockets and aerial dogfights taking place over our heads. My comrades were hidden under their blankets in the dark because the "blackout" was total; and when they heard the commander screaming in the next dormitory, the sound of crying women being slugged haplessly, and the noise of guards running about in their big boots, their blood nearly froze in their veins and they were hard put to believe they were still alive.

As for me, I was lucky enough to have a straw mat that was so thin I could push the sawdust that filled it to both sides and then slip under it in such a manner that my body, combined with the sawdust, gave the illusion of being a normal level mattress of normal thickness.

The commander and his sentinels came running by, knocking on all the bunks with their clubs and shining their flashlights all about. Pity for those women who were found there....

* * *

— In dormitory 3,[1] we all had to get out of the aisle every time an Aufseherin passed. It was really a race for those who were in the back of the top bunks. We had to stand at attention and shout to our neighbor: "Aufseherin!" so that she could assume the same respectful stance. However, one day, when I was sitting sideways on my bed with my back to the aisle, down which an Aufseherin came stalking, I did not hear the signal shouted out by the few comrades who were in the dormitory at that moment. The Aufseherin was furious that I had not come to attention, and she threw herself on me. I raised my arm to protect my head: the unpardonable crime!...We were supposed to let ourselves get beaten up while standing at attention. She continued hitting me until she was tired; and then, more furious than ever, she went over to the administrative offices. After she left, my companions comforted me, but I was in tears....The next day, at work, I saw the big girl from Lyons, "Frédérique," coming toward me; she said I was wanted over in the administrative office. She didn't know why but gently said:

"Maybe they're going to turn you loose!..."

As I entered the office, I passed in front of a row of German Gypsies. The commander and his female counterpart were there. Madame Fusch was also there to translate. She was wrecked with emotion.

"You rebelled against an Aufseherin and you made a menacing gesture...." I protested and told them what really happened. The Aufseherin, who was also present, stuck to her version of the story and continued to heap abuse upon me.

"You are going to receive fifty lashes. It's the punishment you deserve—and it will be put on your record."

1. Unpublished manuscript, Georgette Ducasse. July 1970.

The female commander then told the Gypsies to take turns whipping me. They categorically refused, saying that they were prisoners like me. These poor creatures, many of whom had been arrested up to ten years before, were more pitiful than our torturers.

Meanwhile, I was made to get up on a table and lie on my stomach. And the blows began to rain down inexorably.... When the female commander was tired of hitting me, the male commander relayed her—and showed no remorse.

My companions, Madame Duteich and Madame Arnaud, were waiting for me when I came out; they took me to the showers and massaged me with hot water.

...And then the days began again to pass too slowly for my taste.

One day...the Gestapo came around on an inspection tour of the factory and, unfortunately, several files were opened. One of them came across the annotation which had been added to my record: "REBELLION...."

Again I was convoked; this time I received only 25 blows. That makes 75 blows for having had an instinctive reflex; that's a lot!...Nevertheless, that's what happened to me.

*   *   *

Our "dear commander"[1] not only looked after our health but organized our "recreational periods" as well; these took place on Sundays or during the Saturday afternoon rest hours; they consisted of walking and running, in all types of weather, between the walls of the factory and the electrified strands of barbed wire—next to which there was a path so narrow that we were almost electrocuted if we should stumble. Actually, one such accident happened. A young Polish girl touched one of the wires; she instantaneously began making horrible

---

1.   Unpublished manuscript Juliette Colliet (Janine Dennery).

convulsive movements. Not being able to help her, we all
began screaming at the top of our voices. The current
was cut off and I believe the prisoner slowly got back on
her feet after undergoing this terrifying experience. These
"excursions" took place with the "Aufseherinnen" and
the "Kapos" furiously chanting "links, zwei, drei, vier" in
rhythm because we French intentionally broke the
cadence of the Gypsies who, at the head of the column,
were singing German military songs.

KOMMANDANTS, KOMMANDANTES, AUFSEHERINNEN, KAPOS

We had four commanders in succession.

The first, nicknamed Arthur, was young—and he was
never without his bicycle; he mocked us all the time and
kept giving ironic stares as he went round and round us
on his bike, like a sheep dog circling his flock.

ARTHUR
(To the tune of "Malbrough s'en va-t-en guerre"[1])

Arthur is off to war,
Not on foot, always on his bicycle,
Arthur is off to war,
But he'll hardly be back (twice).

Off to war against women,
Not on foot, always on his bicycle,
Off to war against women,
In a Berlin camp (twice).

He's tall, and he's ugly,
Not on foot, always on his bicycle,

1.   Popular French song.

He's tall, and he's ugly,
He has the air of an idiot (twice).

He told Alice,
Not on foot, always on his bicycle,
He told Alice,
That he loved us all very much (twice).

So we asked him,
Not on foot, always on his bicycle,
So we asked him,
To calm our hunger (twice).

Give us some good soup,
Not on foot, always on his bicycle,
Give us some good soup,
And also some good bread (twice).

And what did we get in the end,
Not on foot, always on his bicycle,
And what did we get in the end,
Some excellent horse manure (twice).

Perhaps in his flower beds,
Not on foot, always on his bicycle,
Perhaps in his flower beds,
He could gather some cumin (twice).

But soon on his land will be,
Not on foot and not on bicycles,
But soon on his land will be,
Russians and Americans (twice).

They will come to make war on him,
Sound the cannons and machine guns!
They will come to make war on him,
And to kick him in the rear (twice).

And in the big factory,
It will be the end of making rounds on a bicycle,
And in the big factory,
Arthur will be hanged (twice).

At the end of a little cord,
Dear Arthur, say goodbye to your bicycle,
At the end of a little cord,
You will pedal no more (twice).

The second commander, a Hungarian S.S. trooper, seemed to be older. There was a very unsympathetic air about him but, right away, we saw that he was not necessarily mean; in fact, he very often cancelled punishments and annulled the interminable roll call that the female commander and the Aufseherinnen imposed upon us. Unfortunately for us he did not stay long.

The commander that succeeded him was called "Schwein"—after the name he gave us. He had a hideous face and was a real brute. He could handle "the schlague" with dexterity, and he brutalized us with it. His specialty was to kick people in the fanny, and I don't think there were many prisoners who could say they had escaped such thumps of his boot; and when he hit, he hit hard.

As for the fourth commander, he was a "gigolo" type. In civilian life, he had been a hairdresser; and he could never make a decision. On his left sleeve he wore the inscription: "Adolf Hitler"—of whom he was very proud (but he promptly got rid of the jacket as Russian troops approached....) He was fairly interesting when he gave us his daily lecture after the evening roll call; here are a few extracts:

"All those who do not want to go down to the shelter with their two blankets during the air-raid alerts will be immediately shot...."

or else:

"You must obey the orders given by the Aufseherinnen, and it is forbidden to give them nicknames—at the risk of being hanged...." Then there was this extract (early April, 1945):

"There are those among you who have told their comrades that in fifteen days or so the Russians will be here" (the Russians had advanced past the Küstrin Fort, which was about 60 kilometers away; as a matter of fact, they entered Berlin on April 23).

"I want you to know that this is absolutely false," and then this simpleton added: "And even *"if that did happen,"* not one of you here will leave these walls alive."

He was the maestro of the schlague. It was he who, every night, after the Aufseherinnen had handed in their reports, distributed from three to thirty-five blows all around—according to how he felt.

Six sentinels, machine guns at the ready, guarded the doors of the factory and accompanied us when we went outside; when we went over to the barrels to find some rutabaga or turnip peelings, they beat us severely with the butts of their rifles. And when we worked at night, for a week, or when we had swilled down our soup, which consisted of a liter of water, an overwhelming desire took hold of us and we had only one thought: to sneak out into the courtyard (out of sheer meanness, the Aufseherinnen had closed the doors to the latrines). But the sentinels always caught us, and when we went back to work, we were black and blue.

As for the female "personnel" staff, it was made up of a commander and twelve Aufseherinnen.

We went through four such female commanders, each less "recommendable" than the next. They left us to go to prison because they had been caught stealing clothes, which they sold on the black market—as well as rations of bread, sausages, margarine, etc. that was supposed to have been distributed to the prisoners.

The one who "greeted" us upon our arrival at the factory was a physical tramp with very large teeth. She was brutal, and made vulgar gestures; she also gave us blow upon blow. It was she who gave us our bread ration—exactly as if we were animals; and if, by some chance, we had a half teaspoon of jam and a half slice of sausage on our piece of mildewed bread, which varied in size according to whether it was cut in seven or ten slices, we could be sure that the jam and sausage would be intentionally smeared together all over the bread— making it almost indistinguishable.

This commander left one day to perform, so it seems, some important function in the camp. I feel for the poor girls who had to put up with her.

Here is the little ditty that we composed about her, to the tune of "Son voile qui volait" (Her veil that flew):

> She was a Führerin,
> Who wasn't yet thirty,
> Who had a dirty mug
> With very large teeth,
> Her peaked cap facing here, facing there,
> The peaked cap falling here, falling there,
> The peaked cap falling all the time.
>
> Who had a dirty mug,
> With very large teeth,
> A blue sweater,
> On a white shirt,
> The sweater twisted here, twisted there,
> Wrinkled sweater here, wrinkled sweater there,
> Wrinkled sweater all the time.
>
> A blue sweater,
> On a white shirt,
> A hussy's skirt,
> Over disgusting underwear.
> The skirt going this way, and that way,
> The skirt that slipped, that slipped,
> The skirt that slipped all the time.

A hussy's skirt,
Over disgusting underwear,
And masculine boots,
Covering calves too white,
Boots facing this way, and that way,
Boots that walked, and walked,
Boots that often walked.

But our Führerin
Also has, my children,
Lovely caressing hands,
For our pretty little faces,
Hands going here and going there,
Slaps handed out, slaps handed out,
Slaps handed out often.

And a divine voice
And great strident cries,
When she jabbers
It starts one trembling,
Cries over here, cries over there,
Her voice that bellows, that bellows,
Her voice that bellows often.

But soon, my friends,
We're going to beat it out of here,
See our homeland again
Which waits for us,
A husband here, a husband there,
Let's sing, and think only of life,
Let's sing, and think only about that.

The second female commander was a veritable brute, but luckily her male counterpart was calmer. She was strong, with the head of a real German, square and common. She spent her time beating us up, with the help of the Aufseherinnen, and leaving us outside after roll call; and, naturally, we saw our poor soup

ration cancelled. Ah! Why do we have to eat anyway....

The third commander was a dishwater blond who
looked like a "circus rider." Small, she always wore
varnished boots, a green military cap, and a white wool
sweater that came up to her chin. Sometimes she wore a
horrible-looking pair of pants made out of military cloth,
and a matching vest; she would parade in front of us,
thinking she was very seductive—even though, in our
eyes anyway, she looked more like a serpent that had
crawled out from under a rock. Her language was
unimaginably vulgar and crude. Everyone got kicked and
slapped around during her reign, and that of the male
commander.

I cannot say much about the fourth commander
because we did not know her well. She was a tall, skinny
woman. When she walked, all the bones in her body
looked like they were about to detach themselves from
the rest of her frame. She was not very nice, but she was
more humane than the others; however, she stayed
hardly a month with us.

The first thing she did when she arrived was to call our
work squad together to tell us that she considered us
workers and not prisoners, and that she would do all she
could to do away with the interminable roll calls and the
various kinds of punishment inflicted upon us. Personally, I don't think she realized that we were no longer
able to do anything—physically—and that we were just
barely able to drag ourselves around; after all, we were
totally worn out, and only our nerves and our willpower
kept us going; nor did she realize that there was too
much work and too many privations; and we were in no
shape to undergo punishment after punishment.

Now I shall say a few words about the Aufseherinnen
who guarded us; there were twelve of them, and we had
given nicknames to almost all.

The first, "Miss Pipi," was in charge of the toilets—
where the male commander often came to give her a

hand—or rather a foot—in chasing us out. Miss Pipi had her hair in a large plaited bun; she was red-faced, massive, and she hit like a horse.

"The Flying Louse," or "The Cur," was the worst of the lot: she was small, strong and—as we used to say—had "the rear-end in Paris and the bust in Berlin." She was blond; she didn't speak, she barked. It was like being in a bad hailstorm when she started slapping women around; and she used to twist our noses until the blood flowed.

She was the one who inspected the dormitories, and when we finished our work at night, dead with fatigue, there was no question of having a moment's rest. Do you know what it is like to work in an atmosphere of infernal noise, night and day (it doesn't cease for a second)? What it's like not to be able to speak normally, having to shout to make oneself understood? Only a thin partition separated the dormitories from the factory, and we even had to sleep in the middle of all this racket.

Do you know what it's like to have to stand for about eighteen hours at a time—in an icebox, without being able to get warm, and being maltreated, brutalized and cursed?

Do you know what it's like to have to work like a madwoman at a dizzying speed, to keep looking to see what time it is without stopping, to always say to yourself: "The assembly line is moving and I haven't finished yet, what's going to happen to me?"

Do you know what it's like to have your head and stomach empty, your eyes all foggy, your legs so weak you're ready to fall down?

The cruel light of the projectors hurt you; the light is so harsh and penetrating that it gives you the impression it is piercing your eyes, going through your head, and coming out at the back of your neck.

No! You don't know what all this is like—happily. But you can easily understand how, after such nights, a person really needs a little rest. I'm not talking about sleeping, because, when "The Cur" was around, that was out of the question; I'm talking about just lying down for a few minutes on your straw mat and relaxing your nerves, letting yourself get carried away with your thoughts, and, of course, away from this slave-ship—to be near those you love, near those who are dear to you, those that you have left back in beautiful France.

What has become of them? Where are they? It doesn't matter! They'll be saved, and one can think ardently about them....

Well I say: No! We haven't slept for months and months; we haven't even rested because this damn S.S. Aufseherin keeps getting us up all the time. Any excuse is a good one: a badly folded dress (or its number can't be seen), a dress not in its place (not exactly on the foot of the bed). Then there were the inspections of our straw mattresses, to see if we had hidden anything under them. One of my good friends, called "Zozo," was feeling sick; so she picked up an empty bottle in the factory and put a little lukewarm water in it to place in her bed to keep it a bit warmer. The poor woman was literally bowled over with blows. And as for my good friend "Samson," with whom I shared a bed, she was so beaten up one morning that she bled for more than eight days—and you could see the coagulated blood down on the floor.

"The Flying Louse" simply disappeared one day. She was pregnant and boasted that, although not married, she was expecting a child.

"I'm not like these French pigs," she said, "who would do anything to have a miscarriage; I'm German and I'm proud to carry around a child that I will give to my country."

We later learned that the child was born prematurely, and had died; she was flat on her back in bed, suffering from severe attacks of rhumatism, and that she was in such pain that she asked to die....

The third Aufseherin was nicknamed "The Viper"; she slithered about like a snake—slapping and cursing and beating people. Her face had become hideous, and what hair she had was straight and disheveled; when she slapped our faces, her arms and hands flapped in the air. But after the bombing attack on Oranienburg, during which she was badly shaken up—she was that scared— she finally dalmed down.

The fourth, "Maria," was very small. Her husband had died at Stalingrad; she was the mother of five children. She never beat us. Some of my friends even went so far as to say "she was nice"; she was a phoney, as far as I was concerned; but, two-faced as she might have been, she was not a sadist.

The fifth Aufseherin, "Star-Gazer," was a kid in her early twenties; she had blond hair, and always had her nose up in the air (whence her nickname). She used to wear a blood-red sweater, with a roll-collar. She detested the French, and when the commander beat us, she would stand around and laugh as we suffered.

Then there was "Love Doll," a 17-year-old little blond who quickly learned how to cuff us about.

And there was "The Ex-Future Commander." We gave her this nickname because, with each change of commander, she filled in for a few days until the new one arrived. She was usually in charge of the kitchen, and we ate, or did not eat, according to how she happened to feel.

In the kitchen were about a dozen prisoners—half of whom were French. Every day a few women were chosen to peel the vegetables. I must say we would have liked taking turns doing this job because we could always take away a little food. But if the French took some for their favorite friends, they didn't want the others coming into their private kingdom—where the women sat down to work—and it was warm. There was always the smell of good food—not coming from the soup prepared for the prisoners, but from the meals served to the Aufseherinnen and the commanders. Our French comrades in the kitchen did not suffer physically as much as we did; they all came back big and fat and, of course, did not realize how much we had suffered. We were a little irritated with them because they could have done much more to help us. But I would like to make clear that this little accusation does not apply to Madame de L...who was always charming and understanding; we owe her a lot.

But let's get back to "The Ex-Future Commander." One of this Aufseherin's great satisfactions was to dish out the soup in the refectory. When the kettle was almost empty, she took it to the back of the room; then, without serving it, she would very slowly drag it to the other end. The women would get up, with their plates in hand, pushing and shoving. Begging and lamenting, they would cry out: "Aufseherin bitte." The outcome of it all was a general melee—with 300 women throwing their spoons and plates at each other. When the Aufseherin saw that the fight was in full swing, she put the lid on the kettle, and even tipped it over; then she had us slapped and kicked out of this frightful refectory, amid screams and screeching.

There were another half-dozen Aufseherinnen who had no nicknames; none is worth mentioning. However, I don't want to end this chapter without saying a few words about "The Redhead," "The Rumanian," and "White Earrings."

"The Redhead," as her name indicates, had flaming red hair. She was small in height. Of all our watch dogs, she was certainly "the least bad." She said her father was German and her mother was Alsacian. When, as of January 1945, we were made to work outside the factory, building roads, cutting down trees and digging ditches, we did everything to get her as a guard. She knew perfectly well that "the jig was up" and tried her best to "pull the fat out of the fire." On her right wrist she wore a little gold chain from which hung a blue, white and red enamel trinket, which represented France. One

day she lost the bracelet; unfortunately, it was a Yugoslav who found it—and returned it for a supplementary
bread ration.

"The Rumanian" was right out of Dubout's humoristic
cartoons: a big fat woman with dark auburn hair and
thick ankles that tapered down to little feet perched on
high heels. It is said she was of Rumanian origin and
that, before becoming an Aufseherin, she had worked in
a factory where, having made one error too many, she
was given the choice of being a prisoner or an S.S.
Aufseherin. When we were all obliged to leave the
factory, before the Red Army arrived, she jumped
the convoy in Berlin—in the middle of a fight—and
swapped her military clothes for "civies"; and disappeared.

As for "White Earrings," she was the most hysterical of
the lot. One day she threw a fit right in front of us; she
was in such a state that we had to carry her on a
stretcher. A few days went by before we saw her again;
but then she came back—and not even calm: she was in
a state that bordered on being half-mean and half-mad.
She drank, and sometimes she could not keep from
staggering. She'd even fall into the ditches we were
digging. Then she'd holler like hell and we'd reach down
and pull her out of the hole. She'd let herself be a
deadweight, which made it very difficult to extract her.
Some of the foreign girls laughed at this ridiculous scene,
but I got away as far as possible, finding the whole thing
odious and morally depressing. She would cuff us
without reason, or jump on some poor woman for God
knows what reason. All day long we felt we were being
hunted down—and then the blows and kicks would
begin! Her language was vile; she would curse you, and
then laugh, and then crack you across the face with
violence. She'd send you back to work by striking you
with her fists and boots. This monster had a French
name, the only one I ever met who did; her name was
Gertrude Lefebvre.

Finally, all these women had deplorable morals; they were always on the outlook for male factory workers or German soldiers. At night, when we went down into the shelters, and everything had been plunged into darkness, we could hear the female German Gypsies murmuring "mein Lieber" to them, as well as the muffled noise of women kissing—accompanied by the little laughs that vicious, excited girls make.

I will end this chapter by describing "the kapos" for you. Fortunately, there were no Frenchwomen among them. These evil-minded beings numbered eight or ten.

In the way of Russians, there was "Edwige"; she was a volunteer who had come to Germany to work and earn money and who, as the result of some dishonest "dealings," had been transferred to this prison. She spoke German very well and, among other privileges, she held the grade of "Blockowa"—a rank which gave her the right (and the pleasure) to mistreat the women under her. When the terrible bombardment of Oranienburg occurred, she was with a young Yugoslav girl that she was supposed to bring to this camp—about 40 kilometers from ours. The bombing runs caused panic and terror, and when these two prisoners sought shelter, they became separated from the camp and the German S.S. If I remember correctly, this happened toward the month of March, 1945; German civilians provided them with shelter and "civies" because their clothes were burned and dirty. Escape, therefore, was extremely easy; this German family would have gladly helped them. But Edwige did not want to take advantage of this unique occasion and obliged her companion to follow her, threatening to denounce her if she didn't. You can well imagine the felicitations this bitch received from the German S.S. after she had returned and recounted her adventure. From that day on, she became so proud of her authority that we feared her as much as we did the female commander.

There was also a girl called "Vera," a licentious and thieving animal who used to spy on us and have us beaten constantly. However, one day she went too far and the male commander had her beaten up in turn; she never again was quite as haughty.

I'll end these lines by telling you about a frightful Gypsy called "Julot." She had close-cropped hair like a boy and, thanks to cosmetics given to her by one of the Aufseherinnen, she lathered herself with make-up; but the Aufseherinnen liked her and she was continually seen clasped in the arms of one of them. She had kind of a beauty mark right on the end of her nose, which made her look even more disgusting; however, the S.S. went for her in a big way—even authorizing her, in the latter months, to wear men's pants. This girl, who used to play the accordeon in a whore house in Poland, could neither read nor write; when she lined us up in ranks, we found she could not even count to five. In fact, she was the one who assaulted my comrade "Zozo" who, outraged by her brutality toward me, screamed at her one day:

"Ein Moment, Schmutz, American hier in einem Monat...." (Hold it, garbage-head, the Americans will be here in a month.)

As it turned out, this proved to be false because it was the Russians who saved us in the nick of time.

We would so much have liked to wreak revenge upon them, but, with the arrival of the Allies, they had, alas, all hidden or fled.

LIFE IN THE FACTORY

— Auf-stehen! Auf-stehen! screamed the Aufseherin.

A few strident blows on the whistle, and a few blows with a club for the unfortunate girls who had not got down fast enough from their straw mattresses.

It's 4:30 in the morning.

Everyone is hurrying, shoving and pushing.

Those who sleep on the top bunk (the third) are trying to make their beds quickly so that bits of straw will not fall on the bunks of their comrades below. Blankets are hastily folded. When turning around, the hands of some girls are stepped on. Others get an unintentional boot in the face. Then we all run to the toilets. Damn! There's already a line, and what a line! We'll never be ready on time.

We hardly wash, and we can't find our things because, if you leave them even for a few moments, they are immediately stolen.

"Appell," "Appell," "Schnell," "Schnell," "bistro," "game," "Appell," "Appell," "Schnell," "Los," "Los," bellow the Blockowas.

They knock us about and throw everyone outside; the women, their clothes, everything goes out of the dormitory amid great confusion; it's hardly five o'clock.

God! It's cold in this factory! And to think we have to stand up in this icebox, answering roll call, for at least two hours before we begin work!

A tremendous tumult, an awful melee of pushing and shoving; it seems everyone is screaming and swearing and trading punches.

At last we're lined up, five by five, the small girls in front, the tall girls in back. To make the ranks a little less disorderly, the prisoners push their neighbors to fill up the open spaces. Everyone pushes to the right by taking two or three steps in that direction—creating even more open spaces than before. It's boring, fatiguing, and irritating as hell. We get shoved away from our French comrades with whom we had hoped to exchange a few words.

Finally the column is formed in ranks of five; on my left is a gypsy gnawing a bone that stinks; on my right is a Russian who keeps blowing her nose and spitting on the ground while, in front of me, is a Polish woman chewing on some turnip peelings—coughing out what she can't swallow; they all smell; what horrible promiscuity....

It's just barely six o'clock. Another hour to wait. The Aufseherinnen pass before us, behind us and between the ranks. Some comrades make the sign of the cross; they are praying. So am I; I am thinking about my loved ones, too; despite the noise, the bellowing, and the cruel light of the projectors, I am still able to think. I see my little girl saying to me: "Good-bye," for the last time. She was so cute in her little red coat, white gloves, and pretty little brown curls! "Give Daddy a big kiss, for me..." she said.

Poor little thing, her father was arrested; she still didn't know...my husband, what became of him?...where is he?...arrested in Paris five days before I was, what have they done with him?

I never found him in any of the "interrogation offices" on the Rue des Saussaies. I hope to God they have not killed him!...Have courage, my darling...have courage, you also...you have to hold on no matter where you are...no matter what they do to you...courage, courage, courage....

Imperceptibly, one tear, followed by another, and then by many others, cloud my eyes. How sweet it is to see again those whom one loves through this fragile veil. And ever so softly, I wipe the tears from my face. All of a sudden, my head is given a tremendous thump, and I almost fall to the ground because I wasn't expecting it. The commander had just come by and said that my arms were not resting along the length of my emaciated body. In just a few seconds, I was brutally jerked back to reality.

It's 6:30.

In front of us is the wing assembly line—with its powerful projectors, its compressed air hoses, its pneumatic hammers, which make such an ear-shattering noise, and drills of all dimensions.

Our comrades who worked all night are hurrying to clean up the floor and put away their hoses and tools before the assembly line begins to move again—in about ten minutes. There goes the bell. Off it starts.

Ten minutes to seven; the machines stop. What silence!

A whistle blows. The prisoners get into ranks of five; off they march. They are not as numerous as we are because, at night, only the wing assembly line functions. They line up in front of us and, though dead with fatigue, hunger and cold, they stand at attention in a straight line when the commander comes by.

Then a series of orders ring out: "Arbeit! Arbeit! schneller, Mensch!"

We make a half turn to the left and march in ranks to our work. Some stop at the wings and immediately take the place of comrades who have just gone off duty. Others go up to the first floor, composed of two sets of nine steps: it's the store room; it goes along the whole side of the factory. That's where the spare parts to be put on the wings are made. Still other women go to the extreme left of the factory, where the soldering equipment is kept; there are about twenty of them. They quickly put on their black glasses. They are seated—the welding torch in the right hand and the piece of metal to solder in the left. A little flame coming out of the end of the gas hose will turn into a brilliant sparkle in a few seconds.

Many women are working underneath the storeroom gallery; they pierce long tubes, put in rivets, and manipulate heavy and highly complicated machines with dexterity—as though they had done this work all their lives.

It's true that one quickly learns a job well when the S.S. is lurking in the area; and it is in the best interests of the poor deportees to do so because, if they don't accomplish the work given to them to the S.S.'s satisfaction, their lives are in dire danger. Me, I'm on wings. The rails on which they slide are in the center of the factory and go from one end of the building to the other. On one side there are 18 stalls, from numbers 1 to 18; then the wing pivots and returns to its point of departure, following the second rail from stall number 19 to 36.

It would be fastidious to describe the work done at each stall; I will just say that, at stall number 1, the left wing of the Messerschmitt 109 is reduced to its simplest form of expression. There is nothing. My French comrades bring over the wing's central element, which weighs more than 80 kilos, to which—little by little—the innumerable metal fixtures and pieces which make up the wings of these frightful planes will be soldered.

Drillers work at stalls 6, 7, 8, 9 and 10.

Some eight prisoners at each stall pierce the wing from all directions; bright little sparks jump up all around. If you get one on your face or your hands, it will burn you a little. Once in a while, a worker will get duralumin dust in her eye. She grabs at this opportunity to go to the infirmary. There, though depending on the mood of the two prisoners who work there (having been medical students, they have been chosen to give us medical treatment), a person can get a little rest—particularly if the Aufseherinnen on duty have not accompanied us. And these few minutes of respite even provide us with the opportunity to engage in a little gossip.

Between stall 11 and stall 18 there was always more noise than elsewhere because this was where the riveting was done. It was abominable. You couldn't hear yourself talk, even if you screamed. The only way to communicate was to grab women, push them around or use sign language with them. They looked like a bunch of monkeys.

Riveting also went on between stall 19 and stall 28—but this was done primarily to fix the metal sheets or plates of duralumin on the wings so that they would be absolutely covered and smooth.

Electric wires and cables for the radio, heating, and transparent windows (made out of plastic) were put on in the last stands.

Finally, when the wing reached stand number 36, it was finished.

The German engineers and the factory directors, who for the most part were not much better than the S.S., would gather around the wing and, with a little mirror—which they used like an automobile's rear-view mirror—and a portable lamp, would thoroughly go over the finished product.

They carressed it with the tips of their fingers, these wicked wings which, for them, seemed to be the most precious thing on earth.

This is probably the moment to introduce "The Violet," because I think none of my comrades would forgive me if I omitted mentioning this sorry individual. "The Violet," so named because he reeked of perfume, was a dangerous enemy for us—mean and crafty. Tall, thin, with a cold cruel look, he terrorized us and made us work without stopping. If he didn't strike us himself, it was because—so it seems—he didn't have the right; but he got revenge by having the S.S. beat us up.

The S.S. were brutes and cowards, but they knew nothing about our work; as long as we were bent assiduously over our machines, they concluded we knew what we were doing—and were doing it well; they did not harass us. But "The Violet," an engineer from the Heinkel factories, knew the work well and never missed a chance to send in his report to the S.S.—who knew how to make us understand that this tiring job had to be done conscientiously, even if it were beyond our physical capabilities.

I will leave you the choice between the diverse punishments that were irreparably inflicted upon us: either the "schlague" or the roll calls—standing in the cold for periods of time that, I assure you, could exceed ten hours; or else we were flatly denied our soup ration.

At long last, the wing left stall 36—and the rails on which it had slid through so many hands, necessitated so much work, and caused so many hundreds of unfortunate girls to go to the brink of fatigue and endure so much physical punishment and emotional anguish. When the time came to put on the finishing touches, we lifted it onto a kind of rolling platform that we pushed to the paint shop, which took up the width of a hall to the extreme right. The paint shop had a glass roof, and it was very warm there. My comrades placed the wing in a horizontal position and began polishing it energetically; then they put a coat of grey mastic on it. At this moment, the wings were attached to each other in Indian file. They were drawn by a cable—advancing very slowly between two high metal sheets equipped with drying projectors. Sometimes, although rarely, alas! we were able to slip between two wings where we would spend a quarter of an hour warming up.

When we came down from our perch we were red and flushed—but at least we were nice and warm. It was so good to feel warm between two and three o'clock in the morning, particularly when, since five in the afternoon, we had been shivering in a factory that had not one pane of glass in the window frames, and where the heating had broken down (as the result of massive bombing attacks, there wasn't much left of these buildings). However, when our "mobile steam bath" arrived, there stood an Aufseherin, club in hand. En route, it was impossible for us to come down from our roost between the two heating walls, thus it was that we arrived at the end of our "ride" feeling softened up by all that warmth; however, we quickly realized how hungry, tired and sleepy we were when the guard cracked us across the back with a magistral whack.

In a few moments we again became the poor, weak and disjointed beings that crawled across the floor like puppets.

Next, the wing came under the spray of a paint gun. The Germans were not fussy about the color of the wings; mighty Germany was no longer even capable of producing paint, and we used what we could find in stock. The wings were either silver or green; some were even blue. Of course, an immense swastika covered them, as well as an inscription in German. They were also painted in diverse colors of indefinite hue, and in tones of brown, in order to camouflage them.

When they left the paint shop, they were considered finished. A large crane transported them in the hall where, after being lined up (six facing one way and six the other), they were left to dry—separated from each other by pieces of wood and carton paper. We could see five or six hundred wings stacked in the hall—ready to disappear one fine day.

At nine o'clock, we had a fifteen minute "break period." For the last few months, the Aufseherinnen and the Stubowas distributed half a dipper of blackish liquid that some called coffee; its great advantage was that it was hot. Later, however, the coffee was done away with completely; we sincerely regretted its absence because this fairly detestable brew momentarily comforted us. But a person had to fight so hard to get any that many of us preferred to forget it. A hundred or so white bowls were on a sort of rickety stand. You can imagine what happened when five hundred women all ran at the same time to get a bowl.... Many of them were smashed on the floor, while others were used as projectiles.

Then the work period began again. An immense clock that struck the hours was, in short, along with the few little birds who lived above it, or next to what were once glass windows, our only distraction—and the only real pleasant memory many of us have of our stay in Germany. At noon, a bell rang. The prisoners formed into ranks, always five by five, under the vigilant and brutal eye of the S.S.

No count was made, but it was simply another measure to make us understand that not for a single instant did we have control over ourselves.

We marched from the middle of the factory, right to the end. We had to line up by two's. Obviously the change-over from the single file we were in a few minutes earlier to the double file we now had to form brought on fights; girls fought and insulted each other.

The Aufseherin broke them up with her schlague. We knew very well that it was time for soup and it would be better to try to get to the table first in order to get a seat on the bench and have a plate more or less full. In any case, it was wiser, at that particular moment, to take off your glasses, if you wore them, because if they weren't broken by blows, it was a miracle.

Then the column slowly moved off. We had to go down a flight of stairs, as the refectory was in the basement. It wasn't difficult to tell (by the smell) that we were going to have turnip soup. Sometimes it was cabbage soup, sometimes beetroot soup; on Sundays we had soup made from carrots.

The Frenchwomen grouped together in order to relax and feel less isolated. This made it easier for the Block-owa to serve us at the table; she would empty her cans on the "Francouzes" side, stirring the contents as little as possible. We were served hardly a ladleful of bad gruel, vaguely greasy, which left a bitter taste in our mouths for the rest of the day; sometimes, right at the bottom of our plates, we came across a few vegetables which must have asked themselves what they were doing there; but these occasions were rare.

At quarter to one, a bell rang three times—and the factory went back to work until seven o'clock in the evening.

At twenty to seven, we quickly started to put away the tools and the machines. The "Meister" took their inseparable leather brief cases out of their drawers, changed their shoes and went to the toilets that were reserved for them, to smoke a couple of cigarettes. The wing assembly line, which a few moments before had been scattered with bits of metal, screws, nuts and rivets, became tidy, clean and even polished.

At ten to seven, another bell, and we got into ranks of five, impeccably lined up in front of the "Führerin" and the "Kommandant." He remained still and measured us with his dead eyes; meanwhile, she counted and recounted us, followed by the Aufseherinnen. Then she returned to the side of the camp commander and, after giving him the Hitler salute, handed over the list of workers present at the evening roll call, or in the infirmary. The Aufseherinnen, in turn, handed in their reports for the day, which meant giving the numbers of the girls to be beaten. Finally, the "Blockowa" arrived with a paper on which were marked the numbers of the prisoners who had not made their beds properly (blankets not straight) or who had disobeyed. When a non-German-speaking Frenchwoman was involved, we had to fall back on our "Dolmetscherin" (interpreter). This disagreeable job caused a lot of anguish to our dear friend, Madame F., who ended up not knowing what to do, nor what to say, to help us. She didn't escape the S.S.'s fury, and even though she had done nothing wrong, she generally received her fair share of blows.

The girls who were called came out of the ranks, lined up next to each other in front of us, and patiently waited to go in to the commander's office to be beaten. Very often, they were deprived of their soup ration. Generally speaking, the seven o'clock roll call meant the end of work for the "Tagschichten" (day shift), and the beginning for the "Nachtschichten" (night shift).

If, on the whole, the work was satisfactory, the roll call lasted no longer than twenty or thirty minutes. But any pretext was a good one to stretch out the roll call, and often, very often, alas! we stood there like poles for hours on end. Then came the second distribution of soup. We got back into line, two by two; this second service was always arduous because it was frequently interrupted by alerts—at which time all the lights went out. The sirens started to scream. The night shift, who had just started work, ran to shelters on the opposite side.

As for us, we pushed each other around like mad-women. If a girl fell, it was absolutely useless for her to try to get up because the uninterrupted flow of bodies could not stop. It advanced like a solid wave, feeling about in the darkness to find the staircase, which was very difficult to go down. The ones holding onto the bannisters were saved, but the others found themselves pushed up against the opposite side—horribly crushed against the wall and dropping the poor can which they held in their dirty hands. The little bag in which they carried their minuscule bread ration, and which they had made with so much difficulty, was often snatched away.

One could hear cries, screams, sometimes "thief"; or feel some girl's hot breath on the back of your neck, murmuring incomprehensible phrases, from which emerged words like: "meine Liebe"; then a hand grabbed your breast. What could be done? One could fight, and in the scuffle try to poke an elbow into the aggressor's stomach; but if the blow misfired, the girl would hit you back. And if you were lucky enough to have a "Kopf-tuch," a headscarf, it disappeared like magic. On the other hand, if you wore nothing on your head, then the little hair you had, or what was regrowing, was torn out.

Once we got to the shelters, we had to wait because we never ate during the alerts. We were tired, but our fatigue was nothing compared to our anguish. Why? It's easy to explain: when the alert sounded, the lights went out; when the lights went out, everything disappeared.

So, what was going to happen to our soup? Our bread? and our ration of margarine and sausage? Because it was in the evening that our daily bread ration was given to us—or I should say, thrown at us. We knew quite well that at least a quarter of the food would have disappeared into thin air...but, what could be done? Wait, wait until the end of the alert. If not too much had been stolen, we would get our soup; but if, on the contrary, the soup cans and the bread had disappeared, there would be new roll calls with searches and, of course, nothing would be found.

Suddenly, the sirens started screaming again. Short blasts at first, to announce that the danger was over, then a last long blast which signified the end of the alert. As food had been stolen, we were again lined up, and after one or two hour's wait, or even more, we finally heard the "Ab-treten" (end of the roll call), which was always so long in coming. The result: we had a quarter or half a ladleful of soup, or little or no bread.

Finally, we were going to rest.

The commander came by for her inspection, followed by her faithful watch dogs. We quickly tidied up our things as best we could on our bunks and stood at attention.

"Achtung! achtung!" here she is at last. To this woman, who seemed to be so happy looking at us, what a sad spectacle we must have been, for her eyes...with our poor shirts, our hair, which was either shaved off or growing back—or straight and still full of duralumin, our dirty, hardened hands, our thin arms and our haggard countenances, especially our eyes, which continually tried to show a little vivacity and expression. Rarely did her inspection tour go off without some drama taking place....At last she left.

Presto! Into bed; let's sleep a few hours while waiting for the next alert—which will certainly occur in the middle of the night. It's such a bore to have to get up in a few hours to go down into the sinister shelters and shake with cold, but I assure you that it does not bore our hearts because we know that, when the bombs fall like hail, they will jump with joy.

(To the tune of "Lili Marlène")

When the alert sounds
We go down in the night
To have a little sleep

In the bottom of the shelters.
We hear the bombs fall
And it really makes us laugh
To know that everything is being destroyed
In this damned country.

The work done by the night shifts and the day shifts was the same. However, the one-hour break granted the day shift was cut to 45 minutes for those working at night because, as they were less numerous, it only took a half hour to serve them their soup, instead of three-quarters of an hour for the day laborers. Still, both night and day seemed interminable to us.

On the second and third Sunday of the month, the factory was closed, and, theoretically, we rested. It was the same for two Saturdays when the day shift worked from seven in the morning until one in the afternoon, and the night shift from four until nine.

It was these periods of "time-off" that we feared the most, and not a day went by that we failed to discuss these sad moments that lay ahead of us.

On those days, we were turned over, bag and baggage, to the S.S. Not one civilian present to witness, should he ever be given permission, the scenes that took place in the camp. I know that the S.S. mocked the advice of the civilian workers, but for us, it nevertheless constituted a vague support for us; and in any case, the factory had to operate; that's why we were there, and we knew it—and some very extraordinary event had to occur for the factory to come to a complete halt. However, these Saturdays and Sundays were spent doing all kinds of chores; cleaning the Schlafsäle and the mattresses, not to mention the tedium we went through having our clothes inspected and our sacks searched. This last operation made our hearts jump into our throats on more than one occasion because, despite the vigilance of the Aufseherinnen and the little liberty at our disposal, we still managed to make a lot of little odds-and-ends that we wanted to take back to our families at all costs.

It's astonishing how the absence of everything that could give a semblance of civilization to our lives made us almost ingenious. For example, in addition to our cook book, we made combs, safety pins, and brooches. We made a lot of other objects, much more artistic—like rings cut out of transparent plastic used in the manufacture of airplanes. Almost all my French friends returned home with, among other souvenirs, some form of ring which, I assure you, lacked neither originality nor harmony. We also made trinkets. At the risk of boasting, this was my speciality: little dogs, pigs, Christmas trees, fish, etc. Many of my French and Yugoslav comrades took them as souvenirs. For my birthday, my charming friend Samson gave me an adorable little wooden fork that all the Frenchwomen admired; it gave me such joy. We also made little hearts, out of duralumin, on which the dates of our arrest and the names of the cities where we had lived during captivity were engraved.

Of course, all of us owned a little knife with a rubber handle. With a material that felt like straw, I also made some charming dolls which I painted and dressed up in ballet skirts—as well as some cowboys, complete with a lasso and a horse, and some tri-colored bouquets of flowers; I even made a pair of slippers for my friend Léa with a little tool that I had bent into the form of a hook.

I found a map of Germany in a magazine, and I carefully copied it; thus it was that we could follow events almost daily. But the searches were true terror for us. Where could we hide all these precious marvels? After looking all over, we finally found an ideal hiding place. In the dormitory to which we were ultimately assigned was an immense washbasin, fifteen to twenty centimeters wide, that extended along the entire length of the room; underneath it, there was an empty space between the basin and the wall; we were saved; thanks to this hidden niche, we were able to take home almost all our precious souvenirs. Once the searches had ended, we were ordered to form ranks, as we were always having to do, and, singing German songs, and with the Gypsies leading the way, we marched for hours in the courtyard of the factory—always right along the building, and in any and all weather.

We were also deloused periodically; often this operation ended with our heads being shaved. Or else we had to fall out for a "special" roll call that lasted all day; as punishment, it seems, for working badly during the week....

In the other part of the building was a large room where garments were sewn and mended. Those that were hiding, holed up there, although none were French. Next door was the infirmary—cleanly kept and well-lighted by a huge window. It contained five white beds; the mattresses and blankets had been slipped into large bags made out of a blue-and-white checkered material. Beside each bed was a chair, and in the back was a little wash basin. Every day the male and female commanders came by to inspect the sick. If, at the end of 18 days, the prisoners were not back on their feet, they were automatically evacuated to the Ravensbrück camp. We never saw even one of them again. These poor women were all assassinated.

I stayed for a month in the infirmary. When I reached the end of the second week, I knew that I was definitely lost because I was going to be forced to leave, too. However, sometimes a miracle happens during one's existence; a miracle happened to me at Schoenfeld. At that extremely critical time, the camp commanders were changed—which saved my life. As a matter of fact, the new commander only calculated the number of days I had spent in the infirmary from the time of her arrival— which gave me another 18 days of respite and the possibility to get well and get up out of bed....

Thus did the days go slowly by, interminably, awful days when, in addition to our strenuous daily work schedule, an order affecting one's entire life would suddenly appear out of the blue. For example, some women were obliged to leave their labor battalion and return to camp. With tears in their eyes and their hearts full of anxiety, we watched our comrades, with pain in our souls, as they left our ranks, lined up in a column, and, without pronouncing a single word, went off in the distance—perhaps forever; a few, those who felt immense sorrow, would turn around and, with a forced smile on their faces, make a little sign of "good-bye" with their hand, or simulate a farewell kiss with their lips.

DISINFECTION

Once a month we underwent a disinfection treatment, during which we again suffered intolerable humiliation. It took place in a camp several kilometers from the airfield, where the only prisoners were Russians (of all ages). After waiting in line around the building for several hours, we entered an overheated room to undress; we hung our clothes and blankets on hooks suspended from a rolling stand; they were disinfected in a special room while we were in the shower. We only had a few minutes in which to wash from head to toe, and there were three or four of us under each spout; then we went to a nearby room to wait for our clothes.

Once there, we had to wait for hours, sitting naked against each other; occasionally, Germans dressed in white overalls would come in to examine us—for their personal pleasure. They made fun of the thin women whose limp and dried-up skin hung in folds; on the other hand, young women and girls who were still attractive were made to stand in front of them; they ran their revolting fingers over the frail bodies, much to the disgust of the prisoners who would have liked to slap their insolent faces. These gentleman were accompanied by Russian prisoners whose sole job was to look after the

clothes and the furnace, but they could not help giving us the eye. Sometimes they were young Russian boys, about sixteen years old. They faced two hundred naked women blushing with shame. The windows were at shoulder height, and dozens of heads pressed up against them, much to the joy of the sadistic Germans.

Finally, our clothes were given back to us; as for the blankets, they were mixed up on purpose; in any case, the Frenchwomen were given the most disgusting ones, those belonging to the Gypsies.

MEMORIES

We taught our country's customs to the foreigners in our dormitory. For example, to celebrate Epiphany, we decorated little sandwiches made out of the bread, jam and sausages allotted us; some were in the form of staircases. We put plastic charms in each sandwich and passed them around. For a few happy minutes we were able to smile at last.

On November 11, all the Frenchwomen observed Armistice Day with a minute's silence.

One afternoon, a French friend and I had a hassle with a Gypsy to whom the Germans had given a coat belonging to a Jew (who had been sent to the gas chamber). Two decorations were still on the coat: the "Legion of Honor," and the "1918 Croix de Guerre." We explained to the German Gypsy what these two decorations meant to us, and we asked her to return them to us. She ignored our request and went on strutting about in the coat. A few days later, I went looking for her, and we had a real ding-dong battle; unfortunately, she was stronger than I was, and I had to give up—but only after getting in some hard kicks to her stomach. She came away from the fray with a black eye and scratches on her face. My friend was smarter and, by keeping a constant eye on her, managed to quickly unsew the decorations when the Gypsy took the coat off. That evening in the dormitory, she showed me the two ribbons; we cut them in two, she kept one half and I kept the other. Of course the Gypsy noticed their absence—but we both ganged up on her and gave her a good thrashing.

After a hard day's work, during which the Germans were as spiteful to us as possible, we met together in the dormitory on the evening of December 24, 1944. Our comrade Denise, a pretty twenty-year-old brunette, whose fiancé had been shot by the Germans, climbed up to the third bunk and, kneeling down, recited in a lovely voice the little poem called "Christmas 44," written especially for the occasion by our good friend Vonvon. We were deeply touched by this.

* *

Schoenfeld lived through an event which was probably unique in concentration camp history: a soup strike. It was organized by the clandestine committee for the defense of Yugoslav deportees.

— Upon being contacted by the Yugoslavs,[1] I said I agreed with the strike and promised to go along with it. Though thoroughly worn out by dysentery, I prayed to myself: "My God, help me! Help me not to eat my soup, I'm so hungry."

— Exhausted by an interminable day's work,[2] we decided, together with the Yugoslavs, to join the soup strike; it was not only a protest lodged against the hot water pompously called "soup," that was served to us, but also an expression of our collective discontent with the inhuman conditions in which we were living and working. This was an heroic act on the part of the deportees (who were already three-quarters dead of

1. Unpublished manuscript, Léa Chandelot. October 1970.
2. Unpublished manuscript, Simone Giraud and Thérèse Gauthier. September 1970.

hunger). After the evening roll call, we went down as usual into the factory's cellar—which served as a refectory. We had a surprise waiting for us: the commander had been warned, and he was waiting for us with a revolver; he was accompanied by guards holding schlagues. All the exits were blocked. The soup was served, but we remained standing as straight as possible in front of our mess kits.

— As there was no more room[1] in the big refectory, I went to the little refectory. There was a spare place at a table occupied entirely by Russians; I silently slipped in among them and did as they did. They are standing up, arms folded, head up and not looking at the soup.

— (In the big refectory) the commander[2] demands an explanation. We reply that, as the soup is made of water, the meal was not enough to enable us to do hard labor. This is where the nightmare began: the commander and the guards threw themselves upon us, striking out at random. Some prisoners went under the tables, others, jumped on top of them. Everything was overturned; a frightening race followed because, as we couldn't get out, we had to keep running around in circles. How long did this madness last? After a good deal of this racing around, some exits were opened and we were able to get out and go back to the dormitory.

— From the small refectory came cries,[3] oaths and shouts in various languages. We realized that the big refectory was being emptied by means of the Schlague. Suddenly an Aufseherin appeared, wildly beating everyone around with her "gummi." We found ourselves at the entrance, a sort of landing leading in to the refectories. The commander is there with his schlague, blocking the passage, and we have to pass in front of him. I realize with horror that my bag (containing all my "treasures") is

1. Unpublished manuscript, Léa Chandelot.
2. Unpublished manuscript, Simone Giraud-Thérèse Gauthier.
3. Unpublished manuscript, Simone Giraud-Thérèse Gauthier.

still in the refectory. I hesitate to go back because what has happened is so terrible. Finally, I go. I was nailed to the spot when I saw what was going on through the open door. After the room had been emptied, certain Russian and Polish prisoners had come back to the refectory (their dormitory was just next door) in the hope of eating some soup, as the cans were still there. They began beating each other up, stealing the plates which were still on the table and, when they had to let go of them, hurling them into the air smashing the electric light bulbs in the process. Several women were fighting on the ground. A Russian running away from a stronger opponent smacked into me—bringing me to my senses. I picked up my bag on the run and got back to the dormitory, frozen with horror at what I had seen.

— Surprising as it might seem, no reprisals were taken; the soup got no better, and that's all.

* * *

— Every day,[1] French prisoners of war came to the factory to do maintenance work. I always tore the black curtains—out of passive defense, as the prisoners had to repair them...and at the same time I got the latest news. I immediately transmitted this information to "Toilet Radio" correspondents, who then diffused it to all the other Frenchwomen throughout the factory.

It was August 15, 1944....My friends arrived to do their daily repair work. They were radiant...behind my back they whispered:

"Fantastic news—we'll confirm it tomorrow—but you can start rejoicing."

Immediately, I passed on the good but unknown news. It was certainly good; our prisoner friends never told tall stories. At the beginning we called them pessimists! The next day was a long time in coming....Alas! when the

1.   Unpublished manuscript, Lise Lesèvre.

two prisoners came near me, an Aufseherin was there, too. I knew from experience that she wouldn't leave before they did: The Germans were very wary of contacts between Frenchmen and Frenchwomen. I really tore at the black curtains so that it would take a long time to repair them...and give me time to gather more news. I hadn't counted on that terrible woman. I couldn't even glance at my friends working up on the big ladder. The job wouldn't take forever! They would go and I wouldn't have any news! They were going to pass behind me...disappearing without saying anything....They remained silent. But then they both started to whistle with enthusiasm; the tune was the well known and comforting: "Everything's going well, Madame la Marquise."

What a relief! I could tell my comrades that the news was true...that it was good! But what news?

It was only the next day that I heard from the two prisoners about the landings at Cavalaire and along the entire Mediterranean coast.

* * *

— An egg![1] Our column was marching by. A hen had just laid an egg. An egg was in the grass. But our guard saw it. So, our whole column of empty stomachs had to file past this poor little egg without being able to touch it.

WORK STOPPAGES IN THE FACTORY

One day,[2] there was an electrical breakdown in the factory; it lasted several hours; it was at the end of December 1944. Then, the same week, the compressor stopped:

"Nicht Licht, nicht Luft" (no light, no air), we were told.

---

1 Unpublished manuscript, Odile Lambolle. May 1970.
2 Unpublished manuscript, Juliette Colliet. Already cited.

Then it happened again; we learned a few days later that, as the Russians had taken Frankfort on the Oder, the factory wouldn't run any more, since the electrical energy came from the Oder. The heating hadn't worked for several months, and three grotesque braziers in this huge factory tried to give off some sort of heat. The Gypsies grouped in a circle around them. To see their dirty, emaciated hands and bodies, with their skirts hitched up so that the heat would penetrate even further, one could visualize them grouped round a miserable little caravan on the side of a bad road. They chanted songs, marking the beat with their hands and feet; one could see their crooked yellow teeth, black stumps from which oozed a disgusting saliva which they spat onto the ground between songs. The promiscuity of the Gypsies in the factory was painful to see. These women, who were mainly of German origin, only knew one thing—how to steal; some of them had been prisoners for many years and they were considered to be a damned race like the Israelites. They were arrested at the same time as the Jews, but none of them were sent to the crematorium ovens. They were imprisoned in order that they could learn a trade and become useful: the period of caravans and carousels was over. Everyone had to be useful to the Great Germany. Among these women, all of whom spoke German, many became dazed and stupid slaves of the S.S.; they would have done anything as long as the S.S. Aufseherinnen gave them extra rations; they had an easier time than we had; they rarely had the worst tasks to do. Their vulgarity and mentality were the same as the S.S. women in charge of us and they had the same background: theft, sexual intercourse and often assassinations.

One lone woman among the Gypsies did not resemble them: she was a pure Bohemian Gypsy, an aristocratic girl who suffered from this horrible promiscuity. Dignified in the face of suffering, she was aghast at the reaction of one of these monstrous Gypsies who, following a mas-

sive bombing on Berlin, learned (a few hours later) that a
bomb had fallen on the house where lived three little
children she had had by a German, killing all of them.
This woman's attitude was revolting: she thanked the
Germans who gave her the news and, rejoining her
group of Gypsies, went on singing, beating out the
rhythm with her hands and laughing her head off....

But to come back to our factory. We spent eight days
doing nothing. It seemed impossible and unbelievable!
The days passed too quickly, alas! We asked ourselves
what would become of us; was this the end of our
torment? Would we have to start work again? Alas!
nothing of the sort! We were given the most exhausting
work you could imagine....The S.S. seemed to have
nothing to do, but every day we felt that something was
about to happen, but what?

It was January 1945.

ROAD CONSTRUCTION

One morning, the roll call was at five o'clock; we were
counted and recounted. Then three quarters of the
prisoners were taken and divided into three groups. We
were full of anxiety: what were they going to do with us?

We were all separated one from another; we looked at
each other sadly. The factory doors opened and each
group, under the surveillance of several Aufseherinnen
and guards, started marching.

Why were we accompanied by sentinels with machine-
guns under their arms? Were they going to shoot
us?...No, that would be too horrible!...And yet we
knew that we had to expect anything and everything. No
one in the world could help us, no one would look for us,
our French families didn't even know our identities.
Many of us had been arrested with false names (which
was the case with me).

What was going to happen?

We were soon to find out. We started to march on the tarred roads which crossed the airfield. We were soon tired by this rapid walking; for more than nine months we had hardly gone out. Finally, we stopped in front of a small building where a load of picks and shovels was piled up.

This was it! We understood everything; we were going to work on the roads.

So, every day, we had the same type of life, the same early start, the same roll calls, the same trip to the building to get our tools, and always this tormenting march. Every day we did a good twenty kilometers to get to the work site. We had to suffer the hard Prussian climate, the wind, the rain, the snow. Our thin clothes, which were almost immediately soaked through, clung to our skin for several days. From January 'til April, we could say we had never been able to warm up for a single instant.

The food sufficed us no longer; we dragged ourselves along the roads, walking in the mud, the snow, in a temperature of minus 28° C, looking for the rare dandelions which might have grown along the way. Then quickly, without leaving the column, we bent down to snatch up this food from heaven; but, however swift we were, the row behind us fell out of step, the shovels we carried on our shoulders were no longer in line; immediately the Aufseherin rushed at us and rained blows on us with whatever came to hand.

The work on the roads was exhausting.

We dug trenches. We even dug them alongside a small lake. Our feet were soaked in icy water that came up above our ankles. It was no longer earth that we were throwing out, but dirty water; clay trickled down the handles of the shovels and splashed over us. We could have cried with rage, with cold, with fatigue and this went on for hours...and days.

After the trenches, we built shelters to protect the airplanes from bombings. They had to be camouflaged.

We cut down trees in a small wood and dragged them over to the new shelters. The Russian girls imprisoned with us were much stronger than we were and for the most part, were used to farm work; even though they were underfed, they kept up their strength; five or six of them could lift a pine tree and carry it easily. They were happy doing this new job; but we managed it so badly. We weren't used to cutting down trees, to digging trenches and, after eight weeks' work, we were at the end of our strength, our courage was gone, even our morale was dying.

It took at least fifteen of us to carry a tree and this brought the anger and the blows of the Germans upon us, and there were irreconcilable differences between the Russians and the Poles on the one hand, and the Frenchwomen on the other. The prisoners never got on well; they were from very different backgrounds, and we knew that the day they had a little freedom would be the day they "got even."

We built the roads because the Germans, in order to protect their planes, no longer left them on the airfields. They towed them by the tail—using our roads and our shelters, which were filled with all kinds of munitions.

When the Germans were satisfied with our work, they had us build a railway track, and to do so they took us to "Mittenwald." I was lucky; I was sent to "Mittenwald" only once: what horrible work it was!

Roll call was at three o'clock in the morning; then we had to take a little train to the east of Berlin. We had to pile up pebbles and fix the rails on wooden ties. The guards hit us with their rifle butts to make us work faster, always faster. The Germans became worried and anxious; things were no longer going their way. They were exasperated by this railroad for it was to be used to evacuate the wounded from the East. The number of wounded was growing; after a fierce resistance, the Küstrin Fort was now in the hands of the Soviet Army, we had reached such a state of fatigue and tension that we feared we could not hold out much longer. Our morale dropped, the weight of our shovels on our shoulders became unbearable, our soaking-wet clothes, which clung to us, no longer dried out. Our bodies were transformed; we were nothing more than a mass of dead, dried-out skin, which flaked off like a snake's; our shoulders stooped. A dry cough shook us. We suffered from dysentery and we walked while holding in our stomachs. Frequent pains wrecked us and caused us intolerable sickness; there was no hope of stopping when the column was marching and we ate chalk to try and stop our pains. It was total confusion and we began to look forward to death with serenity.

Throughout the rest of my life I cannot forget that horrible Easter Monday. In the morning, exhausting work on the airfield, the weather was grey, a strong wind blew us in all directions as if we were reeds. Even the earth was carried away by the wind; every shovelful stuck to our soaking-wet clothes. Then, in the afternoon, we were taken to a little forest of fir trees; the wind had calmed down, but the rain poured down; our cotton dresses stuck to our skin and hurt us when we moved, for we were passing big bricks (weighing two kilos each) down the line without stopping. Our column stretched out over at least a kilometer, starting from the top of a small wood descending to a pond.

For hours we moved bricks at such a rate that, if we dropped one because of our icy and torn hands, we found three or four waiting for us. The Aufseherin rushed up in a fury, pulled us out of the line and beat us; unfortunately we dropped those awful bricks many times....

I can make no commentary on the work we did in Germany because all the words I could find would be too gentle. I only believe that if we miraculously survived all these tests, it is because we fought with all our might. We desperately wanted to live, whatever happened; we tried to keep up a magnificent morale; the tide had to turn and, above all, God protected us.

SATURDAY, APRIL 21

Still in the Schoenfeld factory.

It is seven in the morning; an unusual silence reigns, no noise, no screams. The dormitory doors are still closed. We hear the dull thud of a cannon. However, we have heard the same sound for so many months that we are gradually getting used to it.

However, today, if you listen well, the sound of the cannon is louder; we climb up on the edge of the washbasin and see thick smoke in the distance. All the prisoners are worried; we realize that this time something strange is happening. Rumors spread. Some think that we have been abandoned and want to escape; others think that the S.S. have fled, fearing the arrival of the Red Army, and, what is really depressing, have locked us in; which means that we shall be blown up because the factory is mined.

By eleven o'clock we are all in a state of intense excitement. The dormitory doors open:

"Appell, appell, schnell, schnell!"

Once again we are lined up in this sad and icy hall. The commander arrives at the head of his troops. He climbs up on a heap of old iron abandoned in the corner (in order to appear bigger, nobler and more imposing). From his perch he makes a speech in German, telling us that we are about to leave the factory to go to the camp at Oranienburg, that is if we don't go to the Hitler Youth barracks which is on the way, and where we will all be shot.

With feverish excitement, we pack our bags, which means that we must decide what trophies to take with us. Some have collected pieces of aluminum, others have stolen pieces of blue and white checked material from the infirmary in the hope of making beautiful overalls one of these days; still others gather up little pieces of handiwork which they have made with so much love.

Then, we are again assembled in the middle of the factory and, unbelievably, we are given a whole loaf of bread per prisoner. We literally threw ourselves upon it; since we have been in Germany, we have never been allowed to eat our fill, and we have never held so much bread in our hands. Then, we go down to the refectory where we are given some soup, for the last time at Schoenfeld, a thick soup made with all the leftovers in the factory kitchens.

Finally, we are back again in line, we see the doors open, and, light of heart, we start to march.

By little groups of sixty women we evacuate the factory!...stops...interminable waits...commentaries....

"Did you see, Christiane and Vonvon have gone. Henriette and her sister as well. Oh! I would so much have liked to go with them; do you think that we'll find them?"

We never again saw our friends who left us so suddenly in Germany, and it was only upon our return to France that we had news of them.

* * *

For "those from Schoenfeld," a new, long and cruel adventure started on the roads of collapsing Germany. For Juliette Colliet, it finished on May 2, 1945 when she met the first Soviet Army soldiers; others, many others, never knew this joy.

Those who believed in God and those who did not believe; those who knew why they had been deported and those who did not; those who had a family in their own country and those who had no one waiting for them; those who refused all stupidity, all compromise and those who, by chance, by fear, by stupidity, collaborated by accepting to play a role in the prison hierarchy; those who gave themselves, and the egoist. And the Resistance worker. And the criminal. And the racist. And the prostitute. And the volunteer for Compulsory Work in the Reich factories, punished at Ravensbrück for incapacity, laziness, "intercourse." And the nun. And the servant. And the woman of the world. And the worker and the intellectual. And the peasant. French, Belgian, Polish, Soviets....Women of all races, of all nations, of all political views, of all religions. Women of all ages. Women. All the women of Ravensbrück and its work details. You, deported women, you know the price of happiness and freedom.

TABLE OF CONTENTS

Printed in Spain
Published by Ferni
Distributed by Friends of History

Printer industria gráfica sa   Tuset, 19   Barcelona
Sant Vicenç dels Horts   1978
Depósito legal B. 3361-1978